ONE WEEK LOAN

BEYOND THE LEARNING ORGANIZATION

BEYOND THE LEARNING ORGANIZATION

*Creating a Culture of Continuous Growth and
Development through State-of-the-Art Human
Resource Practices*

JERRY W. GILLEY AND
ANN MAYCUNICH

PERSEUS BOOKS
Cambridge, Massachusetts

Library of Congress Catalog Card Number: 99-068000
ISBN: 0-7382-0073-5
Copyright © 2000 by Jerry W. Gilley and Ann Maycunich

Perseus Books is a member of the Perseus Books Group

Jacket design by Bruce W. Bond
Text design by Jeff Williams
Set in 11-point Times by the Perseus Books Group

1 2 3 4 5 6 7 8 9 10—03 02 01 00 99
First printing, November 1999

Perseus Books are available at special discounts for bulk purchases in the U.S. by corporations, institutions, and other organizations. For more information, please contact the Special Markets Department at HarperCollins Publishers, 10 East 53rd Street, New York, NY 10022, or call 1–212–207–7528.

Find us on the World Wide Web at http://www.perseusbooks.com

To

Bert B. Gilley
October 29, 1919–March 6, 1981

and

Lottie Victoria Gilley
January 1, 1925–November 17, 1998

Your spirits will forever be with us, guiding our lives;
providing influence, support, and encouragement through
the unknown passages yet to come.

CONTENTS

PART 3
HUMAN RESOURCES PRACTICES

7 Human Resource Planning, Recruiting, and Selection   179

8 The Learning and Change Process   207

9 Career Development Strategies   251

PART 4
THE DEVELOPMENTAL ORGANIZATION BLUEPRINT
IN ACTION

12 Building the Developmental Organization   **335**

ILLUSTRATIONS

PART ONE

Introduction

CHAPTER 1

Traditional, Learning, and Developmental Organizations

A virtual certainty in any organization's annual report is a statement of how important employees are to the ultimate success of the business. These organizations claim that their employees are their number one priority. They further assert that their efforts and resources are focused on employee satisfaction and development. In some situations, such statements are absolutely true. Unfortunately, these statements are often a mere collection of words designed to impress potential shareholders. On closer examination, organizational reality is considerably different from the words expressed in the annual report. Typically, employees are treated as disposable resources to be used and disposed of as the organization sees fit, like pawns in a great, competitive contest among the mighty lords of industry. Because of this approach, many of a firm's best employees leave, seeking opportunities for growth, development, and appreciation in other organizations.

In many organizations there exists a disconnect between the perceived importance of employees and their treatment within the firm. When we go beyond the rhetoric of organizational ease and identify the way organizations go about developing their human resources, we discover a remarkable disparity. Let us illustrate. One of the world's largest corporations recently made a conscious decision to adopt the principles and practices of the learning organization. As a result, it renamed its training and development department to the department of organizational learning and changed the name of its executive vice president of training and development to chief learning officer. Close examination of this business revealed that nothing else really changed. Its focus remained on providing classroom training activities. Little regard was given to how learning was ultimately used on the job or how learning could improve the organization's performance capacity. Although the firm's leaders claimed they understood the tenets of learning organizations, they failed to change the overall developmental strategy employed within the firm. In other words, the organization simply applied a new coat of paint to an existing problem, hoping the efforts would change future outcomes. At the same time, the organization boasted that employees were its greatest asset and that it could not achieve its mission without the efforts of its people. In reality, nothing could be further from the truth.

All too often, firms believe that employees are easily replaced. Consequently, they develop policies and procedures that demonstrate a revolving-door philosophy toward human resources (Gilley, Boughton, and Maycunich 1999, 1). Under these conditions, employees are often treated with a lack of dignity and respect because of management's belief that people are disposable and that qualified replacements abound in the marketplace.

When an attitude of corporate indifference prevails, managers often refuse to mentor and develop their employees, tending to wash their hands of any responsibility for their employees' performance. Consequently, as these workers fail to meet performance expectations, they are quickly dismissed. These behaviors degrade employee morale and productivity, severely limiting loyalty and commitment.

Organizations undeniably need qualified, talented employees to produce the products and services demanded by clients. These employees can come from two sources: from the open market and from within the organization.

Gilley (1998, 45–46) believes that:

The overriding need of organizations is clear: an optimal number of qualified, talented employees to produce the products and services demanded by clients. This need can be fulfilled one of two ways. First, organizations can acquire needed resources from the open market given an adequate supply of talented individuals. Second, organizations can grow and develop employees within the firm. Businesses that choose this approach understand that: the specialized knowledge and skills they need are not easily found on the open market; employee knowledge and skills can deteriorate quickly; worker morale can be negatively affected by lack of opportunity or challenges available within the organization; and new employees may need additional development to maximize their performance and productivity.

Regardless of which approach is used, employees thrive on constructive challenges that contribute to their continuous growth and development. Moreover, organizations more easily retain talented employees when they provide career development opportunities. Either strategy requires firms to use developmental activities to achieve competitiveness, productivity, and profitability requirements.

In other words, organizations need a strategic and systematic approach to employee growth and development, one that improves an organization's competitive readiness and renewal capability.

EVOLVING TO THE DEVELOPMENTAL ORGANIZATION

What makes an organization successful? Theories and literature abound—leadership, coaching, efficiency, customer orientation, the list goes on and on. One of the most recent and widely accepted notions is that of the learning organization, characterized by a culture, pervasive throughout the firm, dedicated to improving workers, their productivity, and overall business performance via continuous lifelong learning.

But do the tenets of the learning organization represent the epitome of organizational development? We think not. Although learning is a prerequisite to development, it is not the desired outcome; simply increasing an organization's reservoir of knowledge does not necessarily produce better business results. Taking learning to its highest form—to *development*—enables employees to reach their full potential, while organizations focus on outcomes that produce better business results. Thus, the final phase of organizational transformation is that of the developmental organization. This book examines a blueprint by which organizational leaders and human resources professionals can accelerate beyond the learning organization.

Comparing Traditional, Learning, and Developmental Organizations

There is an evolution that every organization *can* experience—the transformation from a traditional to a developmental organization. This evolution is voluntary; thus organizations have the freedom to remain in their current state of operation or make overt decisions that propel them to greater effectiveness and efficiency.

Three identifiable types of organizations exist along this evolutionary plane: the traditional organization, the learning organization, and the developmental organization (Figure 1.1). What separates one type from another is the importance of human resources in achieving strategic business goals and objectives, the organization's capacity for renewal, and the firm's desire to improve competitive readiness. As with every evolutionary process, it may be difficult to determine exactly where one is at any given period. Often, only when the evolutionary phase has been completed does one know for sure that he or she has passed through it.

Abundant evidence exists for traditional organizations. We believe that more than 80 percent of all organizations currently reside in this phase, producing satisfactory results and achieving sufficient business outcomes. However, their effectiveness could be greatly increased with a shift to a higher, more efficient plane, in which the organization's ability to renew itself and maximize competitive readiness is greatly enhanced while employee importance increases substantially.

The next evolutionary level of organizations is the learning organization. Much has been written recently about the nature of the learning organization, particularly the importance of learning to the development

FIGURE 1.1 Evolution of organizations

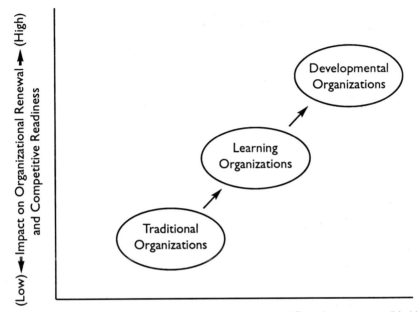

and effectiveness of a business and its people. Learning organizations theoretically maintain a significantly higher capacity for organizational renewal and competitive readiness than do traditional firms because the former emphasize the importance of human resources and achieving desired business results. To effect this emphasis, learning organizations value continuous learning and change (see Chapter 8). However, because they fail to provide a mechanism for achieving renewal and competitive readiness, no vehicle exists to go from theory to practice.

The final phase of evolutionary movement is the developmental organization. In this book, we lay out a practical approach to transforming firms to developmental organizations. Beyond the learning organization lies the epitome of individual and organizational growth and performance. Learning itself does not guarantee employee or business growth and development. Developmental organizations extend themselves further along the evolutionary plane, engaging in activities that promote and reward long-term individual and organizational growth. Consequently, developmental organizations enjoy a heightened capacity for organizational renewal and improved competitive readiness.

One good way to distinguish between these evolutionary phases involves examining their characteristics and issues (Figure 1.2). To do so, we will examine each organization and its perspective of the following:

- capacity for organizational renewal
- importance of human resources
- assumptions regarding growth and development
- expectations of growth and development
- types of developmental activities
- focus of developmental activities
- outcomes of developmental activities
- organizational priorities
- types of leadership most common within the organization
- structure and work climate
- respective roles of leaders, managers, human resource professionals, and employees
- actions needed to maintain the current evolutionary phase or to propel the organization forward

TRADITIONAL ORGANIZATIONS

The most common type of organization is traditional. It can be found in every industry and nation in the world. Although traditional organizations occupy the first phase of evolution, we do not claim that all of these businesses fail to produce satisfactory results. On the contrary, most traditional organizations do generate sufficient revenue streams and profits to continue indefinitely.

Traditional organizations historically move rapidly through the organizational life cycle, with occasional exponential growth and corresponding profitability. Nevertheless, these firms typically fail to account for the dangers of organizational maturity and the subsequent decline that fol-

FIGURE 1.2 Comparing Traditional, Learning, and Developmental Organizations

Characteristics	Traditional Organization	Learning Organization	Developmental Organization
Orientation	Training	Learning	Development
Capacity for Organizational Renewal	Low	Moderate	High
Importance of Human Resources	Not Critical	Critical	Essential
Assumption of Growth and Development	Training will Enhance Organization	Building Capability to Create through Learning	Continuous Development is Key to Competitiveness, Profitability, and Renewal
Expectation of Growth and Development	Improved SKA's	Continuous Learning	Organizational Renewal and Competitive Readiness
Types of Developmental Activities	Accidental Learning Conversational Learning Incidental Learning Anticipatory Learning	Deutero Learning Action Learning	Developmental Learning
Focus of Developemental Activities	Knowledge Acquisition	Application and Reflection	Change and Continuous Growth and Development
Outcomes of Developmental Activities	Comprehension	Mastery and Self-Awareness	New Meaning, Renewal, and Performance Capacity

(continues)

FIGURE 1.2   (continued)

	Market Share, Profits, Productivity, Margin	Learning is Key to Improving Business Results	Achieving Business Goals and Objectives through Employee Growth & Development
Organizational Priorities			
Type of Leadership	Autocratic	Transactional Transformational	Developmental
Structure and Work Climate	Departmental, Formal Hierarchical, Little or No Employee Participation	Team/Project-Oriented Encourage and Reward Individual and Group Learning	Organizational System Approach
Leader Role	Status Quo.	Synergist	Holistic Thinker and Developmental Champion
Manager Role	Status Quo.	Learning Partner	Performance Coach
Employee Role	Status Quo.	Self-Directed Learner	Developmental Enhancer
HR Professional Role	Status Quo.	Employee Champion	Performance Consultant and OD Change Agent
Actions Required to Move the Organization Forward	None	Focus on Learning	Focus on Development

lows. This success often lulls organizational leaders into a false sense of security, preventing them from preparing for the inevitable. Traditional organizations focus on such priorities as increased market share, productivity, and the maintenance of hierarchical structure and leadership style.

Eroding market share, declining productivity, and falling profitability are warning signs of organizational maturity and decline. Warnings often go unheeded as organizations attempt to maintain the status quo so that they may continue to generate the revenue needed for survival. Most traditional organizations maintain their present approach to success because it has paid off in the past. If revenue growth, productivity, and profitability decline significantly enough, traditional organizations tend to take drastic measures to regain their equilibrium. These firms historically are short-term oriented, focusing on quarterly profits and losses rather than long-term strategic plans. Consequently, traditional organizations are unable to renew themselves, thus failing to extend the growth and development phase of the organizational life cycle.

Lack of competitive readiness is the principle reason why traditional organizations are unable to avoid periods of economic decline. Competitive readiness means the ability to adjust to ever-changing market conditions, competitive pressures, and shifts in strategy among competitors. For traditional organizations, competitive readiness is low for many reasons. We contend that the primary reason is the traditional organization's focus on market and product strategies rather than on acquiring the quality and quantity of human resources needed to address competitive challenges.

The vast majority of traditional organizations fail to employ a long-term human resource strategy to enhance their competitive readiness. If a traditional organization does have a human resource strategy, it primarily relies on training as a vehicle to improve workforce skills and knowledge. Traditional organizations assume that training by itself enhances organizational performance, thus improving their competitiveness and profitability. Unfortunately, traditional organizations fail to identify strategies that transfer classroom training to the job. Moreover, they do not connect employee growth and development with competitive readiness or enhanced capacity for organizational renewal.

Type of Leadership

Autocratic leadership prevails in most traditional organizations. The autocratic leadership style focuses on hierarchical structure, power, and control of traditional leaders and managers. The structure most commonly found in these organizations is departmental, which is hierarchically ordered throughout the organization. Traditional organizations consist of various departments that separate employees from one another, depending upon the type of work engaged in and the outputs produced. Formal hierarchical structure typically rules within each department and the organization as a whole.

Communications between departments can occur at any level, although decision making, historically, remains reserved for organizational leaders. Managers function primarily as controllers, gatekeepers, and overseers of performance and production. Employees are relegated to the world of performer or producer of products and services, with little or no participation in decision making, performance improvement, or strategy formulation. Career development strategies seldom exist when little regard for continuous growth and development planning is present. In short, employees are simply another pair of hands used to maintain productivity.

Types of Developmental Activities

Historically, four types of developmental activities are found within traditional organizations. Three are informal activities, consisting of accidental, conversational, and incidental learning. The fourth, and formal activity, is anticipatory development (Marquardt 1996; see also Chapter 8).

Informal developmental activities occur without formal planning or engagements. New employees are on their own to discover the skills and knowledge necessary to perform their jobs adequately. Those who survive in these organizations usually have accidentally stumbled across this information. Accidental developmental activities occur in a haphazard, inconsistent, nonfocused manner. By contrast, conversational developmental activities are slightly more organized, sometimes taking the form of informal discussions between managers and employees. They are often designed to be on-the-job instruction whereby managers or senior

FIGURE 1.3   Developmental activities and outcomes (inside bubbles) by type of organization

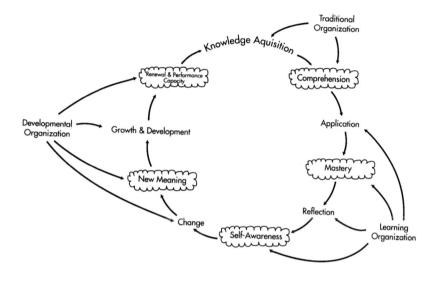

employees quickly describe the tasks to be completed and/or provide overviews of tools to be used to complete an assignment. Incidental learning occurs informally, as one engages in a variety of interactions with fellow employees, managers, and supervisors. While no formal agenda or preset learning objectives may exist, incidental learning can occur as the result of any formal engagement among employees.

When employees participate in planned learning activities to acquire new knowledge and skills so that they may address future opportunities, they engage in anticipatory learning. Through this developmental activity, employees build their skills and knowledge to become better prepared for future performance challenges.

Focus of Developmental Activities

The focus of developmental activities within traditional organizations involves *knowledge acquisition*, defined as the collection of new information useful in identifying, recalling, or recognizing the basic components and steps of their jobs (Figure 1.3). Once knowledge acquisition has taken place, employees should be able to distinguish between correct and incorrect performance procedures. They should also be able to describe, in detail, their job responsibilities, to differentiate between activities, and to compare and contrast their job responsibilities with those of others. The outcome of knowledge acquisition is comprehension. Consequently, traditional organizations have reached their highest evolutionary order when their employees can grasp the meaning of their jobs and differentiate them from other job classifications within the firm.

LEARNING ORGANIZATIONS

The second phase of evolution is the learning organization. According to Marquardt (1996, 229), the learning organization is an institution that learns powerfully and collectively, continually transforming itself to better manage and use knowledge for corporate success, empowering people within and outside the organization to learn as they work and to utilize technology to maximize learning and production. In recent years, several business leaders have begun to focus attention on organizational learning. In companies such as General Electric, Motorola, and Levi Strauss, leaders have concluded that managing, controlling, directing, and facilitating learning is a key role of management.

Marquardt (1996, 19–20) further contends that the learning organization incorporates several important dimensions and characteristics:

- Learning is accomplished by organizational systems as a whole, almost as if the organization were a single brain.
- Organizational members recognize the critical importance of ongoing organization-wide learning for the organization's current and future success.
- Learning is a continuous, strategically used process, integrated with and running parallel to work.
- There is a focus on creativity and generative learning.
- System thinking is fundamental.

- People have continuous access to information and data resources that are important to the company's success.
- The corporate climate encourages, rewards, and accelerates individual and group learning.
- Workers network in an innovative, community-like manner inside and outside the organization.
- Change is embraced, whereas unexpected surprises and even failure are viewed as opportunities to learn.
- The learning organization is agile and flexible.
- Everyone is driven by a desire for quality and continuous improvement.
- Activities are characterized by aspirations, reflections, and conceptualization.
- Well-developed core competencies serve as taking-off points for new products and services.
- The organization can continuously adapt, renew, and revitalize itself in response to the changing environment.

To make the transition from the traditional to the learning organization, Marquardt says that business leaders must alter the environment to support and encourage learning, link learning to business operations, communicate the importance of the learning organization, demonstrate their commitment to learning, transform the organizational culture to one of continuous learning and improvement, establish organizationwide strategies for learning, eliminate organizational bureaucracy, encourage employee involvement, and embrace continuous, adaptive, improvement-oriented learning approaches throughout the organization. Leaders' priorities must focus on improving learning capacity as well as encouraging self-directed learning behavior for all employees. Learning organizations are as concerned about market share, productivity, and profitability as the traditional organization; they understand that learning is the key to acquiring greater business results. Nevertheless, the orientation of the learning organization is simply *learning*.

According to Senge (1990, 191), "learning has very little to do with taking in information. Learning, instead, is a process that is about enhancing capacity. Learning is about building the capabilities to create that which you previously could not create. It ultimately relates to action, which information is not." The principle assumption of learning organizations, therefore, is that if the learning reservoir of individuals is improved, organizational performance capacity also will improve. Consequently, learning takes on several specific characteristics:

- It is performance based (i.e., tied to business objectives).
- Importance is placed on the learning process (learning how to learn) as much as, if not more than, on learning content.
- The ability to define learning needs is as important as the answers.
- Organization-wide opportunities are created to develop knowledge, skills, and attitudes.
- Learning is, in part, a product of the activity and context, and people are more willing and able to learn that which they have helped create.
- A critical survival skill is the ability to know what one must know and to learn on one's own.
- Continuous learning is essential for survival and success in today's world.
- Facilitators can accelerate learning by helping people think critically.
- Learning should accommodate and challenge different learning style preferences.
- Learning is part of work, part of everyone's job description.
- Learning involves a cyclical, cognitive process of planning, implementing, and reflecting on action (Marquardt, 1996, 32).

Boyett and Boyett (1995, 125) focus on the individual's role in learning organizations, maintaining that real, effective learning isn't individual, but social. They also explain that true learning is anything but a passive activity, and the most important stuff for people to learn in organizations is not the explicit stuff of rules, procedures, and so forth, but tacit (intuition, expertise, common sense, core competencies, and the like). They further assert that real learning takes place as part of the work itself, not in sterile training environments or in solitary.

Senge (1990) identified five disciplines critical to the development of learning organizations. These disciplines are the defining characteristics of learning organizations that separate them from traditional organizations:

1. Personal mastery
2. Mental models
3. Shared vision
4. Team learning
5. System thinking

Personal mastery involves the acquisition of individual expertise and proficiency through education, formal learning activities, and work experience. Clifton and Nelson (1992) refer to this as total performance of excellence, whereby people exceed all possible expectations and accomplish great things. A recent example of personal mastery was when Mark McGwire of the St. Louis Cardinals hit seventy home runs in the 1998 season, breaking Roger Maris's record of sixty-one, which had stood for thirty-seven years.

Mental models describe one's fundamental worldview, which is reinforced by structures, experiences, cultures, and belief systems. Mental models guide and direct people as they make decisions, and are used to filter ideas and possibilities. Mental models are very difficult to change because they encompass one's values, beliefs, attitudes, and assumptions. According to Boyett and Boyett (1995), shared mental models, such as those relayed by storytelling and cooperative exchanges, support organizational learning by helping employees make sense out of seemingly random events.

Shared vision is the collective perspectives of employees and evolves from their understanding of the organization's mission. In traditional organizations, shared vision is not commonplace, because little or no effort is made to internalize or understand the firm's mission. Shared vision is, however, a cornerstone of learning organizations because leaders, managers, and employees embrace a common perception of learning in order for it the become paramount within the firm. Shared vision also helps organizations allocate financial, physical, and human resources because they are being used to accomplish the same ends.

Team learning allows people to experience things from a myriad of vantage points, enabling them to expand their horizons, deepen their understandings, amplify their perspectives, and develop a better sense of self. Team learning helps employees improve collaboration, communication, and cooperation, as well as view other organizational members as learning resources.

Watkins and Marsick (1993, 99) believe that the building blocks of team learning involve several activities:

- Framing—an initial perception of an issue, a situation, a person, or an object based on past understanding and present input.
- Reframing—transforming that perception into a new understanding or frame.
- Integrating perspectives—resolving conflicts by integrating divergent views into an acceptable understanding without compromise or majority rule.
- Experimenting—an action undertaken to test a hypothesis or to discover something new.
- Crossing boundaries—two or more individuals or teams communicate to achieve a positive end.

Schon (1983) referred to these components as the interaction of action and reflection.

System thinking requires leaders, managers, and employees to think strategically about all aspects of organizational life, which include the organization's role in achieving its business goals and objectives, its mission and strategy, and its structure, culture, and managerial practices. Thus, examining the organizational system to determine connections, influences, pressures, and dysfunctions among the integrated parts of the organization proves helpful (see Chapter 4). Additionally, system thinking requires reflectivity on the part of leaders, managers, and employees for the purpose of improving understanding and action.

Type of Leadership

The leadership found in learning organizations differs dramatically from that of the traditional organization. The leadership styles most common in learning organizations are *transactional* and *transformational* (Figure 1.2). Transactional leadership occurs when leaders help employees identify what must be done to achieve a desired result. Thus, leaders identify what employees want or prefer, and help them achieve levels of performance that result in satisfying rewards (Gibson, Ivancevich, and Donnelley 1997, 313).

A new kind of leader, called transformational, motivates employees to work toward long-term strategic goals instead of short-term self interests, and toward achievement and self-actualization instead of security (Gibson, Ivancevich, and Donnelley 1997, 314). Consequently, transformational leaders inspire and motivate employees to achieve results greater than they originally planned, with as much emphasis on internal rewards as external. Both leadership styles emphasize the importance of learning in everyday interactions.

The very role of leader within the learning organization is that of synergist, who creates an environment in which the whole is greater than the sum of its parts. Consequently, leaders take on the responsibility for creating an esprit de corps unknown in the traditional organization.

Managers assume the role of learning partner, fostering and encouraging employee learning on an ongoing basis. Within true learning organizations, managers readily accept their responsibility for learning application, mastery, reflection, and self-awareness on the part of their employees.

Human resource professionals assume the role of *employee champion* within learning organizations. They advocate a strategy for learning within the firm to improve and maximize learning opportunities.

Employees accept the role of self-directed learner within learning organizations and become the sole owners of knowledge acquisition, application, and reflection. They understand the importance of learning to themselves and the organization.

Although much more implicit than explicit, a team- or project-centered organizational structure prevails in most learning organizations. Learning organizations historically have attempted to reconfigure themselves to foster group and team performance and learning. In many cases, learning organizations do not break down the formal structure of the organization, relying instead on a simple shift in orientation and operations. In other words, the organization does not attempt a radical reengineering of the firm's operations, structure, and culture. As a result of this inability to re-shape important aspects of the firm, the organization fails to focus on learning as a centerpiece of the organization.

Types of Developmental Activities

Two types of developmental activities are most commonly found in the learning organization: *deutero learning* and *action learning* (Marquardt 1996). Deutero and action learning are conscious efforts by individuals to review and reflect upon their actions or those of others (see Chapter 8). To contrast the two types, deutero learning is as much a process of learning about learning, whereas action learning involves working on real problems, focusing on the learning acquired, and actually implementing solutions.

Focus of Developmental Activities

Developmental activities within learning organizations focus on *application* and *reflection*. Application involves using learned information in new and concrete ways, and applying the steps, rules, methods, concepts, principles, laws, and theories on the job. Employees apply what they have learned in everyday activities (Figure 1.3).

The outcome of application on the job is *personal mastery*—defined as a high level of proficiency in one's area of expertise, skill, or subject matter. Learning organizations encourage integration of new knowledge and skills on the job to enhance and improve an individual's proficiency. Thus, practice brings about perfection.

Another critical focus of developmental activities within learning organizations involves *reflection* (Figure 1.3), which can be any of three types (see Chapter 2). Reflection permits individuals to constantly search for new understanding of how and why they did what they did or believe what they believe. The outcome of reflection is *self-awareness,* that is, gaining a greater cognizance of who one is and why one behaves as he or she does.

Learning organizations focus on application and reflection to generate personal mastery and self-awareness. Furthermore, learning is a prerequisite to the developmental activities of the learning organization. That is, a traditional organization evolves into a learning one when its people begin to utilize all components and respective outcomes from knowledge acquisition through and including self-awareness (Figure 1.3).

DEVELOPMENTAL ORGANIZATIONS

In a recent work (Gilley, Boughton, and Maycunich 1999, 190–191), we describe the evolution from learning organization to the developmental organization:

> Over the past decade a philosophical shift has occurred through acceptance of the learning organization. Many are touting its methods, advantages, and benefits, having concluded that the learning organization is the answer to organizational change and development. We agree that learning is a prerequisite to development, and that it makes sense to focus on the aspects, principles, and policies required to transform a traditional organizational to a learning organization. However, we refuse to accept the notion that the learning organization represents the evolutionary pinnacle of organizational transformation.
>
> We believe that the next evolutionary step in organizational life is that of a *developmental organization.* A developmental organization focuses all of its synergy and resources on enhancing the collective talents of its employees for the purpose of better serving customers in an efficient, effective manner. Ours is a strongly focused philosophical shift that must be made if organizations plan to continue the long, challenging journey toward organizational success.
>
> The transformation from traditional or learning organization into a developmental organization is as much philosophical as pragmatic. In develop-

mental organizations, leaders philosophically recognize that members of the entire organization must be involved in the realization of its mission, vision, and goals for all to enjoy prosperity. Pragmatically, developmental organizations will not be successful unless leaders, managers, supervisors, and employees collectively blend their talents toward achievement of strategic business goals and objectives. Improper treatment and utilization of human resources inhibits performance outputs. Organizational efficiency and effectiveness cannot be achieved without enhancing the skills, expertise, talents, and intellectual capital of all organizational members.

Organizations must embrace and facilitate development to improve their competitive readiness in the marketplace. The organization requires reshaping to foster development and must continually evolve to meet strategic challenges and market conditions. In short, developing a continuous organizational renewal capability helps businesses meet ever-changing market fluctuations, challenges, and conditions.

We recognize that organizations cannot develop people; only people can develop themselves. Moreover, the term "developmental organizations" really means to foster an environment in which employee growth and development is paramount, that is, to create conditions in which employees are encouraged, rewarded, and appreciated for their individual growth and development. Furthermore, the leaders of developmental organizations subscribe to a philosophy that demonstrates their appreciation for employees' contributions—a philosophy that reveals a lifelong commitment to employees and a dedication to their well-being.

Type of Leadership

In Chapter 3, we discuss in greater detail the type of leadership required to make the transition from learning organization to developmental organization. The characteristics commonly found in transactional and transformational leaders are similar to the characteristics needed in the developmental organization. We further focus on the need for a developmental champion within the organization to promote the developmental philosophy and orientation required to truly transform an organization to the highest plane. Developmental organizations require developmental leadership (Figure 1.2) that embraces the following ten principles:

1. Principle of personal accountability
2. Principle of trustworthiness
3. Principle of employee advocacy
4. Principle of employee self-esteeming
5. Principle of performance partnership
6. Principle of organizational performance improvement
7. Principle of effective communications
8. Principle of organizational consistency
9. Principle of holistic thinking
10. Principle of organization subordination

Chapter 4 will examine the organizational system (leadership, culture, structure, work climate, and managerial practices, policies, and procedures) required in a developmental organization, which is best characterized as functional. "Functional organizational system" refers to breaking work down into logical business functions so that projects and activities can be shared across traditional departmental lines to promote efficiency and effectiveness. In that chapter, we will detail the type of business partnerships and relationships necessary to bring about a functional orientation within the organization.

In Chapter 5, we discuss the emerging roles and responsibilities of executives, managers, and employees within developmental organizations. Chapter 6 addresses the same topics for human resource professionals. Leaders must assume the role of holistic thinker within the developmental organization to realize visionary strategic and critical reflective thinking skills. These skills are necessary for organizational renewal and competitive readiness (see Chapter 3).

Within the developmental organization, managers must make the transition from the traditional role of controller or gatekeeper to performance coach. As performance coaches, managers serve as trainers, mentors, career counselors, and performance confronters. Each role is vital in ongoing employee development (see Chapter 5).

Employees must make the transition from self-directed learners to enhancers of development. As developmental enhancers, employees transcend the learning aspects of self-direction to embody the continuous growth and development of developmental organizations. Employees take responsibility for more than mere learning—for higher skills such as reflection, renewal, and growth. Within the employee's role, a distinct difference exists between learning and developmental.

Finally, human resource professionals are required to make one of the greatest transitions within the developmental organization—from traditional program provider to organizational change agent. Change agents facilitate modifications necessary within the business to ensure continuous organizational renewal (see Chapter 6).

Types of Developmental Activities

Within the developmental organization, the most common type of developmental activity is *developmental learning*, which incorporates one's ability to acquire new knowledge and skills and to comprehend, transfer, and integrate them on the job. Further, an individual then analyzes, synthesizes, and evaluates the outcomes of performance, enabling him or her to change and continually grow (Figure 1.3). The result is new meaning and improved organizational renewal and performance capacity.

Organizations utilizing performance growth and development plans, further examined in Chapter 5, have incorporated the interventions necessary to bring about renewal capacity.

Focus of Developmental Activities

The primary focus of developmental activities is to bring about change within an individual (Figure 1.3). Change occurs as a result of gaining new insight, awareness, and understanding of oneself through critical reflection. We define the outcome of change, called "new meaning," as reconfiguration and understanding of oneself. Once an individual changes, whether slightly or significantly, he or she garners a new self-image that filters current realities through an understanding of the person's present state. That is, change that brings about new meaning alters an individual to the point that the person can never return to his or her original state. Consequently, once new meaning has occurred, individuals will desire to change the way they interact on a daily basis. This permanent change propels individual employees to a higher plane. Continually evolving employees fuel organizational evolution.

Another focus of developmental activities is on continuous growth and development (Figure 1.3). Continuous growth is a process of never-ending expansion, taking into account new and different things, the outcomes of which are constant growth are improved renewal and performance capacity. As an individual continues to grow and develop, he or she constantly renews, improving the reservoir of performance capabilities that can be drawn upon when needed. On a macro level, the final outcome is enhanced organizational renewal and performance capacity. As each employee improves his or her personal renewal and performance capacity, the organization's aggregate renewal and performance capacity also increases. Consequently, the business enjoys enhanced competitive readiness and the ability to constantly grow and develop, avoiding the plateau periods of maturity as well as the slippery slopes of decline.

CONCLUSION

It is not enough for organizations to adopt new learning or to employ critical reflective activities. Enlightened firms engage strategies that transform them into developmental organizations, the final step of organizational evolution. The transformation requires organizations to alter their priorities, assumptions, and orientations while instituting new leadership styles, rules, and responsibilities. Organizations must also reconfigure and redesign their culture, structure, managerial practices, and work climate (organizational system) to advocate continuous development. Finally, organizations must embrace change and continuous growth to bring about new meaning and enhanced individual renewal and performance capacity.

When a developmental organization follows these steps, it enhances learning, which in turn increases comprehension, application, and practice. The result is new mastery. Individuals then critically reflect, enhance their self-awareness, and promote change while producing new meaning. New meaning leads to continuous growth and, ultimately, improved renewal and performance capacity. Thus, the cycle of personal renewal is complete.

Adoption of the development approach allows organizations to redefine, reconstruct, and reinvent themselves over and over again. Doing so allows businesses to evolve from the learning organization to the developmental organization.

CHAPTER 2

The Developmental Organization Blueprint

Most organizations desire lasting, meaningful change, the type that helps them avoid decline or continually improve their competitive readiness. Unfortunately, few are capable of achieving it. Many simply go through the motions necessary to bring about change while simultaneously hoping that its catalyst disappears.

Although much has been written about the importance of change and its relationship to organizational viability, occasionally change simply does not work. For example, unfocused, unplanned, superficial change serves as a "cotton candy" approach to addressing real operational difficulties. Although many organizations recognize the need for change, few are able to sustain successful change efforts. According to Ulrich (1997, 157), there are ten reasons why change is not effective: (1) failure to tie change to strategy; (2) viewing change as a fad or quick fix; (3) a short-term perspective; (4) political realities that undermine change; (5) grandiose expectations versus a goal of simple success; (6) inflexible change design; (7) lack of leadership about change; (8) lack of measurable, tangible results; (9) fear of the unknown; and (10) inability to mobilize commitment to sustain change.

According to Patterson (1997), many organizations fail to achieve desired business results because of their inability to adjust to ever-changing conditions. He further contends that many organizations are unable to adapt to change because they maintain faulty assumptions related to change activities. One such assumption is that organizations are rationally functioning systems that adjust strategically to changing conditions. This is simply not the case; organizations operate in their own best interest, often sacrificing long-term, systematic change (which can ultimately improve organizational effectiveness, competitiveness, and profitability) in favor of immediate or short-term results.

Another faulty assumption lies with leadership's belief that organizational change can occur without creating conflict in the system. These unrealistic beliefs increase expectations among employees that cannot be achieved. Ultimately, such assumptions are demoralizing, creating long-term negative effects on employee morale and performance. Consequently, employees are not motivated to grow, develop, or actively pursue career opportunities. When these conditions exist, the type of organizational change required to remain competitiveness is in jeopardy.

Organizational leaders can overcome this dilemma by applying two important tools: the *change process model* and the *developmental organization blueprint*. The change process model provides organizational leaders with a consistent approach for change management and decision-making, while the developmental organization blueprint is a comprehensive tool for creating a developmental organization. Both tools enable organizations to facilitate change and improve its implementation. For best results, these tools should be used in combination, for example, using the change process model to guide decision making while implementing the developmental organization blueprint. By doing so, organizational leaders improve the application of the developmental organization blueprint and ensure long-term success.

THE CHANGE PROCESS MODEL

We believe that for substantial change to occur, a firm must adopt the change process model, which consists of five activities: identifying as-

FIGURE 2.1   Change process model

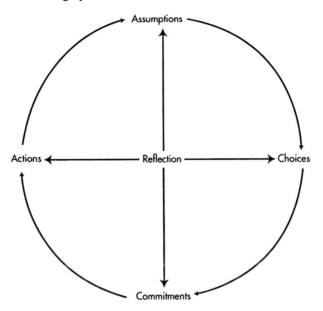

sumptions, analyzing choices, making commitments, selecting appropriate actions, and engaging in critical reflection (Figure 2.1). Additionally, the model guides leaders in the quest for valuable activities that enhance organizational renewal.

Identifying Assumptions

In order to genuinely precipitate change, organizations must first identify their assumptions. According to Brookfield (1992, 13), one way of thinking about assumptions is to consider them as "taken for granted" beliefs that one has about reality. Another way is to view assumptions as the rules of thumb that guide one's actions. A third way involves seeing assumptions as a common set of beliefs and conventional wisdom that one invokes when asked why one did something or why one thinks or believes what is believed.

Schwinn (1996) believes that assumptions are an explicit set of conditions, principles, ethics, and expectations taken to be true about the basis for choosing actions and studying the consequences that follow. In other words, assumptions are the anchors to which most decisions are linked. Therefore, it is critically important to identify one's assumptions about circumstances or events before engaging in change activities. Unless the assumptions are isolated and understood, individuals or organizations will have difficulty fostering and accepting change. This is especially important when adopting a radical change such as organizational transformation. Once assumptions have been identified, it is easy to conclude why organizations make the choices, commitments, and actions that they do.

Analyzing Choices

Analyzing organizational choices remains one of the best ways to understand the decision-making process. Doing so allows us to carefully construct a rationale for the decisions made. Although apparently a simple concept and straightforward activity, understanding why organizations come to the conclusions they do has invaluable benefits. The process of analyzing choices includes examining how decisions are made, who participates in the decision-making process, what criteria are used to reach a definitive outcome, and what consequences follow the choices made. Once choices have been analyzed, organizations are in a better position to determine whether they have made decisions that brought about desired change.

Making Commitments

When assumptions have been identified and choices analyzed, organizations can then make commitments that bring about real, lasting change. Making commitments may require organizations to choose between two desirable outcomes. When confronted with such a situation, employees and businesses must determine which of the positive outcomes they desire most and to which they are willing to allocate important financial and human resources over a long period.

Occasionally, both the business and its employees are confronted with a decision between a positive and a negative outcome. This decision is often the easiest commitment to make. Regrettably, some situations require organizations to commit to one of two negatives, each possessing little or no perceived value. Under these conditions, organizations must minimize their risk and commit to a choice that they can live with, both in the short and long term.

Selecting Appropriate Action

Organizations take concrete actions to help satisfy their assumptions, choices, and commitments. Selecting appropriate actions may include the allocation of financial and human resources, the restructuring of the organization, the identification of developmental strategies, and so forth, all of which enable individuals and organizations to make changes designed to bring about desired results.

Engaging in Critical Reflection

Perhaps the most important activity of the change process model is engaging in critical reflection. Critical reflection extracts meaning from what is previously unknown or unrecognized, and acts on differences between prior and current expectations (Schwinn 1996).

Organizations engaged in critical reflection are attempting to understand why they have made certain decisions. Critical reflection occurs at the completion of each of the previous four activities (Figure 2.1) and serves as a process by which individuals and organizations discover new meaning regarding deliberate decisions or actions. Killion and Todnem (1991, 14) describe critical reflection as the "practice of analyzing one's own actions, decisions, or products by focusing on the processes involved." It is a means for individuals and organizations to develop a greater level of self-awareness of the nature and impact of their performance decisions, providing additional opportunities for professional growth and development (Preskill 1996). In short, critical reflection enhances a person's awareness of why he or she acted and how to improve upon that action.

Saban, Killion, and Greene (1994) have identified three types of critical reflection. The first, *reflection in action,* occurs when leaders, managers, and employees observe themselves acting out certain thoughts and actions, similar to an out-of-body experience. Reflection in action occurs when people view themselves from the outside, to determine what they are doing from a different perspective. The second—and most common—type of critical reflection is *reflection on action.* It occurs when individuals replay a situation in their minds, allowing for review, critique, and reliving of the experience, as well as for the formulation of opinions and judgments regarding their behavior. Reflection on action focuses on the past. The third type, *reflection for action*, predicts how organizations will use what they have learned from experience. According to Preskill (1996), reflection for action focuses on the future, allowing organizations to better plan and sculpt change opportunities.

Understanding why organizations do what they do remains essential, regardless of the type of critical reflection employed. Critical reflection, a quality improvement step in the change process, enables organizations to truly understand, enhance, and embrace change.

Ensuring the long-term effects of change is a crucial by-product of identifying assumptions, analyzing choices, making commitments, selecting appropriate actions, and critical reflection. These critical steps are extremely useful when building a developmental organization.

THE DEVELOPMENTAL ORGANIZATION BLUEPRINT

A plethora of books, articles, and newsletters promulgate the importance of financial models and asset allocation, but few if any organizations can adequately implement such strategies without a talented pool of human resources. For this reason, no organization will maximize its success in today's global economy without an appropriate human resource strategy that transcends mere acquisition of additional learning (even as a critical job component). Not only must businesses move from a reservoir of knowledge to that advocated by proponents of the learning organization, but they must pragmatically implement that knowledge to enhance employees' continuous growth and development.

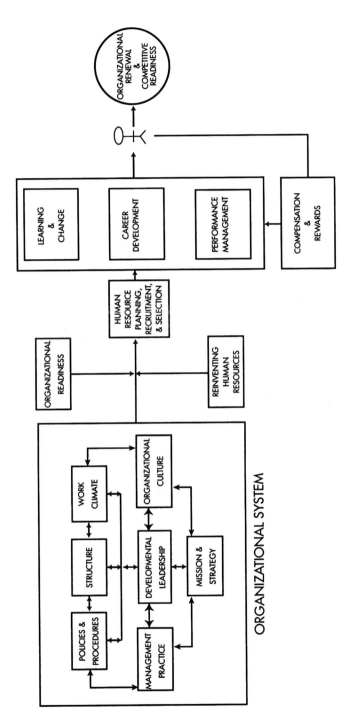

FIGURE 2.2   The developmental organization blueprint

The evolution from traditional to learning to developmental organization can be a difficult journey—one that requires a "blueprint" to expedite the transition and ensure that it is being built correctly and can withstand the harshest of corporate battles. The developmental organization blueprint is such a planning tool (Figure 2.2). It consists of nine interrelated components:

- developmental leadership (Chapter 3)
- organizational system (Chapter 4)
- organizational readiness (Chapter 5)
- reinventing human resources (Chapter 6)
- human resource planning, recruitment, and selection (Chapter 7)
- learning and change (Chapter 8)
- career development strategies (Chapter 9)
- performance management (Chapter 10)
- compensation and rewards strategies (Chapter 11)

The first four components are preconditions to the developmental organization and serve as its foundation. The final five are state-of-the-art human resource practices common in most firms. Although every organization deploys these human resource practices, it is their utilization, unique configuration, and application that produces the synergy necessary to evolve to the developmental level.

Figure 2.2 illustrates the relationships between each of these nine components. The ultimate outcome of the developmental organization is enhanced organizational renewal and competitive readiness.

FOUNDATIONS OF THE DEVELOPMENTAL ORGANIZATION

The four components prerequisite to developmental organizations are developmental leadership, the organizational system, organizational readiness, and the reinventing of human resources.

By prerequisite, we mean preconditions, alignments, changes, or considerations necessary for a successful transformation to the developmental organization. Unless an organization is willing to (1) adopt new leadership techniques, (2) reconfigure its organizational system, (3) reexamine employees' critical roles and responsibilities, and (4) reinvent its human resources, it cannot transform to this higher level. Consequently, these four preconditions must be addressed before an organization can begin its evolutionary journey.

Developmental Leadership

The first step of the developmental organization blueprint is identifying the type of leadership required for transformation (Figure 2.2). In Chapter 3, we examine the role of organizational leaders and the relationship between organizational renewal and leadership; we identify organizational obstacles that must be removed prior to transformation. Ten essential principles of developmental leadership are also outlined. We look at the outcomes of developmental leadership and the importance of leadership in transformation.

Organizational System

Chapter 4 outlines the organizational system (culture, structure, managerial practices, work climate, and so forth) essential to fostering developmental organizations, examining each carefully and identifying critical ingredients for businesses to manifest developmental environments. Although components of the organizational system are not foreign terms to most, their relationships and interplay are often misunderstood. Cultural components, structure, and the integral relationship between jobs, managerial practices, policies and procedures, and work climate all provide opportunities for developmental improvement.

Organizational Readiness

The next step in building a developmental organization is an examination of a business's readiness for the transformation process (Figure 2.2). To do so, an organization must critically examine the roles and responsibilities of executives, managers, and employees. In Chapter 5, we explore the emerging roles and responsibilities of key players within developmental organizations, outlining individual obligations of each member and defining the respective purpose that each plays in the evolutionary process. An organization's readiness to proceed is directly proportionate to the willingness of its critical players to change and adopt new roles and responsibilities.

Reinventing Human Resources

In Chapter 6, we examine the need for reinventing human resources, which is predicated by the ever-increasing demands of organizations, their customers and stakeholders, and competing organizations. Such a redesign requires human resource professionals to undertake new and exciting roles and responsibilities. Thus, human resources will be an equal contributor to organizational success, which is often attributed to other functions such as marketing, finance, and research and development.

STATE-OF-THE-ART HUMAN RESOURCE PRACTICES

In the book of Ecclesiastes are found these telling words from Solomon: ". . . and there is no new thing under the sun" (Eccles. 1:9). Solomon's statement reveals that the solutions to an organization's performance problems or competitive difficulties lie in the things we already know how to do or in the solutions that we have tried in the past. Simply stated, solutions to organizational problems exist within a firm's own experiences. To demonstrate our point, let us journey to any international conference in human resources, where we will witness an overwhelming effort by hundreds, even thousands, of consultants to solve complex problems with simple, painless, often instantaneous solutions. These solutions are packaged in the most technologically advanced way, consisting of colored brochures and materials. They are presented with enough emotion and enthusiasm to make an evangelist blush. Wrapped in the newest, fanciest, attention-grabbing slogans and names, the solutions simply sparkle. Sounds great? There is only one problem—most of these solutions simply do not work. They are like the many dietary programs being advertised today that promise immediate results without exercise or a healthy, sensible diet and thus fail miserably. Such solutions neither address the serious issues facing firms nor help them solve their problems. Like cotton candy and funnel cakes, they taste great, have no nutritional value, and, as if that were not bad enough, give you cavities.

Organizations do not need "creative, innovative, simple, and painless" solutions that promise guaranteed success with little or no effort or commitment. What organizations do need are serious, workable solutions to their problems, ones that will help them improve their competitive readiness and enhance organizational renewal. Organizations need to do as Solomon says—return to proven, commonsense, even boring solutions that help them get the results they need. While these solutions are not spectacular techniques with cute names and slogans, they are at the heart of achieving results through people. They have been with us for decades and have proven their worth, but have been overlooked as organizations attempts to find the magic potion that will cure all ills. These solutions are simple human resource practices common to virtually every organization:

- human resource planning, recruiting, and selection
- learning and change
- career development strategies
- performance management
- compensation and rewards

Certainly, organizations must offer state-of-the-art products and services while serving a well-defined mission, vision, and strategy in order to bring about financial success. Equally important are human resource practices enabling organizations to have the right people in the right places at the right time. Consequently, developmental organizations cannot evolve without implementing state-of-the-art human resource practices.

Although these practices are not new, they work especially well when organizations are committed to execute them efficiently. Firms must be enthusiastic about their application, be dedicated to their success, and be willing to implement these practices passionately and forcefully. One important difference today is that these practices must be state-of-the-art. That means they must be *best practices*, executed at the highest possible level.

Each of these human resource practices has, at some point, been perceived to be an organizational panacea, although no singular practice has brought about permanent change. When these five human resource practices are performed at their highest level of proficiency and appropriately combined, they transcend organizational barriers and internal resistance to change, enabling organizations to enhance their competitive readiness and improve their renewal capabilities.

Human Resource Planning, Recruiting, and Selection

Organizations can and do acquire talent on the open market, a tactic requiring a comprehensive, well-designed human resource planning strategy that maintains organizational continuity (Chapter 7). This focus identifies an optimal number of employees along three planes: today's human resource needs, short-term requirements, and long-term obligations. Human resource planning includes job analysis, career planning, and other activities designed to identify what is best for the organization as a whole (Figure 2.2). The input and recommendations of employees are welcome, particularly in their areas of expertise, although organizational leaders continue to make final decisions regarding planning activities.

Another component of the acquisition strategy is recruiting and selection, a science in and of itself. Determining how to obtain essential employees and assessing where they might be in the future takes tremendous planning and thought. Once human resource needs have been identified, the selection of the most competent, capable employees begins. Developmental organizations comprehend that recruiting and selection is not short-term oriented, but concerned instead with the firm's future performance needs. Employee selection for the right reasons is critical, followed by integration within the organization and development to such an extent that they become positive, contributing business members.

The pure developmental approach to obtaining optimal numbers of qualified employees constitutes the remaining four human resource practices (learning and change, career development, performance management, and compensation and rewards) within the developmental organization blueprint.

Learning and Change Process

Developmental organizations clearly understand, encourage, and support learning and change actions that bring about individual employee improvement and growth. These actions include self-directed learning events, action learning, and renewal capacity approaches (Figure 2.2). The primary purpose of this human resource practice is to improve employee knowledge, skills, and attitudes, making certain these are transferred to the job and integrated into an individual's daily work life. Chapter 8 examines the various phases and principles guiding learning and change, along with their contributions to learning renewal that enhance employee growth and development.

Career Development Strategies

Career development is a long-range strategy useful to employees and employers, providing workers with a professional road map while enabling organizations to prepare for a future punctuated with an optimal number of talented employees (Chapter 9). Career development helps employees identify their career interests, set career goals, and take a proactive, long-range approach to their professional lives. These activities combine employee goals with appropriate career plans, balancing worker interest with the organization's need for a certain number of employees available at specific times to ensure competitive readiness. The ultimate career decision, however, rests with employees, who bear the responsibility of planning their own careers. Management's role is to mentor, guide, and develop staff. Consequently, businesses must forge partnerships that enable managers and employees to work in harmony on successful career development activities.

Performance Management Process

As we asserted in an earlier book, every organization faces the challenge of developing management systems that view employees as its greatest asset. To meet this performance challenge, firms must develop and implement a management system that improves performance and competitiveness. This process must also incorporate an organizationwide approach that combines the entire performance improvement process into one cohesive operating system. Developmental performance management links performance to compensation and rewards, strategic business goals and objectives, and client needs and expectations (Chapter 10).

Developmental organizations embrace performance management processes that enable employees to become their greatest asset. When managers function as performance coaches, they become trainers, confronters, mentors, and counselors, providing positive feedback and reinforcement to improve skills and competencies that ultimately enhance overall employee performance.

Performance management functions as an integral part of a comprehensive development strategy, although too few organizations subscribe to this philosophy. Hence, the business world overflows with mediocre, stagnant, or failing organizations that stubbornly or ignorantly overlook their employees' potential. We believe that well-designed and well-executed performance management provides an excellent vehicle for promoting continuous employee and organizational growth and development.

Compensation and Rewards

Developmental organizations attribute their success to their employees, compensating and rewarding employees for their achievements, growth, and development (Figure 2.2). As a result, employee growth and development, performance improvement, and compensation and rewards form a trinity designed to bring about organizational success.

Barriers to Creating a Developmental Organization

Organizational neglect of employee development is nothing new. Most businesses fail to adequately plan for their workers' long-term developmental needs or incorporate them into strategic human resource planning. Consequently, many organizations have no strategy focused on long-term career development and performance enhancement. Obviously, these firms are short-term oriented when it comes to developing their employees.

A number of circumstances prevent organizations from developing their employees. First, many fail to value their workers' contributions, skills, and abilities. As a result, employees are treated as disposable resources that, when used up, are discarded.

Second, many organizations embrace and demonstrate the belief that employees are easy to replace. This attitude retards organizational responsibility to mentor and develop workers, killing morale while limiting loyalty and commitment.

Third, many firms' practices encourage unproductive, unprofessional, or incompetent managers. We call this phenomenon managerial malpractice (Gilley and Boughton 1996). Managers should be selected for their ability to secure results through people. When this does not occur, development is severely limited or nonexistent.

Fourth, ineffective leadership leads to inadequate developmental strategies. In Chapter 3, we discuss the principles of developmental leadership that aid selection and implementation of appropriate developmental strategies.

Fifth, many organizations maintain poor human resource practices that prevent them from adequately developing their people. We examine this dilemma more closely in Chapters 7 through 11.

Sixth, organizational success often creates developmental blindness. When organizations achieve desired business results without a great deal of difficulty they often become overconfident. Overconfidence leads firms to believe that they are invincible. Their leaders are not receptive to new ideas or ways of improving performance and quality, believing instead in the organization's invincibility. Overconfident businesses tend to relax and take it easy—a fatal mistake against guaranteed long-term competitive readiness. We have all watched sports teams coast with a big lead during the second half, only to be upset in the final waning moments of the ball game.

Seventh, many organizations possess a client-oriented philosophy. Maintaining that customers are their number one priority, these organizations exert all their energies and resources to meet client needs. While we believe that this is certainly a noble strategy—strongly concurring with the notion of meeting or exceeding client expectations—this emphasis is misguided. An organization's greatest asset is its employees. Carlson, in his classic book, *Moments of Truth* (1987), believes that no organization is capable of superior customer service without hardworking, dedicated employees who adhere to and strongly believe in the organization's vision and mission. Employees tend to treat customers the way they themselves are treated. Poor treatment begets the same. Those treated with dignity, honesty, concern, and respect pass it on to the customer, resulting in improved employee–customer relations and satisfaction. Enhancing customer service proves impossible without an adequate, long-term, strategic developmental strategy, one that communicates and demonstrates the importance of employees to the achievement of the organization's vision and mission.

Additional barriers prevent creation of a developmental organization, including the following:

1. Lack of an inclusive problem-solving approach
2. Neglecting to incorporate an organization-wide diversity strategy
3. Failure to link developmental activities and strategies to the organization's business goals and objectives
4. Inability to deal with self-defeating or dysfunctional behaviors

Lack of an Inclusive Problem-Solving Approach

No one, or leader, is an island. He who stands alone falls alone. We do not plan to fail; we fail to plan. Words of wisdom abound, all tribute to personal or organizational failure at one time or another. History reminds us that success is not guaranteed, particularly when individuals or small groups attempt to wield power or make decisions without the support of their organizations.

Excluding employees from the decision-making process wastes valuable talent, breeding mediocrity as employees focus on tasks instead of creative, collaborative, problem solving. Misguided management rarely considers employees as talented, creative contributors to organizational success. Executives focused on seclusion ignore worker concern for the firm's well-being or competitiveness in the marketplace.

Embracing an inclusive approach builds the foundation for continued and continuous development on the part of individuals and the organization. Employee participation at all levels yields a bountiful harvest of insight and imagination, strengthening teamwork, commitment, and organizational focus. Inclusion may be as simple as listening to employee ideas and implementing creative solutions accordingly or acknowledging their ability to solve job-related problems.

Another obstacle to inclusion arises when managers only pay attention to employees with extensive experience. This approach ignores the fresh, unbiased perspectives offered by new employees. Enveloping new employees in an environment of respect and dignity, in which they are valued for their input, fosters synergistic relationships, continuous growth, and development. Caution is required, however, as "newbies" are often considered "outsiders." New employee safety must be assured prior to creating a comfort level that encourages honest exchange of information and ideas relevant to organizational issues.

Neglecting to Incorporate an Organizationwide Diversity Strategy

Organizations waste millions of dollars on ineffective diversity programs that fail to make a difference. Adopting an inclusive approach incorporates open, honest discussions on issues involving fear in the workplace (e.g., AIDS, racism). Since fear occurs at all organizational levels, no one should be excluded. Failure to incorporate an organizationwide diversity strategy hinders the firm's ability to evolve from the traditional to the developmental levels. Management participation and support sends a powerful message throughout the firm.

Organizational diversity should be celebrated! Individual differences make us interesting, revealing areas of specialization, creativity, and unique success. When properly nourished, these differences lead to organizational initiatives that may bloom into new ideas, products, or efficiencies that capture the imagination (and potential customers). Weaving diversity into the organization's fabric enables employees to share their varied experiences and talents without fear of repercussions. The goal is not merely a tolerant workforce accepting of each other's respective differences, but excited, creative employees who challenge one another and demand excellence. This in and of itself demonstrates a developmental strategy.

Failure to Link Developmental Activities and Strategies to the Organization's Business Goals and Objectives

Unless developmental activities and strategies help firms achieve their business goals and objectives, they are of little consequence. To be of value, developmental activities and strategies must be linked to specific business processes as well as organization incentives (Brinkerhoff and Gill, 1994). Developmentally oriented managers and human resource professionals design and implement developmental activities and strategies that strive toward these goals:

- improving business processes
- achieving business goals and objectives
- improving organizational performance capacity and capability
- improving competitive readiness
- enhancing organizational renewal
- upgrading employee skills
- fostering a developmental environment
- encouraging continuous employee growth and development
- creating a reservoir of talented and gifted employees
- encouraging employee commitment

- improving performance, productivity, and quality
- creating organizational synergy
- enhancing developmental readiness
- encouraging togetherness
- advancing continuous lifelong learning
- encouraging organizational unity

When these outcomes have been achieved, developmental activities and strategies have been properly linked to desired business results.

Inability to Deal with Self-Defeating or Dysfunctional Behaviors

Hardy and Schwartz (1996) contend that fear causes self-defeating, dysfunctional behavior. They further believe that organizational fears are emotional responses to outside stimuli that are not filtered through the organization's core values and principles. Consequently, organizations are often reactionary (responding without strategically thinking about consequences), engaging in counterproductive strategies without considering their appropriateness.

Dysfunctional, self-defeating organizations deny their ailment by minimizing the consequences of their actions or blaming scapegoats. Hardy and Schwartz maintain that organizations face two types of fears: realistic and unrealistic. Realistic fears can be managed productively by avoiding overactive, counterproductive responses to unknown or unsubstantiated perceptions. Realistic fears are based on fact and are not destructive or paranoid organizational self-talk. Unrealistic fears have no concrete foundation, often resulting from insecurity or paranoia. Unrealistic fears prove destructive when firms use them to avoid implementing performance improvement and development strategies.

When organizations demonstrate self-defeating, dysfunctional behavior, healthy, capable employees resist damaging policies and procedures. If these persist, workers become exhausted and eventually flee the firm, leaving less capable employees to further the organization's mission. Less capable employees frequently hide within the organization by avoiding conflict or adapting to an unhealthy environment. Passive behaviors do little to facilitate organizational change or improvement, but do enable many employees to survive counterproductive, pathological environments. Moreover, less talented employees become the "organizational bench" while better performers move on to healthier environments where their potential is appreciated and can be maximized.

Overcoming self-defeating and dysfunctional organizational behavior is a difficult task. Developmental organizations avoid unnecessary, negative self-talk by focusing on realistic, supportive, documentable information. In this way, organizations avoid reliance upon unsubstantiated data or unrealistic fears. Another approach involves reflection on organizational decisions and actions to determine whether they are beneficial. Sound businesses isolate and ban actions that fail to produce desired results.

Finally, developmental organizations always remember their pathway to success, avoiding the crippling laws of fast forgetting, slow learning, and organizational stupidity. Some organizations experience fast forgetting when their perceived success causes them to forget the basic management and organizational principles that were instrumental in bringing about financial and operational success. These businesses become short-term oriented, make unwise decisions in an effort to maximize profitability, and fail to appreciate the contributions and sacrifices made by employees for the good of the organization. Fast forgetting prevents organizations from investing in their people or creating developmental environments conducive to long-term success. In short, in their attempt to maximize financial gain or improved market share, organizations forget how they became successful, thus prompting self-defeating, dysfunctional behavior.

Many organizations are slow to learn from their mistakes and are consequently doomed to repeat them. As we detailed previously (Gilley, Boughton, and Maycunich 1999, 204), slow learning occurs when leaders and managers fail to understand the contribution of their decisions and actions toward organizational shortfalls. Lack of comprehension of the conditions that led to crisis situations destines organizations to repeat their mistakes. Typically, many organizations try to minimize losses by denying the situation or affixing blame on others. As a result, they demonstrate self-defeating and dysfunctional behaviors, which results in high absenteeism, high turnover, rising costs, and paranoid work environments.

Organizational stupidity, the worst sin of all, occurs when firms repeat the same decisions, tasks, or activities over and over again, expecting different results. Organizations repeatedly bang their heads against the wall, each time surprised that it hurts. The logical solution is to simply stop doing what is painful. Yet organizations stubbornly insist on repeating behaviors that produce consistently negative results. This exemplifies classic self-defeating and dysfunctional behavior.

Making the transition to developmental organizations requires a cognizance of the importance of people in the success equation; avoidance of self-defeating and dysfunctional behaviors by breaking the cycles of fast forgetting, slow learning, and organizational stupidity; and realization of when fears are realistic versus unrealistic, so that healthy fears may be managed. Following these positive behaviors focuses organizations on a developmental perspective that ultimately transforms the firm, causing it to rely on employees and encourage investment in their ever-increasing abilities. Thus, a developmental organization is created.

BENEFITS OF THE DEVELOPMENTAL ORGANIZATION

Developmental organizations and their employees enjoy several benefits foreign to traditional firms and learning organizations. Some of the benefits are listed below.

Organizational Benefits	*Employee Benefits*
• dynamic, proactive environment	• dynamic, proactive environment
• qualified employees	• personal and professional growth/lifelong learning
• inspired employee commitment	• high satisfaction

Organizational Benefits	*Employee Benefits*
• synergy	• greater involvement/participation
• achieved goals and objectives	• equality of opportunity
• increased employee productivity/ championship performance	• improved self-esteem
• continuous and rapid growth	• greater compensation and rewards
• improved succession planning and career pathing	• broadened entrepreneurial spirit and environment
• enhanced organizational capability	• organizational renewal and competitive readiness
• developmental readiness	• overcoming employee depression

Organizational Benefits

The preceding list of benefits is certainly not all-inclusive. Further, the benefits to the organization will ultimately benefit employees, and vice versa.

Dynamic, Proactive Environment. Developmental firms are proactive, as opposed to reactive, regarding market competitiveness, organizational change, and developmental activities. The developmental approach provides businesses and employees with problem-solving skills that help them develop the ability to identify problems, gather and analyze information, identify and select alternatives, and implement solutions.

Developmental organizations embrace an entrepreneurial spirit that allows them to remain ahead of the competition. They learn to solve problems before they become insurmountable. Besides anticipating and addressing future issues, organizations avoid costly mistakes and time-consuming errors.

Furthermore, changing the roles and responsibilities of executives, managers, employees, and human resource professionals permits them to identify the firm's strategic direction and its strengths, weaknesses, opportunities, and threats (SWOT analysis). Aligning key player duties with SWOT analysis focuses on self-reflection and proactive, long-term decision making designed to guarantee the firm's growth, development, and future viability. The developmental environment exemplifies a culture supportive of change and the vitality of empowered individuals and teams driven to succeed both personally and professionally.

Qualified Employees. Organizations benefit by creating a developmental system that produces qualified, high-caliber people who enable the organization to accomplish its strategic business goals and objectives. This system provides the most appropriate career development interventions and organizational development opportunities to help the firm perform at the highest possible level, now and in the future.

An appropriate mix of talented, experienced, capable employees maintains the business's competitive position. Since recruiting talent for all positions poses an unrealistic undertaking, developmental firms rely on managers, in cooperation with human resource professionals, to develop employee knowledge, skills, and attitudes.

Inspired Employee Commitment. Developmental organizations view their employees as valuable, contributing team members—truly their greatest assets. Individuals treated with respect and dignity while allowed to act as owners feel and exhibit commitment, loyalty, and dedication to their supervisors, leaders, and managers—in essence, to the organization and its mission.

Synergy. Working together, developmental organizations and their employees create a conceptual and functional "whole" that far exceeds the capabilities of its individual parts operating separately. Developmental firms exude teamwork via cooperative and mutually beneficial strategies that create win–win situations for all. The result? Cooperative, supportive environments devoid of power struggles, internal competitions, or self-serving individuals or teams that inhibit aggregate performance.

Achieved Goals and Objectives.   Organizations achieve strategic goals and objectives through developmental activities that allow them to enhance their competitive readiness and profitability. These actions begin with leaders, managers, and employees committed to personal, professional, and organizational improvement. Continued individual growth, development, reflection, and renewal leads to the same in organizations, the way a rising tide raises all boats.

Increased Employee Productivity/Championship Performance.   Developmental organizations provide opportunities and support for employee excellence by virtue of their very philosophy and actions. Advocating personal growth and development as their primary motive demonstrates developmental firms' commitment to their greatest asset—their employees. In return, employees are able to reach their performance peaks—basking in the warmth of supportive, collaborative, nurturing, healthy environments.

Identifying critical competencies required to produce exceptional results (performance outcomes) is yet another benefit of developmental organizations. Setting standards for outputs and designing improvement activities enrich performance, allowing employees to function at championship levels (Chapter 10).

Developing and implementing systematic, well-organized performance management improves employee productivity, quality, performance, and overall development. Increases in employee productivity yield better business results—typically an aim of strategic business goals or objectives.

Human resource professionals provide a valuable service designing, implementing, and managing such systems. At the same time, performance management systems improve manager–employee relations by encouraging supervisors to develop positive alliances with employees via timely feedback and coaching activities.

Continuous and Rapid Growth.   Organizations reaching the developmental level are capable of enjoying rapid, sustainable growth unprecedented by other types of firms. Traditional and learning organizations, because of their focus on issues such as short-term results and learning, as opposed to growth and development, fail to create environments that can sustain continuous growth. Their internal systems simply are not designed to accommodate individual or organizational factors such as entrepreneurship, risk taking, reflection, and renewal, so critical to lifelong growth.

Improved Succession Planning and Career Planning.   Well-designed career development programs provide managers with a framework for succession planning and career pathing—critical elements for organizations that desire to not only survive but grow. Proactive, developmental firms plan for the future, with human resource needs instrumental in the success equation. Human resource professionals are often those responsible for assisting employees with career planning and helping them make critical career development decisions. These activities foster employee growth and development, as well as a sense of accomplishment. Career development programs improve employee retention rates, reduce turnover, and lower recruiting costs. These programs improve the working environment, increasing employee morale, loyalty, and sense of belonging.

Enhanced Organizational Capability.   According to Ulrich and Lake (1990, 40), organizational capability is a business's ability to establish internal structures and processes that influence its members to create organization-specific competencies and, thus, enable the business to adapt to changing customer and strategic needs. They contend that organizational capability includes people management, and the means through which organizations implement policies and procedures to develop and sustain employee commitment.

Organizational capability depends greatly on teamwork and the ability of a firm to capitalize on synergy to produce results. In this respect, Ulrich and Lake have captured the essence of the developmental organization. We believe this is a fundamental benefit of the developmental organization, building ongoing success provided the firm establishes the structures (foundations) and processes (human resource practices) needed to facilitate the required competencies that ensure organizational competitiveness (Figure 2.2).

As previously mentioned, a rising tide raises all boats. Although organizational capability increases as employee productivity improves, mere outputs are not sufficient to ensure long-term business viability. Developmental organizational capability improves as a result of the aggregate enhancement, growth, development, reflection, and renewal abilities of employees. Organizational members who are healthy, in spirit as well as body, are far more qualified to lead the firm to success on all planes. As employees maximize their knowledge, skills, and abilities, these are transferred to the organization—which ultimately benefits.

Organizational Renewal.   Every spring the earth reawakens after the long winter. Nature's ability to rebuild after a long dormancy or a catastrophe is astounding. Furthermore, organisms able to survive the test of time or catastrophe are often stronger than the year before.

In the same way, organizations experience cycles of prosperity and misfortune. Those able to renew themselves by incorporating new ideas, processes, or procedures rebuild their empires—emerging stronger and wiser than before. Hence, an organization's ability to renew itself is an indicator of its ability to survive. Further, renewal activities (e.g., creative exercises, entrepreneurial ventures) are exhilarating, providing firms and their employees with creative, safe outlets through which to test their talents. As anyone afflicted with spring fever can attest, rebirth is a time characterized by innovation, heightened activity levels, and productivity.

Competitive Readiness.   The ability to lead the competition, not simply respond, is a hallmark of developmental firms. Dynamic, proactive, entrepreneurial work environments propel organizations and their employees to the forefront, illustrating their ability to innovate, create new products, and develop processes and efficiencies that enhance competitive status.

Developmental Readiness. Developmental organizations are masters at preparing people for change, which is also known as individual developmental readiness. Employee developmental readiness occurs as a result of a concentrated, continuous, nurturing effort on the part of organizations to convey the importance and benefits of change to employees and the organization, create an environment that encourages risk taking and allows mistakes, provide employees with the knowledge and skills necessary to facilitate positive change, correlate change with growth and development, and reward personnel for change efforts. As explained previously, developmental firms understand that individual actions (such as change, growth, and development) lead to similar actions at the organizational level.

Overcoming Employee Depression. Developmental organizations are able to overcome employee depression, which is a psychological condition brought about by underutilization, apathy, and alienation of employees who feel they are not perceived to be vital, contributing members of the firm (Ulrich 1997). Other psychological dimensions of employee depression include feeling overwhelmed, lost, or fatigued as a result of excessive work demands or productivity requirements. In either case, employees feel unappreciated or less energized.

Ulrich contends that to address these feelings of either inadequacy or excessive demands, organizations must strike a balance between the two. One solution is to adopt a philosophical approach to employee enhancement—that of the developmental organization. In this way, employees exert control over their careers, reestablish commitment to the organization, participate in challenging work, engage in collaborative, team-oriented activities, share in a culture that fosters personal improvement, and receive the performance feedback and support necessary to motivate continuous growth and development. All these strategies, says Ulrich, address employee depression. Further, we assert that these actions constitute a core component of the developmental organization.

Employee Benefits

Employees, the developmental organization's greatest asset, enjoy numerous benefits as a result of being affiliated with firms embracing this philosophy.

Dynamic, Proactive Work Environment.   Just as developmental organizations gain from positive, ever-changing, innovative atmospheres, so do their employees. Dynamic work environments challenge employees, supervisors, managers, leaders, and human resource professionals to the fullest. Never a dull, mediocre moment passes in these firms. One of us had the pleasure of working with a truly developmental manager (Nora Ruder, zone vice president of Foremost Insurance) whose department was a pleasure to work in. Each day brought new work challenges yet offered exciting outlets for creativity and camaraderie with team members.

Personal and Professional Growth and Lifelong Learning.   One's personal and professional growth and development are enhanced by increased knowledge, skills, and better attitudes. The developmental approach encourages employees to engage in lifelong learning for their own personal enjoyment as well as to further the organization. Educated, well-rounded employees possess insights, qualities, creativity, and unique experiences that enhance their self-concepts as well as their performance on the job.

Developmental organizations help employees recognize performance strengths and deficiencies via the utilization of feedback (Chapter 10 and 11). Analysis of this type is a starting point for performance improvement, growth, and development, providing employees with an accurate reflection of their competencies in relationship to other employees as well as providing them with a baseline for improvement. Self-knowledge breeds confidence on and off the job.

Personal and professional growth manifested in improved performance opens the door to career and advancement opportunities. Promotional opportunities yielding additional responsibility, authority, and rewards appeal to motivated employees with an eye toward the future.

Greater Involvement and Participation.   In developmental organizations, employees are valued as partners. As such, their input is solicited at all levels and regarding all products, processes, and procedures. After all, employees, particularly front-line personnel, constantly interact with customers, suppliers, and competitors—making them invaluable sources of information, ideas, and input critical to organizational growth, development, competitive readiness, and renewal. When viewed as participating partners and esteemed for their contributions, employees act as owners, taking responsibility for individual and organizational success as well as failure.

High Satisfaction.   Developmental organizations are a pleasure to work for. Challenging, demanding, goal oriented—yes. Supportive, participatory, rewarding—also yes. Developmental firms position their employees for success by providing the knowledge, education, skill training, tools, change, reflection, and renewal opportunities necessary for success. Employees in organizations such as these are partners in success.

Individuals successful in their endeavors are happy with their accomplishments and themselves. Developmental employees recognize their organizations' (and co-workers', supervisors', managers', and leaders') contributions to their personal and professional achievements, which results in greater satisfaction with the firm, work environment, peers, and so forth.

Equality of Opportunity.   Employees, managers, and leaders are treated positively, uniquely, and with respect for and appreciation of their individual talents in developmental organizations. Further, developmental firms seek to maximize the potential of each employee, regardless of level or position within the company. Individualized growth and development plans and career planning emphasize one's unique knowledge, skills, abilities, and potential. Developmental organizations realize and appreciate the important contributions—past, present, and future—of each firm member while proactively engaging systems to ensure the continued unique success of each.

Improved Self-Esteem.   Employees who participate in learning and change activities, career development, and performance management interventions realize that their efforts contribute significantly to the organization's success. This involvement and understanding greatly enhances worker satisfaction, sense of accomplishment, and self-esteem, ultimately improving teamwork and cooperation. High job satisfaction encourages future growth and development of employees, furthering organizational success.

Developmental organizations create what we call a "self-esteeming" environment within the firm (Gilley, Boughton, and Maycunich 1999). Self-esteeming is the complementary, synergistic relationship between managers and employees, where the whole is greater than the sum of its parts. This relationship is based on the enormously powerful need of managers and employees to feel good about themselves and their experiences, skills, and abilities. In short, self-esteeming is the sum total of how managers and employees feel about themselves.

Self-esteeming is similar to a debit and credit account from which employees draw to build up or tear down their self-concept. The account balance fluctuates based on interactions within the organizational environment (i.e., their experiences). Thus, self-esteem is the net of an employee's experiences, forming a positive or negative self-concept.

Managers are responsible for improving their employees' self-esteem. Each interaction enhances or depletes an employee's self-concept; thus, work assignments or interactions can energize and engage employees or diminish their self-concept. Via successful interactions, employees continuously grow and develop, which encourages them to tackle increasingly difficult challenges and assignments. Conversely, negative interactions can promote dependency or self-doubt, severely limiting an employee's potential.

Developmental organizations engage employees in interactions that ultimately enhance their self-esteem. Partaking in developmental activities can and will provide employees with opportunities to enhance their personal dignity and respect within the organization. Consequently, the developmental organization, by design, fosters self-esteeming behavior.

Greater Compensation and Rewards.   Rewards and recognition are natural, common occurrences bestowed generously in developmental organizations, whose employees understand that their growth, development, and performance will be celebrated and recognized appropriately. Financial rewards may include incentives, raises, fringe benefits, profit sharing, and the like. Recognition comes in many forms, such as informal managerial congratulations, participation in awards banquets, employee-of-the-month celebrations or certificates, highlights in newsletters, and so forth. Developmental firms understand that appropriately rewarded performance typically results in increased employee job satisfaction and efforts.

Broadened Entrepreneurial Environment.   As previously mentioned, developmental organizations exhibit dynamic environments characterized by vision, spirit, creativity, and drive—in summary, an entrepreneurial atmosphere. As employees grow and develop, developmental organizations help them cultivate reflection and renewal skills—critical to helping improve the organization's renewal capacity. To fully maximize renewal capacity, employees are given the freedom to be entrepreneurs. According to Meyer and Allen (1994, p. 5), an entrepreneur is one who organizes and owns a business with the intent of making a profit. One who operates within an existing firm is an "intrapreneur" (Pinchot and Pellman 1999).

Entrepreneurship provides powerful intrinsic rewards for employees, from self-esteem and confidence to responsibility and authority. Feelings of ownership further bind employees to their developmental employers, who allow workers the opportunities to apply their skills or experiment in safe, supportive environments.

CONCLUSION

When organizations have adequately prepared for the transformation from the traditional to the developmental organization, as well as implemented state-of-the-art human resource practices, they have created a condition that enhances organizational renewal and improves the performance capacity and capabilities of the organization. This allows organizations to maintain their viability and youthfulness, perpetuating the growth and development phase of the organizational life cycle while enhancing their competitive readiness. Developmental organizations are able to address any market condition, competitive challenge, or threat that might confront them in the near or distant future.

The developmental organization exemplifies a firm's philosophical shift in its treatment of human resources, requiring the business to examine the roles and responsibilities of all employees and making adjustments that bring about enhanced organizational renewal and performance capability. Developmental organizations transform the organizational system so that it contributes to employee development and rewards their contributions accordingly, while leadership adopts new and exciting ways to guide the firm.

There are many barriers to creating a culture of continuous growth and development. Some prevent change altogether, whereas others limit its effectiveness. Regardless, barriers must be addressed through strategies designed to overcome them. When this occurs, organizations and employees benefit significantly, which fosters greater and greater growth and development. If allowed to continue, the cycle will continuously enhance organizational renewal and competitive readiness.

Developmental benefits are numerous to both employees and the organization. Perhaps the most critical benefits involve enhancement of organizational capabilities, achieving strategic goals and objectives, the creation of a self-esteeming work environment, and fostering personal and professional growth. The learning organization falls short of true growth and development; the developmental organization does not.

PART TWO

Foundations of the Developmental Organization

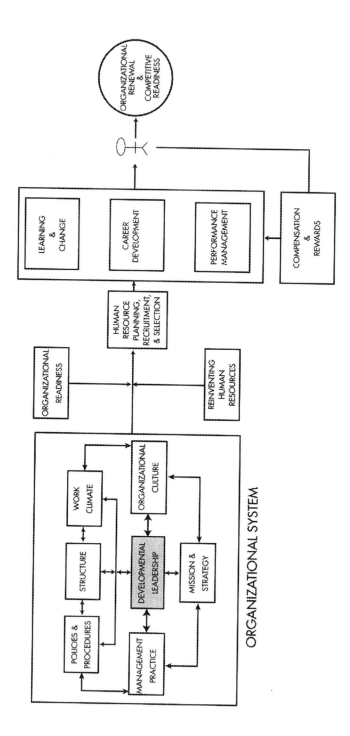

ORGANIZATIONAL SYSTEM

CHAPTER 3

Principles of Developmental Leadership

One of the most popular topics of research is leadership. In fact, Internet sites such as Amazon.com, Barnes and Noble.com, and Borders.com list over 1,250, 1,100, and 1,175 books on the topic, respectively. The subject has been researched extensively since the early 1950s; however, little agreement has been reached on whether leaders are born or developed, or what constitutes effective leadership. One area of agreement involves leadership styles (e.g., autocratic, charismatic, transactional, and transformational) and their corresponding strengths and weaknesses.

Our aim is not to develop a treatise regarding what constitutes leadership or discuss the advantages of one style over another, but to examine the importance of leadership in transforming organizations. We look to identify the leadership philosophy needed to establish a developmental organization, review the unique roles and responsibilities of developmental leaders, and explore the principles of developmental leadership. Each of these components reveals the importance of leadership in bringing about organizational renewal and enhancing competitive readiness.

Above all, one point remains clear: Making the transformation from the traditional to the developmental organization *cannot* occur without the support, guidance, and efforts of organizational leaders. Organizational renewal is forever linked to leadership. The only question that remains unanswered concerns what type of leadership is needed to help transform organizations. As discussed in Chapter 1, autocratic and charismatic leadership styles are commonly found in traditional organizations, whereas transactional and transformational leadership are required to make the leap to the learning organization. Although transformational leadership is a considerable improvement over autocratic and charismatic forms, we believe that the developmental organization requires a new type of leader—one who realizes that organizational renewal and competitive readiness are totally dependent on employees prepared for future challenges, new work assignments, ever-increasing competition, continuous lifelong learning and change, and continuous growth and development.

Each of these conditions requires innovative approaches to problem solving, creative solutions to complex issues, and new knowledge, skills, and competencies to meet competitive challenges. Developmental leaders constantly embrace change as a positive opportunity, spending most of their time creating conditions favorable to managing and implementing change. Consequently, developmental leadership is about influence—nothing more, nothing less (Maxwell 1998, 17).

LEADERSHIP: THE NAVIGATOR IN THE EYE OF THE STORM

"Anyone can steer the ship, but it takes a leader to chart the course" (Maxwell 1998, 33). Navigators see the path ahead and make midcourse corrections to avoid dangerous water, relying on past experiences as a source of information and wisdom. They solicit the advice of others, examine conditions before making commitments, and have faith in others while dynamically balancing optimism and realism, intuition and planning.

Maxwell's navigator analogy summarizes the difference between developmental and traditional leadership styles. Developmental leaders understand that leadership is a twenty-four-hour, seven-day-a-week job. Effective leaders inspire employees and encourage their continuous growth and development, constantly attending to every minute detail, daily nurturing and promoting growth, trust, respect, intuition, sacrifice, shared power, mutual success, and accomplishment.

Maxwell developed an excellent acrostic that helps developmental leaders remember the importance of leading as navigators:

Predetermine a course of action.
Lay out your goals.
Adjust your priorities.
Notify key personnel.

Allow time for acceptance.
Head into action.
Expect problems.
Always point to success.
Daily review your plan.

PHILOSOPHY OF DEVELOPMENTAL LEADERSHIP: SERVANTSHIP

The story goes that in 1863 the British ambassador to the United States called on President Abraham Lincoln at the White House. Upon arrival the ambassador was escorted to the president's private office, where he found President Lincoln shining his shoes. The British ambassador was shocked by what he witnessed and blurted, "Mr. President, you can't shine your own shoes." President Lincoln paused, slowly looked up and calmly replied, "Then whose shoes should I be shining?"

This story clearly reveals the inappropriate perceptions that people have of leaders. It also demonstrates the humility needed to be a *servant leader* (one who puts employee needs, growth, and development above one's own).

As the Appalachian saying goes, "Be careful not to grow too much above your raisin'." Interpreted, this means that we must remember where we came from and not vault ourselves too high above those we were raised with. Thus, we can remember the important principles and ideas that shaped our personal philosophies, values, and beliefs. Further, we are grounded upon reflection of our background, ideals, and goals, which keeps us humble and focused on the needs and expectations of others.

By remaining humble, leaders actually become more influential and powerful because employees are drawn to leaders who are approachable, open, and friendly. Accessible leaders enable employees to remain at ease during interactions. With this improved communication, employees feel closer to their leaders and more willing to support their thoughts, ideas, and suggestions. The mental wrestling match so common in leader–employee relationships simply disappears.

A servantship approach is critical when leaders ask their employees to produce business results and outcomes requiring tremendous dedication and personal sacrifice. Most employees are willing to participate but are more so when their leaders experience the same hardships and exert similar effort.

Boyett and Boyett (1995) discuss several characteristics of servant leaders:

- They are servants first—driven by the need to learn and serve.
- They lead by listening to their followers.
- They help people articulate their own goals—and that of the group by reaching consensus or a common will.
- They inspire trust via their actions, their beliefs, and the value placed on followers.
- They take people and their work seriously, exhibiting commitment to employee growth, development, and ability to be self-led.

During the past several years, a favored topic of discussion has been the importance of empowerment. Interestingly, when all the fancy arguments are stripped away, empowerment is simply helping others see their own potential for greatness and arranging conditions by which they can become successful. Empowerment thus sounds a lot like servantship.

In an earlier work, we argue that the term "empowerment" interferes with the intent of the act (Gilley and Boughton 1996). Empowerment implies granting *power* to one's employees to become more responsible or to achieve greater levels of performance. While this definition seems harmless enough, it reinforces the old paradigms of authoritarian leadership. We contend that leaders cannot grant power to others, because the supposed power being granted already resides with each employee. In a leader–employee relationship, the employee allows the leader to lead him or her. Think about it. Employees *allow* leaders to lead. If employees individually or collectively refuse to accept a leader's direction, what can be done? The employees be could fired, yes. But in this case, have leaders demonstrated true leadership abilities? No. Where is the leaders' so-called power to lead and get things done? It lies with employees.

Empowerment is based on granting control that leaders do not really possess, because employees hold the power and then willingly relinquish it in a leadership situation. Remember, employees choose to follow; leaders cannot control the thoughts, actions, or behaviors of their people. We also assert that empowerment, as typically taught, is a one-way process, from leader to employee. Again, this is the old, authoritarian model of leadership, not a new approach to leadership.

Recognizing that power and control rest with one's employees, developmental leaders exercise servantship to help employees become all that they can be. Well-served employees realize that they have the power to achieve great things—to grow and develop, to become masters of their careers, and to achieve professional success.

Truly developmental leaders possess the heart of a servant—willing to put the needs, expectations, interests, and success of their employees above their own. Developmental (servant) leaders advocate, support, and promote their employees; accept their overall and career development responsibilities by working tirelessly to help employees grow and develop; assist workers as they struggle to become the best they can be; share organizational success with subordinates; make certain that other decision-makers in the organization are aware of employee contributions to achieving desired business results; accept responsibility for their employees' failures and; celebrate their successes. Above all, developmental leaders operate without regard for their own well-being or career advancement because they believe their employees are the organization's most valuable asset. Most important, developmental leaders are servants because it is the right thing to do.

Jack Welch, president and CEO of General Electric, is often touted as an exemplary servant leader, one who values employees and makes their growth and development a prime directive. Welch, for example, regularly devotes his time to facilitate employee training, proving beyond a shadow of a doubt the importance of employees to the organization and its success.

To embrace servantship, leaders must be willing to let their employees grow and develop above and beyond themselves, perhaps the most difficult aspect of becoming an effective developmental leader. Maxwell (1998, 215, 221) calls this the law of legacy, whereby a leader's lasting value is measured by succession. He further asserts that "a legacy is created only when a leader puts his/her organization into position to do great things without him/her."

Servant leaders delegate tasks and responsibilities to others because they are secure with themselves and realize that such opportunities for growth and development stimulate employees. These leaders also understand that they will receive credit for a job well done since part of their job was being delegated.

Another characteristic of servant leaders is personal involvement, the willingness to engage employees by becoming personally involved in their careers and professional lives. As a result, employees are willing to discuss important issues openly and honestly, without fear of negative repercussions or reprisals, and are willing to become vulnerable and exposed rather than guarded and controlled. When this type of behavior is exhibited, honesty and openness will be mutual on the part of leaders and employees.

A servantship approach does not mean that leaders are weak or unable to make difficult decisions. It simply implies a personal philosophy of humility and a willingness to work for the betterment of others. Moreover, servant leaders help their organization by advocating, assisting, growing, and developing its most important asset: its people. Simply stated, servantship means being a caretaker without regard for one's own personal needs or the rewards typically afforded leaders responsible for the professional lives of others. Servant leaders bear a tremendous responsibility, one that should not be taken lightly.

MYTHS OF LEADERSHIP

To understand leadership, we must dispel its myths and misconceptions. First, management and leadership are not the same thing. Leadership involves influencing people to follow, whereas management focuses on maintaining systems and processes (Maxwell 1998). Second, entrepreneurs are not necessarily leaders, even though they possess persuasive abilities. Entrepreneurs are often independent, lacking the long-term influence over others that leaders enjoy. Third, leaders are not always the most knowledgeable people in an organization. In fact, most effective leaders realize that their employees are more knowledgeable than they are regarding certain organizational issues and processes. Consequently, leaders are subordinate to their employees, reinforcing the servantship philosophy so critical to developmental leadership. Fourth, leadership is not about the position one holds but about influencing others to contribute their expertise, to perform beyond their abilities, and to continually grow and develop. These conditions of true leadership are what separates developmental leadership from management and other leadership approaches.

ROLES AND RESPONSIBILITIES OF DEVELOPMENTAL LEADERS

Throughout this book, we discuss the elements of the developmental organization. Each of these correlates with the roles and responsibilities of developmental leaders, which include the following:

- adopting the principles of developmental leadership (Chapter 3)
- sculpting an organization system that fosters development (Chapter 4)
- increasing organizational readiness for learning and change (Chapter 5)
- reinventing human resources (Chapter 6)

- building organizational capacity and capability through human resource planning, recruiting, and staffing (Chapter 7)
- enhancing organizational renewal through learning and change (Chapter 8)
- implementing career development strategies (Chapter 9)
- applying the performance management process (Chapter 10)
- encouraging development through effective compensation and rewards strategies (Chapter 11)

The primary role of developmental leaders is servantship. Developmental leaders help employees grow and develop without regard for their own selfish interests.

DEVELOPMENTAL LEADERSHIP ASSUMPTIONS

Developmental leaders make several assumptions that guide their actions and behaviors. According to Maslow (1998), developmental leaders make the following assumptions about their employees:

1. They can be trusted to perform to the best of their skills and abilities.
2. They have the right to be informed about the decisions of the organization, its mission, and its strategy.
3. They prefer to be an involved contributor rather than a passive observer.
4. They are willing to take risks if the organization establishes a safety net.
5. They enjoy teamwork and group harmony.
6. They can be improved.
7. They want to grow and develop.
8. They prefer to feel important, needed, useful, successful, proud, and respected.
9. They desire to develop a positive relationships with leaders, managers, and co-workers.
10. They prefer meaningful work.

11. They desire to be appreciated and recognized for their accomplishments.
12. They prefer responsibility to dependency and passivity.
13. They prefer a self-directed leadership approach to that of an authoritarian approach.
14. They want the organization to become successful and to meet its strategic business goals and objectives.

TEN PRINCIPLES OF DEVELOPMENTAL LEADERSHIP

To achieve a servantship approach, leaders must apply the ten principles of development leadership. These leadership responsibilities are critical to the developmental organization. The ten principles are clustered into four categories:

1. intrinsically oriented principles
2. employee-oriented principles
3. performance-oriented principles
4. organizationally oriented principles

Intrinsically Oriented Principles

Personal accountability and trustworthiness are the two intrinsically oriented principles that surface when leaders work closely and harmoniously with managers and employees. These principles forge interpersonal relationships, demonstrate trustworthiness and respect, foster collaboration, and build teamwork.

Principle of Personal Accountability. Far too many organizational leaders simply wash their hands of responsibility for their own worlds. Developmental leaders, on the other hand, understand that they are personally accountable for their own behavior, actions, and business results, including the policies, procedures, incentives, interventions, and plans they advocate and implement. Moreover, developmental leaders live by the Truman philosophy "The buck stops here" and behave accordingly.

Personal accountability is more than a mere slogan used by leaders who want to manipulate a situation or event. This is a guiding principle that leaders live by every single day of organizational life. In other words, personal accountability is part of their personal fabric and remains constant during good times and bad; it is not abandoned when leaders are caught with their hand in the cookie jar, as happened with Presidents Nixon and Clinton.

Personal accountability is a way of thinking, guided by the deeply internal forces of every organizational leader. It causes managers and employees to believe in their leaders, making them vulnerable by trusting in leaders' words and deeds. In short, personal accountability bridges a connection with leaders so that employees are willing to grant them power and control, without which leaders could not direct their organizations. Developmental organizations embrace this principle as the ingredient necessary to foster continuous employee growth and development.

Principle of Trustworthiness.   Without trust, employees do not take risks. Absent trust, employees will be less likely to participate in growth and development activities or engage in projects and interventions to improve their skills and competencies. Trust is an essential element of the developmental organization and one of the most important components of developmental leadership.

Leaders have power and authority over employees, yet this does not guarantee that employees trust them. Establishing trust is a time-consuming, difficult undertaking based on truth, respect, character, and integrity. Truth implies open, honest, and direct communication, and avoidance of hidden agendas that discourage positive working relationships. Respect involves believing in leaders and holding them in high regard. Leaders lacking respect will also lack trust. The true test of a leader's character is what he or she does when no one is looking. Obviously, trusting employees believe that their leaders will do the right thing. Integrity is essential because employees follow leaders who do what they say they are going to do, and in an honest, trustworthy fashion.

In a previous book (Gilley and Boughton 1996), we outlined five preliminary steps to establishing trust:

1. Create a work environment free of fear.
2. Develop a solid communication pattern with employees, both in terms of frequency and depth.
3. Discover the unique characteristics, personality, life experiences, and professional paths of each employee.
4. Engage employees by accepting them as positive contributors and worthwhile human beings.
5. Become personally involved with employees, spending significant time with each.

Trust is granted when leaders have successfully accomplished each of these steps.

Peterson and Hicks (1996) believe that significant surprises, unpredictability, and stress in the work environment seriously diminish the trustworthiness of a leader. Other conditions and behaviors that erode a leader's trustworthiness include the following:

- lack of a sense of safety and security
- fear of losing something important
- uncertainty about other peoples' intentions
- inconsistent behavior, actions, or decisions
- indecisiveness
- inconsistent policies and procedures
- lack of expectations and performance standards
- inadequate performance reviews and reward systems
- favoritism
- blaming behavior
- inappropriate criticism and threats

These conditions and behaviors can be referred to as "trust killers."

Peterson and Hicks identified four questions that serve as a personal audit of one's trust level:

1. Do employees know what to expect from you?
2. Do employees believe that you do what you say?
3. Do employees believe that you pay attention to their interests?
4. Do employees believe that you are competent to carry out what you say?

The answers to these questions determine one's trustworthiness, and can be used to create a growth and development plan for leaders.

Employee-Oriented Principles

Employee-oriented principles demonstrate that employees are the organization's most important asset. These principles reaffirm that without employees and their contributions, organizations could not achieve their strategic business goals and objectives. Thus, it make sense that organizational leaders serve as employee advocates and as conduits of employee self-esteem.

Principle of Employee Advocacy. The true test of leadership is legacy—not so much in terms of how one will be viewed by others, but rather in what the leader accomplished. Did the leader develop others to assume his or her role and responsibilities? What will be the lasting impact that others will make as a result of a leader's developmental efforts? What impact did a leader have on the lives and careers of others? Finally, how did leaders help others grow and develop?

All too often, organizational leaders are selfish, concerned only about their own careers and how they will advance in the firm. Since little regard is given to the careers of their employees, it should come as no surprise that these leaders abdicate their development responsibilities. Consequently, their employees are on their own when acquiring or developing the knowledge and skills needed to ensure adequate performance and productivity or to advance their careers. In fact, most employees are simply hoping to survive.

Developmental leaders realize that employee growth and development fuels their own long-term career success and advancement. "Getting results through people" is their job, not using people as stepping stones on the journey to professional utopia. Developmental leaders understand that their success depends on the contributions of each employee. Realizing that the sum of the parts is greater than the whole, they advocate and encourage a synergistic approach to problem-solving, strategic planning, organizational development initiatives, change intervention, and so forth.

Developmental leaders practice the principle of employee advocacy every time they delegate work tasks and responsibilities to their subordinates. Delegation is a process of appointing someone to operate on your behalf implying that employees and leaders are interchangeable parts used to produce desired results. Employees and leaders serve as replacements for each other and assume each others' tasks and responsibilities. In essence, delegation forces leaders to rely on others to help achieve desired business results.

Delegation is the ultimate growth and development strategy but is seldom viewed in this light. Delegation is most commonly seen as a way of dispersing work tasks and responsibilities throughout the organization to improve performance efficiency and productivity. Although this aspect of delegation is certainly true, delegation also allows more experienced employees (leaders and managers) to relinquish tasks and responsibilities to those less experienced, giving both delegator and delegatee the opportunity to acquire new knowledge, skills, and competencies. Over time, the delegation cycle enhances an individual's performance capacity to such a point that he or she is able to take on even more difficult and challenging tasks and responsibilities. When the delegation cycle is complete, leaders, managers, and employees grow and develop, becoming more important assets within the organization. Consequently, as we assert in a recent book, "delegation is quintessentially a growth and development strategy" (Gilley, Boughton, and Maycunich 1999, 126).

When the principle of employee advocacy has reached it apex, organizations have established policies that prevent a person from being promoted within the organization unless an adequate replacement has been developed. In other words, a *promotional linkage* exists between a leader's career growth and development and the preparation of others to assume the leader's vacated position. In this way, career-minded individuals are required to develop a replacement before they can be advanced within the organization. This ensures that every employee, manager, and organizational leader desiring career advancement advocates and prepares another to replace himself or herself. This is what a developmental organization is all about.

Principle of Employee Self-Esteeming.   A primary purpose of developmental leadership involves enhancing the self-esteem of employees. Developmental leaders have opportunities to enhance employee self-esteem through interactions including work assignments, growth and development activities, one-on-one meetings, performance appraisals, projects, discussions, presentations, proposals, and so on. Collectively, these interactions make up employees' "private and public world," which they draw upon to enhance their self-esteem. Conversely, this world can seriously diminish and deplete self-esteem with negative interactions, which cause feelings of depression, anger, and resentment (Gilley, Boughton, and Maycunich 1999).

The aggregate of employees' interactions produce a positive or negative net balance. When positive, employees feel comfortable with themselves and are motivated to take risks. They are willing to grow and develop; they feel unique, expressive, courageous, and self-assured. Positive self-esteem is the foundation of career growth and development. When their net balance of self-esteem is negative, employees are often defensive, frightened, reclusive, critical, bitter, resentful, and mistrusting. These attitudes cause employees to be reluctant to take risks, accept new challenges, take advice, or receive constructive criticism. As we have described, "their attitude toward growth and development activities is often negative, as these actions are perceived as additional work instead of a challenge or growth opportunity" (Gilley, Boughton, and Maycunich 1999, 122). Moreover, employees fail to look inwardly, instead finding fault with the organization, its managers, their job, and their co-workers.

Developmental leaders maintain the critically important responsibility of improving employees' self-esteem because every interaction has the potential to enhance or deplete an empoyee's self-concept. Consequently, leaders discover and implement activities that have profoundly positive effects on employees' self-esteem. Interactions that help employees grow and develop or encourage them to accept increasingly difficult and challenging assignments can have the most positive impact.

Bradshaw (1981) identified four additional ways to enhance employees' self-esteem:

- promoting achievement, accomplishment, and mastery (e.g., encouraging employees to acquire new skills and knowledge and to participate in creative endeavors, granting employees new and exciting responsibilities, encouraging participation in visibly important projects, and requesting employees' opinions and insights regarding the organization's strategic direction)
- sharing power, control, and influence (e.g., providing employees with opportunities to have influence over decisions or authority over others; appointing employees to be members of decision-making committees, task forces, and teams; asking employees their opinions regarding upcoming changes; and asking for suggestions for improving organizational efficiency and effectiveness)
- caring for and valuing employees (e.g., giving employees positive affirmation for their existence, and acknowledging employees' contributions, recommendations, and achievements)
- allowing action on values and beliefs (e.g., allowing employees to make decisions based on their values and beliefs, and allowing employees to act on their values and beliefs)

Each of these four steps channels positive interactions into employees' "self-concept buckets," which raises their self-esteem. The more positive interactions employees experience, the higher their level. When employees experience negative interactions, developmental leaders need to find activities that replenish their employees' self-esteem levels.

Performance-Oriented Principles

Developmental leaders rely on performance-oriented principles to help their organizations achieve the business results needed and to improve employee performance and productivity through continuous growth and development. These three principles—performance partnership, organizational performance improvement, and effective communication—provide a foundation for excellence by allowing leaders to communicate their expectations in a clear, motivating, and inspirational manner.

Principle of Performance Partnership.   Developmental leaders, managers, and employees must work closely together in creating an environment the fosters continuous growth and development. Leaders are required to create performance partnerships that enable employees to acquire new knowledge and apply it to the job. When fully developed, this partnership is a mutually beneficial relationship allowing employees to acquire critical skills and competencies to improve their performance and career development opportunities (see Chapter 9) while helping organizational leaders and their firms achieve better business results. Performance partnerships are based on the belief that employees are more willing to participate in growth and development when they are activity involved in their establishment.

The principle of performance partnership is based on seven requirements. First, employees must want to change their performance. Second, growth and development must be linked to employees' needs for performance improvement. Third, developmental leaders must identify the barriers and cultural issues that prevent knowledge acquisition and transfer. Fourth, developmental leaders must identify conflicting job tasks and activities that reduce employee motivation for learning and change. Fifth, leaders must provide performance feedback, reinforcement, encouragement, and support in order to improve employee performance and productivity. Sixth, employees must accept their responsibility for acquiring new knowledge and skills and transferring them to the job. Seventh, developmental leaders must recognize and reward employees for their participation in growth and development activities.

When these seven requirements for behavioral change are achieved, most employees will participate in growth and development activities. Over time, employee performance and productivity will improve, helping organizations achieve better business results, improve their competitive readiness, and enhance their organizational renewal.

Principle of Organizational Performance Improvement. Developmental leaders are responsible for achieving business results through people. Some believe that failing to achieve desired business results means that leaders have failed to lead. Although we believe that developmental leadership consists of other important characteristics (such as the principles discussed in this chapter), achieving desired results is a pinnacle of effective leadership and should be considered a critical measure of leadership aptitude and ability. To this end, developmental leaders create work environments where employees are

- challenged to perform at maximum levels
- encouraged to demonstrate creative solutions to complex problems
- engaged in quality initiatives
- asked to participate in continuous organizational improvement activities
- required to participate in growth and development interventions

We believe that achieving these high standards requires developmental leaders to understand how organizations operate, the needs and expectations of shareholders, and how to construct well-designed, long-term solutions to difficult problems. In short, developmental leaders must possess business acumen. Each of these skills provides leaders a vehicle by which to improve the organization's strength and viability. Thus, having a keen awareness and a potent operational understanding of the business leverages one's knowledge and expertise to improve the organization's performance.

Developmental leaders demonstrate appropriate work styles to meet the needs of their people and the organization. These leaders are aware of their employees' maturity, skills, aptitudes, and preferences, and appropriately adjust their work style to guarantee organizational success. The three most common types of work styles are directive, supportive, and collaborative.

A directive work style is appropriate when employees lack experience or when time is limited. This approach works best when there is a "best way" of performing a job or task. It is also appropriate when direct commands will save time and money without jeopardizing the relationship with employees. For example, new hires are often subject to directive work styles as they "learn the ropes" in their new organization.

When developmental leaders encourage creative, innovative solutions or entrepreneurial approaches, they are demonstrating a supportive work style. In most cases, this style enables leaders to function as employee advocates, encouraging their contributions, efforts, and actions. A supportive work style is best used when employees are very experienced, capable, and confident. Field sales personnel, for example, thrive under conditions that prompt creativity in developing new approaches.

A collaborative work style best represents the type of work environment found in developmental organizations. Collaboration is best exhibited when leaders and employees work together to accomplish the organization's business goals and objectives. Under these circumstances, true "performance synergy" can be achieved as the talents, skills, abilities, and expertise of each employee are utilized for the betterment of the organization (Gilley, Boughton, and Maycunich 1999, 167). Collaborative work environments are conducive for sharing, caring, supporting, and encouraging. They can generate creative, energetic solutions to complex problems facing the organization. Organizations that embrace collaborative work environments are characterized by a high degree of internal stability, maturity, and professional leadership. When collaborative work environments dominate, employees are aware of and understand the organization's mission, strategy, and long-term approach to business success.

Possessing business acumen and creating performance synergy are two components of improving organizational performance. Respect, the third element, binds these components, creating a powerful trilogy. Without respect, leaders cannot lead; nor can they motivate their employees, produce desired results, or be effective long-term. Earning respect is a difficult undertaking, requiring hard work, fairness, honesty, consistency, and adherence to the organization's guiding principles. According to Maxwell (1998, 161), developmental leaders earn respect by "making sound decisions, admitting their mistakes, and putting what's best for their followers and the organization ahead of their personal agendas." Building respect requires leaders to create work environments that are free of fear, based on open communications, engaging and accepting, personally involving, trustworthy and honest, self-esteeming, and focused on employee growth and development. Leading with respect is one of the most effective ways of motivating and inspiring employees. It will be rewarded by better business results, enhanced competitive readiness, and continuous organizational renewal.

Principle of Effective Communications. Developmental leaders possess effective communication skills that enhance their ability to deliver performance feedback, conduct performance appraisals, confront poor performance, and provide career counseling and mentoring. As a result, their communication skills improve employee performance, productivity, and willingness to participate in growth and development activities that enable the organization to achieve desired business results.

Developmental leaders acquire the ability to skillfully communicate with others throughout the organization. Communications is not just the expression of ideas or rhetorical choices made during an interaction, but the ability to use all communication mechanisms available to stimulate and challenge employees to growth and develop as well as to perform to the best of their abilities. Developmental leaders communicate efficiently and effectively, making certain that they are understood by their employees. They have a command of the communication process and understand that information is often misunderstood due to inference and distortion. Developmental leaders understand nonverbal messages when interacting with employees and use such techniques to emphasize their meaning.

Developmental leaders ask pertinent questions to enhance their understanding and to demonstrate that they are paying attention to their employees. They also listen intently to employees to solicit meaning and understanding while working intently at minimizing distractions that interfere with their comprehension and awareness. In this way, developmental leaders avoid misinterpreting information.

Developmental leaders utilize the most appropriate technology when communicating, understanding that technology is sometimes used as an excuse to avoid interacting with employees face-to-face. Hence, they avoid using voice-mail and e-mail when personal communication proves more effective.

Organizationally Oriented Principles

Organizationally oriented principles help leaders create work environments and organizational cultures that foster employee growth and development. The three principles are organizational consistency, holistic thinking, and organizational subordination.

Principle of Organizational Consistency. A hallmark of the developmental organization is organizational consistency. At first glance, consistency appears to conflict with the principle of continuous employee growth and development common in developmental organizations. Although change is essential to competitive readiness and organizational renewal, a closer examination reveals that employees want their leaders to demonstrate consistent behavior and decision making—they want their leaders to avoid the latest fads and trends typical of so many organizations. Workers want their leaders to filter decisions through a set of guiding principles that control and influence their actions.

Although continuous change is inevitable in today's world, most of us look for equilibrium—where our current state is consistent with our desired state. Equilibrium is a type of utopia that most people strive for, like a calm lake in the early morning when the stillness is deafening. Organizational equilibrium may be the only way of achieving the peace and serenity necessary for personal and organizational renewal. Finally, equilibrium is necessary because it allows employees to "catch their breath" between episodes of growth and development, not unlike the winter season that allows nature to pause and slow down before a period of rapid renewal.

One way of guaranteeing that the principle of organizational consistency reigns involves conducting what we call a values alignment, a process by which leaders' guiding principles are integrated with those of the organization. First, leaders identify their personal values and beliefs, comparing them to those of the organization. Second, they determine the amount of agreement between personal and organizational values and beliefs. Third, leaders identify how their personal values and beliefs impact employees daily. Fourth, they make adjustments that align their personal guiding principles with those of the organization.

Conducting a values alignment helps developmental leaders identify what that they consider important—an essential element in making decisions that impact the well-being of the organization. Through values alignment, firms maintain organizational consistency, which keeps them appropriately anchored in the rough seas of corporate life.

Principle of Holistic Thinking.   Developmental leaders articulate a vision for their organizations, identify an achievable game plan designed to achieve this vision, and reflect upon their actions as a means of improving and maximizing future opportunities. When these three components are presented, developmental leaders are applying the principle of holistic thinking. Holistic thinking consists of three types of thinking: visionary, strategic, and critical reflective.

Visionary Thinking.   Developmental leaders have clear visions for their organizations in both human and financial terms. This vision allows employees to focus on a common set of goals and outcomes that give their daily activities serious meaning and determine an organization's success or failure. Furthermore, developmental organizations clearly know what they want to achieve and how employees can better serve their customers. In short, visionary thinking identifies the purpose of one's organization.

Developmental leaders are successful in communicating their organization's purpose and creating an environment built on employee support and involvement. Because developmental leaders use an inclusive approach when designing and developing organizational vision, employees participate in the creation of this vision, share their opinions and ideas, and accept the responsibility for activities that help the organization realize it dreams. Developmental leaders generate the support necessary for the collaborative vision to resonate throughout the firm, thereby creating an environment of employee and organizational success.

Strategic Thinking. The ability to direct one's attention to the organization's future is called strategic thinking. It includes the ability to anticipate business trends and processes and to break them down into manageable units for others to understand and implement. By dismantling business trends and processes into manageable components, developmental leaders generate a variety of solutions that narrow the gap between what is needed and what is delivered, making the necessary adjustments to ensure organizational success.

When developmental leaders use strategic thinking skills, they forge an organizational direction dedicated to ensuring competitive readiness and organizational renewal. Strategic thinking is a conceptual-level activity requiring organizational leaders to establish business priorities. Developmental leaders possesses the ability to look to the future and navigate uncharted waters, thus demonstrating visionary and strategic thinking simultaneously.

Critical Reflective Thinking. Developmental leaders continually examine their behavior, decisions, and beliefs, making appropriate adjustments as needed. As a result, they are able to reinvent themselves over and over again, looking inward to discover new awareness and insights. This skill is essential for leaders to understand who they are, what they believe, their strengths, their weaknesses, and their growth areas.

We define critical reflectiveness as the ability to understand one's values and beliefs, and to know why one behaves in a particular manner. Critical reflectiveness implies that developmental leaders understand why they alter their behavior and when the changes violate their guiding principles. Thus, developmental leaders know when changes are consistent with their guiding principles and when they are not. Without this self-awareness skill, developmental leaders have difficulty maintaining personal integrity with employees, who may view their behaviors as manipulative or insincere. Over time, employees lose confidence in their leaders' intentions, which severely damages professional relationships and in turn diminishes organizational productivity, quality, and efficiency.

Leaders transform their firms into developmental organizations by thinking holistically. This requires them to create a vision for their organization and identify the role that continuous employee growth and development plays in organizational success. Next, leaders demonstrate strategic thinking skills by developing strategies and implementing initiatives that enable the organization to achieve its vision. Establishing work climates, environments, organizational structures, and a culture receptive to and supportive of continuous employee growth and development indicates strategic thinking, as does developing policies and implementing procedures that encourage, recognize, and reward employee growth and development.

Developmental organization leaders insist that the relationship between managers and employees exudes synergy, fostering growth, development, and managerial acceptance of their developmental responsibilities. Developmental leaders advocate and support growth and development as a means of achieving strategic business goals and objectives.

Principle of Organizational Subordination. It was once said, "Put a good employee against a bad system, and the system wins every time." This simple statement explains why most organizations never really evolve to the developmental level and demonstrates a firm's attitude toward its employees.

When organizational leaders allow their firms to "get in the way" of employees' positive contributions, ideas, and efforts, the employees' importance and value diminish. In reality, organizational leaders are communicating that the organization is more important and valuable than their employees, setting up a confrontation that results in increased employee turnover, disloyalty, mistrust, poor performance and productivity, low morale, and, ultimately, organizational sabotage by some employees. These undesirable outcomes are inconsistent with developmental organization philosophy and practice.

The "organization first" approach must be reversed if organizations wish to evolve to developmental status. Developmental organization leaders understand that the way they treat their employees determines performance, productivity, loyalty, growth, and development. Put simply, organizations become subordinate when leaders place the contributions, involvement, and loyalty of employees above those of the organization, striving to guarantee organizational subservience to employees' efforts to improve productivity, efficiencies, and approaches essential to competitive readiness and organizational renewal. Moreover, developmental leaders "get out of the way," allowing employees to work effectively and efficiently. In this way, workers can demonstrate creative, insightful, and innovative approaches to business problems and performance difficulties.

Developmental leaders demonstrate organizational subordination in several ways:

1. Eliminating policies and procedures that interfere with, prevent, or discourage employee growth and development
2. Eliminating organizational structures that inhibit two-way communication
3. Eliminating organizational structures that discourage or prevent employee growth and development
4. Eliminating negative and personally demeaning work climates
5. Creating organizational cultures where employee growth and development are encouraged and sponsored
6. Creating performance management systems that foster employee growth and development
7. Creating work environments where continuous learning and change are the norm
8. Transforming performance appraisals into developmental evaluations designed to foster employee growth and development
9. Creating compensation and reward systems that recognize and reward employee growth and development
10. Selecting managers and supervisors for their employee development and interpersonal skills, rather than their personal performance records

11. Eliminating political favoritism in favor of a performance-oriented promotion system based on continuous employee growth and development

12. Encouraging employee career development and linking it with long-term human resource planning initiatives

13. Selecting employees based on their readiness to learn, change, grow, and develop

14. Linking employee growth and development to the organization's mission and strategy

CONCLUSION

The questionnaire shown in Figure 3.1 summarizes the questions that leaders might ask themselves to determine whether they have mastered developmental leadership. Making the transformation to the developmental organization cannot occur until senior managers and executives adopt the philosophy of developmental leadership, accept the responsibilities and assumptions of developmental leaders, adopt the servantship philosophy of leadership, and apply the ten principles of developmental leadership. When these elements are working in harmony, executives will be immediately transformed from traditional autocratic "bosses" to developmental leaders, ready to lead their organizations in competitive corporate wars, armed with a secret weapon—the developmental organization. When fully developed, this organization is a force to be reckoned with because its strategic approach gives organizations a significant competitive advantage. Read on, more exciting information lies ahead.

FIGURE 3.1   Principles of Developmental Leadership Questionnaire

Scoring the Developmental Leadership Questionnaire:

Once the questionnaire is completed, transfer your responses to the **Competency Scoring** sheet. Enter the point value (1–5 points) on the Points line, which is below each of the numbered *Items*. For example, if you respond "Sometimes" to item number 1, then a "3" (point value) would be entered directly below the number 1 on the scoring sheet. Total all points recorded for this skill area and enter the cumulative score on the *total* line. Repeat this process for all four skill areas.

After calculating the total for each of the four skill areas, total **all** four skill areas and enter this overall score at the bottom of the page on the **Developmental Leadership Mastery Score** line.

Principles of Developmental Leadership Questionnaire

	Never	Infrequently	Sometimes	Frequently	Always
1. I demonstrate personal accountability for my decisions and actions.	1	2	3	4	5
2. I delegate work tasks and responsibilities as a way of helping employees grow and develop.	1	2	3	4	5
3. I create work environments to encourage employees to produce creative solutions to difficult problems and to participate in continuous organizational improvement.	1	2	3	4	5
4. I do not allow others' negative perceptions to affect my performance or decisions.	1	2	3	4	5
5. I look inward to discover new awareness and insights.					
6. I openly communicate with employees to help them improve their performance.	1	2	3	4	5
7. I create performance partnerships that foster employees' growth and development.	1	2	3	4	5
8. I make a list of my values and beliefs to make certain they align with those of the organization.	1	2	3	4	5

	Never	Infrequently	Sometimes	Frequently	Always
9. I request feedback from my employees regarding my performance and behavior.	1	2	3	4	5
10. I enhance the self-esteem of employees by delegating work assignments that are rewarding and satisfying.	1	2	3	4	5
11. I identify and eliminate conflicting job tasks and activities that reduce employee motivation and performance.	1	2	3	4	5
12. I make certain that my personal guiding priniciples are integrated with those of the organization.	1	2	3	4	5
13. I encourage employees to share their opinions regarding the direction of the organization.	1	2	3	4	5
14. I provide advancement and promotion opportunities for my employees.	1	2	3	4	5
15. I work collaboratively with employees to accomplish the organization's goals and objectives.	1	2	3	4	5
16. I have a clear vision of my organization, both in terms of its financial condition and human resources.	1	2	3	4	5
17. I attempt to develop trust with employees.	1	2	3	4	5

	Never	Infrequently	Sometimes	Frequently	Always
18. I link employees' promotions and advancements to their growth and development.	1	2	3	4	5
19. I am long-term focused, resisting quick-fix opportunities or short-term decisions or solutions.	1	2	3	4	5
20. I allow employees to participate in the development of the organization's vision.	1	2	3	4	5
21. I create a work environment free of fear.	1	2	3	4	5
22. I give employees assignments that provide them opportunities for achievement, accomplishments, and mastery.	1	2	3	4	5
23. I work collaboratively with my employees in order to improve their performance.	1	2	3	4	5
24. I anticipate business trends and processes, and break them down into manageable units for others to understand and implement.	1	2	3	4	5
25. I develop a solid communication pattern with employees both in terms of frequency and depth.	1	2	3	4	5
26. I allow employees to enhance their power, control, and influence within the organization.	1	2	3	4	5

	Never	Infrequently	Sometimes	Frequently	Always
27. I help employees improve their knowledge and skills so that they can enhance their careers and improve their performance.	1	2	3	4	5
28. I know what my organization wants to achieve and how to accomplish it.	1	2	3	4	5
29. I discover the unique characteristics, personality, life experiences, and professional paths of each employee.	1	2	3	4	5
30. I provide positive affirmation for employee participation and provide positive feedback for their contributions, recommendations, and achievements.	1	2	3	4	5
31. I communicate the organization's purpose and vision to ensure employee support.	1	2	3	4	5
32. I know when an organizational change is consistent with my guiding principles (values and beliefs).	1	2	3	4	5
33. I engage employees by accepting them as positive contributors and worthwhile human beings.	1	2	3	4	5
34. I encourage employees to discover ways of integrating their values and beliefs on the job.	1	2	3	4	5

	Never	Infrequently	Sometimes	Frequently	Always
35. I immediately point out employees' performance shortfalls before they become serious.	1	2	3	4	5
36. I can identify and eliminate the barriers to employee performance.	1	2	3	4	5
37. I become personally involved with employees, spending significant time with each.	1	2	3	4	5
38. I enhance the self-esteem of employees even when their performance does not warrant it.	1	2	3	4	5
39. I provide a communication climate that is non-threatenening, comfortable, and conducive for sharing.	1	2	3	4	5
40. I help employees to work effectively and efficiently by minimizing organizational interference.	1	2	3	4	5

Competency Scoring Sheet

Intrinsically Oriented Principles

Item:	1	5	9	13	17	21	25	29	33	37	Total
Points:	–	–	–	—	—	—	—	—	—	—	—

Employee Oriented Principles

Item:	2	6	10	14	18	22	26	30	34	38	Total
Points:	–	–	—	—	—	—	—	—	—	—	—

Performance Oriented Principles

Item:	3	7	11	15	19	23	27	31	35	39	Total
Points:	–	–	—	—	—	—	—	—	—	—	—

Organizationally Oriented Principles

Item:	4	8	12	16	20	24	28	32	36	40	Total
Points:	–	–	—	—	—	—	—	—	—	—	—

Grand Total ___

Developmental Leadership Mastery Score

40	60	80	100	120	140	160	180	200
20%	30%	40%	50%	60%	70%	80%	90%	100%

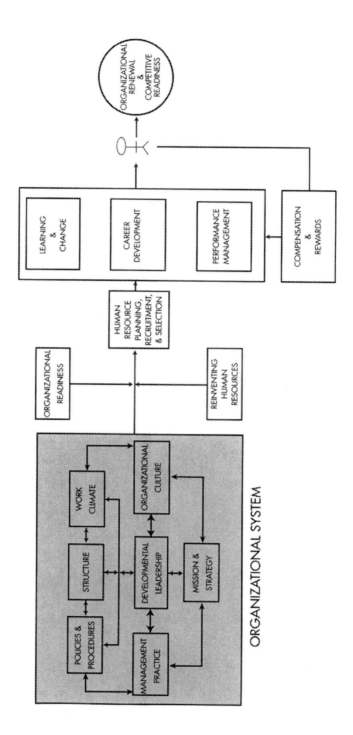

ORGANIZATIONAL SYSTEM

CHAPTER 4

The Organizational System: Its Impact on Transformation

As we contemplate transforming organizations from traditional to learning to developmental, we must consider what constitutes an organization. Many view organizations as complex, hierarchical structures composed of impersonal relationships organized to produce products and services. We often forget that organizations are made up of people. People constitute all aspects of organizational life—without people organizations cease to exist. People do not haphazardly reside within organizations; each has his or her selected purpose for existence and has responsibilities for producing outputs necessary for the survival of the firm.

Occasionally, it is useful to think of organizations as icebergs—we only see the part above the surface. This represents the formal components of an organization—the perceived image, business logo, or what senior management want people to think the firm represents. Beneath the water's surface—unseen, unknown, undetected—lies the real organization, consisting of hierarchical layers, departments, units, functions, policies, procedures, practices, managerial relationships, and so forth. The global community has little firsthand knowledge of most informal operations within organizations. An outside community cannot observe interactions or activities that take place in order for businesses to achieve their goals.

Viewing organizations as icebergs allows for a simple description of their formal and informal natures and both their visible and unseen components. Capturing the real essence and complex nature of organizations, however, requires more in-depth consideration. In a previous book (Gilley and Maycunich 1998a, 64), we likened organizations to human organisms:

> . . . humans have digestive, circulatory, skeletal, and nervous systems; organizations have similar subsystems that enable them to remain alive. Typically, organizations are diagrammed in such a way to describe connections between various departments, both vertically and horizontally. On the horizontal plane, various departments are indicated that represent functions such as finance, marketing, manufacturing, customer service, and so forth. On the vertical plane, organizations are divided into subparts of various departments, usually indicating individual titles and specific reporting relationships.

Because firms are organized both vertically and horizontally, they create divisions of labor, departmentalizations, spans of control, and levels of authority. Deeply imbedded within these vertical and horizontal intersections is a culture, a work climate, and managerial practices that reflect the interactions between executives, managers, and employees. As we examine these intersections more closely, we discover that all organizations have policies and procedures that help structure interactions while providing input in decision making, communications, and accountability. Integral to any organization is a leadership that provides organizational direction, articulates the organizational mission, and lays out strategies to accomplish that mission.

Taking our biological analogy one step further, we see that human beings are the outward manifestation of several internal systems working in harmony. If we strip away the outer skin and muscle that house the human body, we are left with a skeletal structure and vital organs that constitute the essential components of the human body. The outer skin and muscular frame of an organization represent what we perceive an organization to be—what gives it its texture, depth, and breadth. The ability to see, touch, and feel leads to understanding. Organizations, like the human body, consist of vital organs and structures that give them strength, rigidity, form, and function—components critical to an organization's life.

Figure 4.1 (page 99) provides an overview of the organizational system, which consists of interdependent functions upon which the firm depends to remain viable. These seven interdependent functions include and are compared to the corresponding systems or body parts within the human body:

1. Leadership—heart and circulatory system
2. Organizational structure—skeletal system
3. Organizational culture—digestive system
4. Mission and strategy—eyes and brain
5. Managerial practice—muscular system
6. Policies and procedures—nervous system
7. Work climate—respiratory system

As indicated in the figure, each of these seven functions is dependent on the other (as represented by arrows). Yet each function is an independent component of the organization, not unlike the vital organs of the human body. The arrows in both directions convey an open-system principle—what changes in one factor will eventually impact others (Burke 1992). Connection points exist between the organization system and other components of the organization, such as the performance management system (see Chapter 10). That is, the organizational system must be intact, healthy, and vibrant to positively impact other systems within the firm. If an organization is healthy and producing positive results, these seven interdependent functions are working in harmony. When an organization fails to achieve desired results or is ill equipped to meet the competitive demands of the global marketplace, it is helpful to look within each of these functions and/or their relationship to one another to determine whether their symptoms are those of decline, inadequacy, or failing. Thus, organizational leaders in concert with human resource professionals can analyze the relationship between various functions within the organizational system to reveal potential breakdowns or areas of weakness, or both.

Change interventions can be targeted to improve various functions for the entire organizational system. Thus, organizational leaders and human resource professionals will have a systematic approach to examining weaknesses as well as looking for opportunities for continued growth and development essential to organizational renewal.

ELEMENTS OF THE ORGANIZATIONAL SYSTEM

As previously discussed, an organizational system consists of seven distinct yet interdependent functions, each of which is dependent upon the others yet can function quite successfully on its own. Regardless of one's orientation or responsibilities within an organization, be it marketing, finance, manufacturing, distribution, or so forth, these seven functions are constants. That is, regardless of one's organizational vantage point, each of these seven functions clearly exists. The difference lies in one's perception of function and one's understanding of the interdependence and relationship of each.

As shown in Figure 4.1, the center of an organizational system is leadership. We believe that the heart of every organization is its leaders. Their skills and abilities impact the firm's direction while energizing, exciting, and influencing its workforce. Hence, leadership directly impacts the four most important functions within the firm: structure, culture, mission and strategy, and managerial practice. These functions are like the skeletal, digestive, muscular systems, eyes, and brain of the human body.

Leadership indirectly influences policies, procedures, and work climate, which are greatly affected by such things as organizational structure, culture, and managerial practices. The distance between various functions also has some bearing on how the functions interrelate. For example, changes in organizational structure may not directly affect its culture unless leadership and work climate change simultaneously. At the same time, structural changes might not influence the firm's mission and strategy unless leadership deems it necessary. Similarly, improvements in managerial practices may not significantly affect an organization's work climate unless the structure, leadership, and culture are altered to reflect these improvements. Changes in policies and procedures might have no

FIGURE 4.1   Organizational system

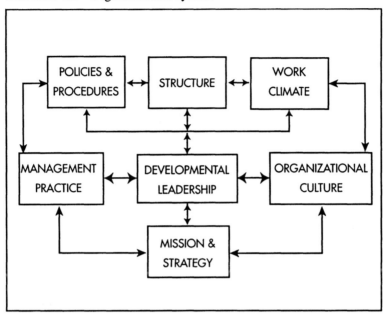

effect on work climate or culture unless structural considerations and leadership are fully supportive of these changes. Although policy and procedural changes are blessed by leadership, in reality many changes occurring deep inside individual departments are rarely fully disclosed to senior management. Consequently, departments may vary drastically in their interpretations of organizational rules and regulations. The result of this varied interpretation may be a somewhat schizophrenic work climate and culture. These examples illustrate the complexity of an organizational system and its various interrelated functions. Understanding these complex interrelationships is important in creating an organizational system that promotes renewal and increases performance capacity through growth and development.

Leadership

Leadership is at the center of every interaction, decision, communication, and action within an organization (Figure 4.1). Gibson, Ivancevich, and Donnelly (1997) define leadership as an attempt to influence or motivate individuals to accomplish some goal. We define leadership as a process of making decisions regarding how to interact with employees to motivate them, then translating those decisions into actions. Burke (1992, 130) describes leadership as the behavior of managers and executives that provides direction and encourages others to take needed action. Effective leadership is like the human heart and circulatory system, on which all human life depends. Each definition reinforces the concept that leadership is the nucleus of an organization's universe, around which all activities revolve. These definitions further reflect leadership's primary purpose as a motivator of others to take action to accomplish a predetermined objective.

Without leadership, an organizational system would cease to have a center of influence. Hence, it is important to understand leadership's impact on other components within the organizational system. In Chapter 3, we discussed the principles of developmental leadership, describing several leadership theories and analyzing how different types of leadership theories apply to traditional, learning, and developmental organizations. Another outlook is to consider leadership as the catalyst by which things are done within an organizational system. We will further examine the relationship between leadership and other components of the organizational system.

Structure

The term "organizational architecture" is sometimes used to describe an organization's structure. By "architecture" we mean the foundation upon which the firm is built and the structure that gives an organization its character. The structure of an organization is analogous to the human skeletal system; organizational structure provides the rigidity necessary to support the firm's weight and strength during periods of uncertainty or crisis. Like a human skeleton, a firm's structure provides definition and organization—there is a place for everything, and everything in its place. Structure for departments and divisions supports the firm's ultimate objectives.

In an earlier book (Gilley and Maycunich 1998a, 71), we explained that structure also refers to the arrangement of work functions and employees in specific areas and levels of responsibility, to decision-making authority, and to the relationships for the business to achieve its strategic business goals. We proposed that creating an organizational structure involves four important variables:

1. Division of labor: the process of dividing work into specialized areas
2. Departmentalization: the process by which a firm is divided by combining jobs in accordance with shared characteristics
3. Span of control: the number of employees who report to specific managers or executives
4. Authority: the power to make and execute decisions within the organization

Most organizations are divided into centralized or decentralized operations. However, we are witnessing the emergence of project-based and customer-based organizational structures designed to be more responsive to client needs on a short-term-project orientation or long-term customer-satisfaction emphasis. The degree to which organizations divide into centralized or decentralized project or customer bases depends largely upon communication, structure in place, and the organization's reliance on formal policies and procedures when making decisions.

Boyett and Boyett (1995) maintain that the strongest structure has no walls—no barriers between people, departments, or customers. Developmental organizations, too, by virtue of their changeable, free-flowing nature, are boundary-free, breaking down the walls that separate people. In fact, says Burke (1992, 63), the developmental organization structure

has no boundaries . . . [and] has been compared to a solar system, a symphony orchestra, a spider's web. . . . It is open, adaptive, and infinitely flat. It is both centralized and decentralized, and perhaps most importantly, it is virtual. . . . It is fluid and free-form. It is hard to depict with lines on a chart. It requires motion and movement, because it is constantly changing and reforming itself. . . . [I]t takes a million different forms, so there is no single "it" to describe.

Division of Labor.   Organizations often divide work into relatively specialized jobs to achieve a differential advantage over the competition. This is also done to enhance the advantage of specialized work functions to increase quality and efficiency. Division of labor within an organization usually occurs in one of three ways.

First, work can be divided into professional specializations, often referred to as occupational professional identity. Thus, employees think of themselves as accountants, engineers, human resource professionals, and so forth.

Second, jobs can be divided into separate activities based upon the sequence of work that an organization completes. For example, insurance companies with claims divisions separate jobs into their natural sequence of handling claims: the claims processor (who takes the initial call, initiates the paperwork, and assigns the claim to an adjuster), the claims adjuster (who examines the claim and determines the amount of the payment), and the claims payable department (which actually cuts the check). Each position handles various aspects of an insurance claim. Gibson, Ivancevich, and Donnelly (1997) refer to this as "horizontal specialization."

Third, jobs can be divided based on a hierarchy of authority, from the lowest to highest levels within the organization. Along this vertical plane is a significant differentiation from a first-line supervisor to that of the CEO, from job responsibility to accountability.

Historically, the division of labor has been a function of what was best for the organization in terms of achieving its strategic business goals and objectives. Although this is an acceptable and often useful means of arranging job specialization, developmental organizations incorporate an additional element. How can jobs be arranged to enhance and encourage employee growth and development?

This simple question often evokes a complex answer. Most employees desire to be identified with some type of professional occupation, even though this practice may be detrimental in the long run. These employees may be cast into groupings that limit learning, opportunities for change, or career development emphasis. Similarly, a vertical or sequential division of labor may be detrimental to the creation of a developmental organization. Nevertheless, no right answer prevails as to how a firm should divide its labor force. What is important is that organizations examine the issues to guarantee that whatever decisions they arrive at are made for reasons that advocate employee growth and development in addition to achieving desired business results.

Departmentalization.   The most common element of organization structure is departmentalization, a process by which a firm is structurally divided when combining jobs in departments according to some shared characteristic. The principle purposes of departmentalization involve maximizing economies of scale, assembling individuals with similar backgrounds or other shared characteristics to improve productivity, performance, communications, employee involvement, and decision making. The main danger of arranging jobs into separate, individual departments is that they become tall, thick, and windowless structures that prevent interaction between peers at low and mid levels. Rummler and Brache (1995, 7) likened these organizations to silos, contending that a silo structure forces managers to resolve low-level issues, taking their time away from higher-priority customers and competitive concerns. A silo structure forces people to adopt cultures, language, and customs common to their department rather than that of the organization as a whole—behavior that inhibits cross-departmental interaction and communications, and deteriorates decision making, performance, and quality.

We believe that organizations operating within silo structures are likely to produce the organization's tower of Babel. Similar to the biblical metaphor, an organizational tower of Babel is indicative of a time when confusion reigns within organizations or society as a result of specialized culturalization. When this occurs, people from different departments (cultures) fail to communicate or maintain a common language, which leads to isolation and operation from a narrow departmental perspective. When the organizational tower of Babel flourishes, employees are prevented from working across departmental lines to achieve desired business goals. Further, organizational decisions are pushed up to the highest level, preventing teamwork and cross-departmental cooperation. Therefore, savvy leaders will guard against inappropriate, illogical departmentalization, which prevents a firm from achieving its ultimate business goals and objectives.

According to Gibson, Ivancevich, and Donnelly (1997), five types of departmentalization occur within organizations. First, businesses commonly organize around functions common to their industry. For example, manufacturing firms may include production, marketing, finance, accounting, and personnel, whereas hospitals may include surgical units, psychiatry, housekeeping, nursing, pharmacy, and supplies. Divisions such as these perpetuate specialization and division of labor.

Second, some national and international organizations are divided into regional departments whereby geographical areas determine how the business is organized. This practice is very common in large manufacturers, consulting firms, and insurance companies. Under these circumstances, employees in various geographical locations are grouped together and may be separated into functions within territories, although the primary orientation is their regional identity.

Third, organizations are more and more often dividing themselves into product divisions. Recently, 3M divided the organization into product lines. Personnel throughout the United States and the world combined their identity with the products for which they were responsible rather than their job specialization or geographical orientation.

Fourth, some organizations are beginning to divide themselves into customer- or client-based groupings. A common example of customer-oriented departmentalization is the structure within educational institutions. Colleges and universities historically have been broken down into divisions such as business, engineering, education, agriculture, and arts and sciences to meet the needs of specialized clients (students). More and more corporations are also finding it advantageous to be tied around customer bases to improve their customer service and enhance customer-focused managerial practices.

Fifth, some businesses maximize their strengths and minimize their weaknesses by employing both functional- and product-based approaches. These approaches, called matrix organizations, enable firms to be product- or project-based and organized around various functions, vis-à-vis specific products or projects. William M. Mercer, Inc., a large compensation, benefits, and human resource consulting firm has recently moved to this type of departmentalized approach. Because it is a project-oriented organization consisting of several different professional practice areas, it was advantageous for the company to organize around specific projects in which multiple practice areas might participate. For example, a merger or an acquisition consulting engagement might require experts from the pension (defined benefits and contributions), executive compensation, health care, communications, and human resource management practice areas to execute a successful project. Once the project has been successfully completed to the client's satisfaction, these professionals move on to the next project. They may or may not be working together in the near future; however, if certain projects require their expertise, they may be reassembled. The focus here is on the project or product, utilizing the appropriate functions of an organization.

Regardless of how a firm elects to departmentalize, each departmentalization method can be used to enhance employee growth and development. Organizations must guard against selecting a departmentalization strategy based solely on the enhancement of productivity or profitability. It may make more sense from a growth and development standpoint to organize in ways that give employees new, challenging job assignments. If organizations are committed to evolving to the developmental level, electing a functional or territorial departmentalization approach may not be advantageous, even though such approaches may be the easiest to manage or most efficient. The product, customer, or matrix approach may be more appropriate, despite its potential to require more of management's time and care. These three departmentalization schemes allow for cross-departmental cooperation while advocating a synergistic approach to achieving business goals and objectives. A functional or territorial departmentalization approach can be effective, but organizations must make certain that employee growth and development are paramount in a long-term strategy.

Span of Control.   Span of control refers to the number of individuals reporting to a specific manager. The issue generally boils down to how many people a manager can effectively oversee. Thus, will the organization be more effective if its span of control is relatively wide or narrow? William M. Mercer, Inc., had a standard policy that a consulting office should not exceed one hundred members. When it reached this threshold, it was divided into separate operational units. The philosophy behind this approach was that the effectiveness of a senior consultant to manage and interact with other consultants reached a point of diminishing returns at about one hundred staff members. To maintain effective communications, decision making, and interaction, the organization made certain that its offices did not exceed this limit.

From a developmental perspective, the smaller the span of control, the better. This way, managers are responsible for the individual growth and development of the people who report to them; they utilize their performance coaching skills at maximum efficiency (see Chapter 5). In addition, the smaller the span of control, the more frequent the contact with individual personnel. The result is increased opportunity to discuss employees' developmental needs and career aspirations. Equally important to development is the opportunity to communicate face to face with employees. When an organization has expanded to such an extent that face-to-face interaction is no longer possible, the ability to receive reinforcement and feedback is greatly diminished, which hurts employee growth and development in the long term. Building synergistic relationships with employees propels a firm from the traditional to the developmental organization. Consequently, organizations wrestle with the issue of span of control and identify an acceptable threshold for them while meeting their employees' developmental requirements.

Authority.   One hidden characteristic of organizational structure is authority. Although an organization might address the issue of authority when examining its division of labor, departmentalization, and span of control, authority should stand alone as a component of organizational structure. Authority refers to an individual's rights to make important job decisions without approval from senior management or direct obedience to another.

Businesses must decide how much authority should be delegated to each job and each job holder. Most organizations support either a centralized or a decentralized authority. In a decentralized environment, employees throughout the firm are given permission to make appropriate decisions, which encourages them to gain the decision-making skills and problem-solving abilities required of such responsibility. When job specialization is high, decentralized authority is often the most efficient approach, because individuals possess a high level of confidence. Thus, they are often perceived as authorities within a professional practice and are granted a certain level of respect and freedom to make decisions.

When employees are scattered throughout the nation or world, it makes sense to grant individuals the authority to make decisions when and if appropriate. Under these circumstances, the ability to deal with autonomy and freedom is of paramount importance as individuals must feel as though they have the right or justification to make certain decisions in isolation.

Centralized authority is most advantageous in avoiding duplication of effort and in improving the efficiency and effectiveness of decision making. Consequently, centralized decision making may be financially expedient. Further, many senior managers are accustomed to making decisions and resist delegating authority to their subordinates. Finally, reviewing or auditing decisions made by individuals other than those at the top of the organizational hierarchy can be quite expensive. Thus, organizations attempting to manage by saving money will often use a centralized authority approach.

A decentralized authority orientation provides the greatest potential for employee growth and development because as employees participate in the decision-making process they develop analytical and rational skills useful throughout their careers. Employees also enhance their own personal self-esteem and sense of accomplishment, thus increasing their personal job satisfaction and loyalty to the organization. Finally, decentralized authority allows personnel to maintain an involvement level uncommon in centralized authority situations. Thus, employees are challenged to continuously examine new ways of enhancing their knowledge and skills.

Organizational Culture

Culture represents another major area of the organizational system. It is analogous to the human digestive system, through which all things pass to sustain life. Organizational culture is the important artifacts, rules, values, principles, and assumptions that guide organizational behavior. According to Schein (1992, 9), organizational culture can be defined as "a pattern of basic assumptions invented, discovered, or developed by a given group as it learns to cope with the problems of external adaptation and internal integration that all works well enough to be considered valid and, therefore, to be taught to new members as the correct way to perceive, think, and feel in relation to those problems." Schein's definition illustrates that culture involves assumptions, adaptations, perceptions, and learning. More simply, Burke (1992, 130) refers to organizational culture as "the way we do things around here." Organizational culture is indeed a complex topic strongly influenced by history, customs, and practices. Moreover, organizational culture is what employees perceive to be the pattern of belief, values, and expectations that guide behavior and practice within the firm. In short, culture determines the type of institution the organization becomes.

Developmental organizations provide flexible, adaptive work assignments designed to offer employees challenging work that will both improve employee self-esteem and enhance their contribution to the firm. Additionally, these organizations actively identify and retain sincere, person-oriented managers and supervisors with the propensity and desire to create synergistic relationships between themselves and their employees that improve comprehension, decision making, performance, and achievement of business results.

Developmental organizations manifest the optimal organizational culture. According to Burke (1992, 196–197), developmental organization culture exhibits the following characteristics:

1. Growth and development of organizational members is just as important as making profits or staying within budget.

2. Equal opportunity and fairness for people within an organization is commonplace, the rule rather than the exception.

3. Managers exercise their authority more participatively than unilaterally or arbitrarily; authority is associated more with knowledge and competence than role or status.

4. Cooperative behavior is rewarded more than competitive behavior.

5. Organizational members are kept informed on, or at least have access to, information, especially concerning matters directly impacting their jobs or them personally.

6. Members feel a sense of ownership of the organization's mission and objectives.

7. Conflict is dealt with openly and systematically rather than ignored, avoided, or handled in a typical win–lose fashion.

8. Rewards are based on a system of quality, fairness, and equitable merit.

9. Organization members are given as much autonomy and freedom to do their respective jobs as possible, enjoying both a high degree of individual motivation and the accomplishment of the organization's strategic goals and objectives.

When these characteristics are present, the evolution to the developmental organization is complete.

Mission and Strategy

An organization's mission and strategy are greatly and equally influenced by the firm's leadership and culture. Therefore, leaders should answer the following questions when developing an organization's mission:

1. What is our purpose?
2. What direction do we want to strive toward?
3. Who are our customers?
4. What are we trying to achieve?

5. What significance are we attempting to accomplish?
6. What will our purpose be in the future?

When these questions are answered, organizations clearly envision where they are going and how to get there, similar to the eyes and brain working in harmony.

Establishing an organizational mission is a time-consuming, soul-searching process intended to bring about unanimity among all firm members regarding what the business is attempting to accomplish. Ultimate agreement brings about enhanced support within the organization. Gilley and Eggland (1992, 76) believe a mission statement acts as an "invisible hand which guides widely scattered organizational members to work independently yet collectively toward the realization of the organization's strategic business goals and objectives."

Strategy, on the other hand, refers to how an organization intends to achieve its purposes over an extended period. Strategy helps identify the tasks and activities that an organization will undertake in order to demonstrate its purpose and define its direction as it manifests its achievements. Organizations consider strategy as their game plan, to be embraced and executed by all members. It should remain flexible, adaptive, and take into consideration unique circumstances and events, but should always be focused on helping the organization achieve its desired purpose.

In developmental organizations, the firm's mission and strategy are fully communicated to and understood by all members of the firm. It is common for employees and managers to work in concert with organizational leaders to construct the mission and implement its strategies. In this way, developmental organizations are living by the concept that people support what they create.

Management Practices

The normal activities employed by managers to execute organizational strategy are referred to as managerial practices. These practices include the utilization of human and material resources, employee communications, the delegation of work tasks, project management, organizational change interventions, and the management of employee conflicts and poor performance. As the muscular system provides the human body with definition and strength, so do managerial practices accomplish organizational objectives through people.

Most managerial practices are concerned with two dimensions: tasks and people. Managers must be able to achieve desired business results, concerning themselves with accomplishing tasks within the organization. Managerial practice is equally concerned with people, the human resources assigned to bring about the desired business results. Within developmental organizations, managers are equally concerned about tasks and people. Along the people dimension, developmental organizations focus their attention on building positive working relationships with employees and providing them with growth and development opportunities throughout their careers. Developmental organizations are not different from any other organizations in their concern for tasks. Positive business results are absolutely critical. The fundamental difference between developmental organizations and traditional organizations is the utilization of human resources to achieve their desired ends.

Policies and Procedures

Policies and procedures encompass an organization's rules and regulations, much like the human nervous system providing electrical charges that protect and ensure appropriate responses. Policies are the established set of rules employees must follow; procedures prescribe how employees will execute daily work activities (Gilley and Maycunich 1998a, 74). The extent to which organizations rely on written rules, regulations, and predetermined actions of employees is known as formalization (Gibson, Ivancevich, and Donnelly 1997). The more formalization within an organization, the more an organization relies on delegated authority and wide spans of control. High formalization allows organizations to become highly specialized, allowing division of labor to be so specialized as to leave little or no discretion to the job holder. Conversely, low formalization permits tremendous job diversity and discretion but centralized authority and one-to-one supervision. High formalization is most common when organizations have selected a functional departmentalization approach.

When policies and procedures are constructed to reinforce centralization, that is, when managers retain the authority to make decisions, this authority is delegated to individual workers, allowing for wider span of control and greater use of functional departments and jobs requiring higher degrees of specialization. In this instance, policies and procedures are very restrictive, permitting little freedom among employees.

In developmental organizations, policies and procedures should allow the firm to align personnel around its central focus and mission and should govern organizational behavior by providing a normalizing orientation that by no means should restrict innovative, creative solutions to problem solving. Policies and procedures should be flexible enough to allow employees' input, but structured enough to provide guidance and direction for employees when uncertainty rules. There should be a code of conduct and behavior developed and shared among employees that increases their willingness to participate in projects and assignments. In short, policies and procedures in developmental organizations enhance cooperation; guarantee innovative and creative problem solving; enhance professional respect; ensure responsible behavior and rational, mature thought; and reinforce performance accountability and behavior.

Work Climate

Work climate is greatly affected by an organization's leadership, structure, and culture, and can be best determined by examining employees' impressions and expectations concerning the work environment. An organization's work climate is similar to a person's respiratory system, which is essential to life and health. When positive, anything is possible; when negative, poor performance, productivity, and quality follow. Organizational leaders, co-workers, the type of organization, economic factors, and departmental stability all impact work climate. Work climate is a by-product of the organization's culture and structure. In developmental organizations, employees are viewed as important and committed. They are allowed to participate in critical decision making and provide input into business practices. Work climates foster loyalty and involvement, creating both challenging and rewarding work assignments. Managers are encouraged to become involved with their employees' growth, form positive working relationships, create a climate of continuous change and development, and encourage transformational leadership.

In developmental organizations, a positive work climate fosters dialogue between leaders, managers, and employees—between all people within a firm—creating an environment based on respect and reciprocity that encourages collaboration, togetherness, and teamwork. These ingredients promote a sense of belonging among employees, enabling them to adopt a shared reality and purpose. When blended together, these elements produce an environment that allows for active engagement by all employees. In this environment, each employee is a valuable, contributing member of the organization, with an enhanced self-esteem and sense of personal worth.

TYPES OF CONSULTING ACTIVITIES

Developmental leaders and human resource professionals use the organizational effectiveness framework to determine the types of consulting activities in which they may appropriately engage. In fact, these actions are consistent with the human resource professionals' roles discussed in Chapter 6.

For human resource professionals working to improve the organizational system, the most appropriate type of consulting activity is *change management.* Change management reshapes, redesigns, and reengineers the organization (Gilley and Maycunich 1998a, 81). This management activity requires human resource professionals to be organizational experts and employee champions simultaneously (see Chapter 6). The goal is to review the relationship between the seven functions outlined within the organizational system to assess the efficiency and effectiveness with which they work together.

Human resource professionals are occasionally solicited to improve employee performance, productivity, or quality, thus functioning as *performance consultants* (see Chapter 6). Performance consulting involves examining the organization's overall performance capacity and capability, typically by assessing the interplay between the eight performance management system variables and determining how employee performance can be improved. In Chapter 10, we discuss how performance management aids employee growth and development while improving performance, productivity, and quality.

We discern distinct differences between change management and performance consulting. Performance consulting is designed to impact organizational effectiveness by improving the performance system and the behaviors of each employee. Change management consulting examines the organizational system's impact on performance. Both are, however, essential in creating a developmental organization.

Improving both the organizational and performance management systems simultaneously requires organizational development consulting. Organizational development consulting is a holistic, efficient means by which to improve organizational effectiveness. Investigating these two systems allows human resource professionals to determine the impact each has on the other while isolating components that need special attention. This insight enables human resource professionals to design interventions or advocate changes that will improve employee performance and productivity while enhancing growth and development opportunities (see Chapter 6).

THE IMPACT OF THE ORGANIZATIONAL SYSTEM ON WORK DESIGN, LEARNING SYSTEMS, AND PERFORMANCE COACHING

The organizational system greatly impacts the performance management system. Most affected are work design, learning systems, and performance coaching because they are directly linked to components within the organizational system.

Work Design

When an organization fails to achieve its desired business goals and objectives, examination of the organizational system often reveals how it may have affected this outcome. Once each of the seven functions and their relationships have been examined, it may be necessary to further assess work design. Work design is defined as a series of steps used to produce a product or service (Rummler and Brache 1995). When the organization fails to achieve its objectives, reshaping, reorganizing, redefining, replacing, or improving work design may be warranted. It is also important to determine if any of the seven components of the organizational system have hurt the work design process.

In the developmental organization, employees have input in work design analysis. This practice is based on the premise that employees possess a greater knowledge of job-related problems because they perform job tasks on a regular basis and thus are familiar with the components of each. Leaders, on the other hand, have the authority to solve job-related problems and are in a position to exercise control and change related to each job (Gilley, Boughton, and Maycunich 1999, 183). Developmental organizations have two fundamental goals: to increase the leaders' knowledge of job-related problems and to increase the employees' authority to solve job-related problems.

The result of reaching these two goals is more harmony and efficiency within the organization. This increased harmony between leaders and employees improves their collective problem-solving effectiveness, which, in turn, improves the organization's efficiency because leaders are more aware of job-related problems and effectively address them. Conversely, employees are free to respond to job-related problems more quickly because they have been granted greater decision-making latitude by the organization.

In developmental organizations, leaders can increase harmony and efficiency by encouraging risk taking by employees. Larson and LaFasto (1989, 126) assert that to accomplish this, leaders must provide climates supportive of decision-making by the following actions:

- trusting employees with meaningful levels of responsibility
- providing employees with the necessary autonomy to achieve results
- presenting challenging opportunities that stretch employees' abilities
- recognizing and rewarding superior performance
- standing behind employees and supporting them

The presence of these behaviors encourages employees to unleash their talents, resulting in efficient, effective decisions along with employee growth and development.

Learning Systems

An organization's learning system reveals a great deal about how growth and development occur within a firm, indicating how serious an organization is about learning. As stated previously, learning is a prerequisite to development; hence, without learning, development cannot occur. Thus, it is important to scrutinize an organization's learning system to determine the following:

- how employees learn
- why employees learn
- what employees learn
- when employees learn
- where employees learn
- who is responsible for employee learning
- how learning is reinforced and rewarded
- what the barriers are to learning transfer

The type of learning occurring within an organization also reveals a great deal about the learning system. To determine the type of learning present, one must identify the relationship between information exchange, learning acquisition and practice, and transfer and integration.

When placed in a working model, these three dimensions yield eight different types of learning:

1. Content–centered learning
2. Trial and error learning
3. Accidental learning
4. Anticipatory learning
5. Incidental learning

6. Traditional theoretical learning
7. Self-directed learning
8. Developmental learning

Each type of learning will be examined in greater detail in Chapter 8.

The organizational system can have a tremendous impact on an organization's learning system. The types of organizational leadership, structure, culture, and work climate exhibit the value that organizational leaders place on learning (including learning by managers), opportunities for growth and development, and the encouragement, rewards, and recognition that employees received for applying learning on the job (Figure 4.1).

Performance Coaching

In Chapter 5 we examine the importance of adopting performance coaching to overcome managerial malpractice. Further, we discuss the critical subroles—facilitator of learning, mentor, confronter, and career counselor—that managers play to improve employee relations, performance, productivity, quality, growth, and development.

Making the transition from manager to performance coach can be exulted or diminished, based on the policies and procedures employed by an organization, its managerial practices, structure, and leadership (Figure 4.1). To illustrate, some organizations have a long history of authoritarian management practice—in which the *boss* is all-knowing and powerful. Little attention is given to manager–employee relations or to the input of employees. This practice makes it extremely difficult for organizations to employ the principles and practices of performance coaching. Overcoming this hurdle requires organizations to recruit and select managers who possess the characteristics and competencies necessary to become performance coaches—or who are willing to learn these skills accordingly (Chapter 5).

We believe that managers who champion and employ the principles and practices of performance coaching can and will, over time, influence an organization's management practices. The above example demonstrates the interplay between organizational system components and performance coaching. It also explains why it is so difficult to make the transition from the traditional to the developmental organization.

The types of leadership and structure prevalent in an organization impact the policies and procedures used to regulate managers' and employees' decisions and behavior. These organizational system components indirectly influence the use of performance coaching. Conversely, components of the organizational system can positively affect deployment of this approach, greatly enhancing its success and the benefits derived from performance coaching.

Applying the Organizational Effectiveness Framework

One of the best ways of applying the organizational effectiveness framework is to think of it as a troubleshooting guide useful in isolating organizational breakdowns and performance problems. For example, electronic technicians use diagrams (schematics), automobile mechanics rely on diagnostic tools, and building contractors refer to blueprints to provide them direction and to isolate breakdowns and problems. Similarly, human resource professionals and organizational leaders employ the organizational effectiveness framework to isolate problems or identify areas that require examination in order to craft an intervention (Gilley and Maycunich 1998a, 82–83).

When confronted with a performance problem or an organizational breakdown such as the lack of collaborative work environment, human resource professionals and organizational leaders should follow the eight steps to maximize organizational effectiveness (Figure 4.2).

Let us illustrate. First, identify the most logical components to determine the extent of the problem or breakdown, such as management practices, leadership, work climate, or organizational culture. Remember to identify only those components that have a direct impact on the problem. Second, define each component. Third, identify their importance in the organization. This allows human resource professionals and leaders to develop a working definition of each component and prioritize them. Fourth, identify the strengths and weaknesses of each compo-

FIGURE 4.2   Eight steps for overcoming performance
problems and breakdown in a developmental organization

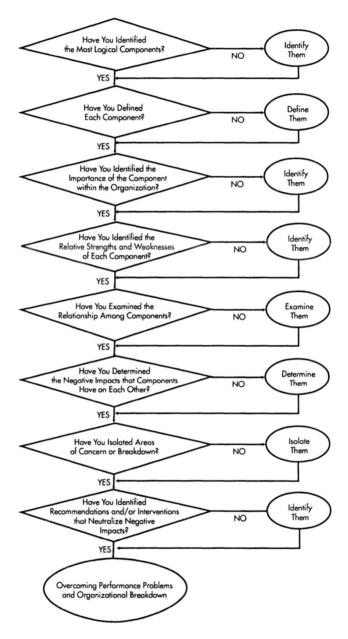

nent. For example, weak, unreliable leadership would be a significant weakness and could contribute to the lack of a collaborative work environment. An organizational culture that fails to encourage or reward cooperation and collaboration would be a weakness and a contributing factor to the problem. Work climates of specific departments may advocate teamwork and cooperation which would be a strength. Fifth, examine the relationship between components to determine their impact on each other. In our example, the four components are closely grouped together; consequently, tremendous interplay exists between them. Thus, a slight change in one component dramatically affects each of the others. Failure to execute a key component will significantly impact the effectiveness of the other components. For example, if leadership changes or encourages self-directed work teams, project teams, or collaboration among employees, the overall work environment changes. Additionally, such a change positively affects work climate, organizational culture, and management practice. Sixth, determine the negative impacts that components have on each other. Seventh, isolate areas of concern or breakdown. Eighth, identify recommendations and/or interventions to overcome negative impacts or build on organizational strengths. Once this has been achieved, seek support for implementing the proposed recommendation or intervention.

Every organizational breakdown or performance problem proves challenging to solve, but applying the eight steps just outlined will help isolate areas of concern so that appropriate action can be taken. We believe the key to this process is determining the negative impacts among components. Once this has been accomplished the real issues emerge; hidden agendas and "zealot" behaviors are eliminated.

STEPS IN TRANSFORMING AN ORGANIZATIONAL SYSTEM

Transforming an organizational system follows a logical process. Leaders and managers serious about becoming developmental will find that the following steps serve as a useful guide.

1. Recruit, select, grow, and develop leaders committed to employee growth and development.
2. Create a developmental work climate.
3. Communicate the vision of a developmental organization.
4. Create an organization-wide strategy to build a developmental organization.
5. Make growth and development a part of all policies and procedures.
6. Encourage management practices that foster employee growth and development.
7. Reengineer the organizational structure to support growth and development.
8. Integrate growth and development into the guiding principles of the organization.
9. Link growth and development initiatives to the organization's strategic business goals and objectives.
10. Create an organizational culture in which growth and development are highly valued and rewarded.

CONCLUSION

Organizations are systems consisting of various components, each working distinctly yet interdependently to bring about desired business results. Within developmental organizations, leadership, structure, climate, mission and strategy, managerial practices, policies and procedure, and work climate align to enhance employee growth and development. When all these components come into play, work design is greatly improved, and the organization is better able to remain competitive in the global marketplace.

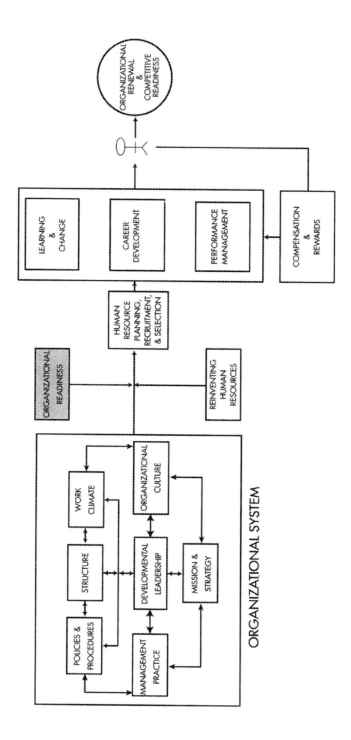

ORGANIZATIONAL SYSTEM

CHAPTER 5

Organizational Readiness: Changing Roles and Responsibilities

A primary characteristic of the developmental organization is the emerging roles and responsibilities of executives, managers, human resource professionals, and employees. The shift in roles and responsibilities reveals whether an organization has evolved to the developmental level. We will examine each respective role (summarized in Figure 5.1) in detail, concentrating on the emergence of responsibilities for executives and managers. We will address human resource professionals' shifting roles and responsibilities in greater detail in Chapter 6.

EXECUTIVES' ROLES AND RESPONSIBILITIES

In most organizations, executives are by definition the firm's leaders. While this has been true for many years, Hesselbein, Goldsmith, and Beckhard (1995) believe that there are a number of shifts occurring within organizations regarding leadership. Many of their contentions apply to the evolution of organizations from traditional to learning to developmental. Several contentions are most applicable to the developmental organization:

FIGURE 5.1   Roles and responsibilities of leaders, managers, and employees
in the developmental organization

	Executive	*Manager*	*Employee*
Roles	Change champion Advocate for development	Facilitator of learning Mentor Performance confronter Career counselor	Personal change agent Career advocate Career planner
Responsi- bilities	Initiate and maintain organizational transformation Foster change	Build synergistic relationships Enhance employee performance Conduct developmental evaluations Create growth and development plans Link compensation and rewards to growth and development Create learning partnerships Foster change	Foster change

- Leadership will be shared throughout an organization rather than only at the top.
- Team leadership will be the primary emphasis in tomorrow's organization.
- Leaders will be more likely to ask questions than give answers or provide solutions.
- Leaders will focus on learning and the implications it has on organizational renewal.
- Although thinking and interventions will replace exclusively domestic focuses, leaders will shift from reliance on purely analytical tools to integrating analytical approaches to problem solving.
- Leaders are less likely to accept simple solutions to complex problems in favor of identifying interventions and solutions that will impact the organization throughout its life.

Ulrich (1997, 242) believes that systems must be created to mold future leaders. These systems might include designing and using competency models, tracking present leadership quality, finding creative models for leadership development, and involving senior managers in serious leadership development.

Executive Roles

Executives assume two principle roles as initiators of organizational transformation: champions for change and advocates for development.

Champions for Change. If change is to occur within an organization, leaders must accept their role as its champion, identifying key success details for building change capacity. Ulrich (1997) identified seven critical factors of success in building capacity for change. He included specific questions useful in determining the extent to which these factors exist within organizations:

1. Leading in change: "Who is responsible?"
2. Mobilizing commitment: "Who else needs to be involved?"
3. Changing systems and structures: "How will change be institutionalized?"
4. Monitoring progress: "How will change be measured?"
5. Making change last: "How will change be started, and how will it last?"
6. Creating a shared need: "Why do it?"
7. Shaping a vision: "What will it look like when we are done?"

Ulrich contends that these seven factors are not particularly new and can be identified by most leaders in a few minutes of reflection. Unfortunately, few leaders employ these factors when contracting change. He further argues that change presents a paradox, one that requires the utilization of a clearly defined change model to be resolved. Although leaders are responsible for guiding change, managers and employees also have their respective responsibilities, as we will discuss later in this chapter.

Advocates for Development. During every evolutionary transformation, someone serves as an advocate, acting as a guide during the evolutionary process, providing and interpreting information, identifying problems, facilitating solutions, and evaluating outcomes. Advocates serve as "scouts," discovering how the organization can implement initiatives that continue the evolution to the developmental organization. As scouts, executives focus on the success of developmental interventions designed to improve organizational renewal and performance capacity. Thus, scouts serve as change ambassadors within the firm.

To become developmental advocates, executives must possess credibility with other decision makers, stakeholders, influencers, and human resource professionals within the organization. Credibility is essential because advocates ask the business to take risks that may seriously impact its competitiveness and financial viability. Consequently, this role requires executives to be perceived as influential, visionary leaders dedicated to the firm's ultimate success rather than advancing their individual careers.

Executive Responsibilities

The primary responsibility of executives in the developmental organization is to initiate organizational transformation. Organizational transformation is the re-creation, redesign, and redefinition of a firm to meet continuous, ever-changing competitive challenges. Within this definition it is assumed that leaders will be responsible for initiatives that cause organizations to shift their culture, structure, work climate, job and work designs, and fundamental identification of products and services necessary to enhance a firm's competitive readiness. Although these leaders will integrate managers, human resource professionals, and employees into the transformation process, it is still the leaders' sole responsibility to identify the firm's future vision, strategies, and tactics necessary to reach its destiny.

Organizational transformation may be accomplished when executives shift their human resource efforts from activity-based to outcome-based solutions. Developmentally minded executives demand that human resource professionals focus on outcomes instead of activities. Ulrich (1998) believes that four approaches accomplish this change. First, executives should communicate to all organizational members that personal skills, cultural change, and intellectual capital are critical to business success. Executives must stress the importance of soft skills, demonstrating this belief in words and deeds.

Second, executives explicitly define the deliverables for human resource professionals, holding them accountable for results. This accountability is similar to that for other departments, divisions, and units. Thus, human resource professionals will track, measure, and evaluate results, and be rewarded accordingly.

Third, executives invest in innovative human resource practices. Human resource professionals must utilize new technologies and practices to transform the organization to the developmental level. By promoting new human resource practices, executives signal to the organization that its human resources are worthy of the organization's investment, attention, and time.

Fourth, executives must improve the professionalism of human resources practitioners, which is perhaps the most important thing that executives do to transform the organization (see Chapter 3). Firms need human resource professionals who know the business, understand the theory and practice of human resources, can manage culture, can make change happen, and possess personal credibility (Ulrich 1998, 133–134).

Fostering Change.   Leaders are ultimately responsible for bringing about change through these seven factors, although they rely on managers and employees to ensure that change happens. Although leaders initiate and guide change, employee participation is necessary to create a shared need and shape organizational vision. Managers sponsor change by mobilizing commitment, modifying systems and structures, monitoring progress, and making change last. We will examine the questions that help leaders, managers, and employees assess and accomplish the key success factors for change in their respective sections in this chapter.

Effective leadership drives lasting change. Moreover, evolving to the developmental level requires organizational leaders willing to follow certain practices (Ulrich 1997, 160):

- own and champion change
- publicly commit to making change happen
- obtain the resources necessary to sustain change
- make a personal commitment to follow through with change

The organization's responsibility is to determine whether leaders possess "the right stuff" essential to championing the changes needed for evolution to the developmental level.

Managers' Roles and Responsibilities

One of the great debates within organizations involves who should be responsible for employee development. In many firms this responsibility has been delegated to human resource professionals who are skilled in adult learning, instructional design, and the facilitation of learning (Gilley 1998). Although this may be a convenient solution to the developmental dilemma, it raises serious considerations given the primary responsibility of managers—to secure results through people.

Achieving greater and greater results requires employee development. Although some argue that the development process is a complex one requiring specialized expertise, we contend that development revolves around manager–employee communications designed to enhance employees' knowledge, skills, and competencies for their current job or in preparation for future assignments.

For development to be successful, complex skills and activities should be broken down into "microsteps" and communicated to less experienced workers. Employees learn to perform these tasks one step at a time, achieving proficiency that eventually increases their performance and productivity. As this process plays out over time, employees improve their overall development.

Development aims to improve employee knowledge, skills, and competencies for current or future jobs. Since employee performance and organizational productivity are impacted by developmental activities, it makes sense to hold the same people responsible for all three areas. Who is the organizational player accountable for performance, productivity, and overall development? The answer is obvious: managers.

Human resource professionals (training and development practitioners, specifically) are not held accountable for employee performance and productivity because the organization does not ask them to explain why performance, productivity, or quality decline. Logically, then, development should be managers' responsibility since they are the only organizational members held accountable for employee performance and firm productivity (Gilley 1998, 26).

Additionally, managers judge their subordinates during formal performance appraisals, evaluating quality, measuring performance, and discussing strategies for improvement and development. Given these responsibilities, it makes sense that managers are held responsible for development. Again, human resource professionals do not conduct performance appraisals for the individuals they train; they simply provide training activities, at the conclusion of which employees return to the workforce to apply what they have learned.

In essence, managers are responsible for the transfer of new knowledge, skills, and behaviors on the job by their employees. Currently, human resource professionals inhibit the transfer of learning by advocating an inefficient model in which training occurs off the job, in formal training activities. At the conclusion of these training sessions, employees are on their own to apply what they have learned. Because human resource professionals do not interact with employees on a regular basis they are unable to provide feedback, reinforcement, support, or additional instruction necessary for employees to integrate what they have learned on the job. This model creates a barrier to learning transfer, as it prevents the efficient, effective application of new learning on the job. The individuals best positioned to reinforce and provide feedback, support, and instruction are managers. Consequently, the very grouping of developmental activities around an inefficient model offers another reason that development should be every manager's responsibility.

Managerial Roles

The developmental organization requires managers to dramatically shift their roles to accommodate and encourage employee growth and development. Managers are the heart of every organization, whether large or small, because they are responsible for securing results through people. They are the decision makers, energizers, guides, and directors for their employees, serving as conduits for organizational change and development.

Many of us have experienced the "manager from hell." You know the one—he or she is abusive, angry, indifferent, fearful; assumes a superior attitude; has poor interpersonal skills; will not delegate; and cannot develop their people, conduct performance evaluations, or establish priorities. When firms place managers such as these in positions of power they are guilty of *managerial malpractice.* We define the term as simply allowing, encouraging, or supporting practices that produce unprofessional, unproductive, or incompetent managers (Gilley and Boughton 1996). Various symptoms of managerial malpractice can occur within organizations:

1. Keeping managers who are not good at securing results through people
2. Promoting to management individuals who do not know how to manage
3. Selecting new managers because they are the best performers or producers, without regard for their people skills
4. Spending valuable time "fixing" managerial incompetence instead of hiring qualified managers
5. Keeping managers who preach the importance of teamwork yet reward individuals who stand out from the crowd
6. Allowing managers to say one thing and do another

Performance Coach.   To cure the proliferation of these symptoms, an organization needs a dramatic shift. This shift requires managers to assume the role of performance coach, who must establish rapport with employees, encourage face-to-face communications, be an active participant with workers rather than a passive observer, and rely on good listening, questioning, and facilitation skills to achieve the desired business results. Performance coaching is *person-centered management*; that is, a series of one-on-one exchanges between managers and their employees that solve problems, improve performance, and achieve results through personal growth and development (Gilley and Boughton, 1996). Performance coaching consists of four roles—facilitator of learning, performance confronter, mentor, and career counselor.

Facilitator of Learning.   As previously discussed, the responsibility of developing employees lies with managers. As learning facilitators, managers are supportive yet directive, operating as partners in performance improvement and using feedback and summary techniques to make certain that employees fully grasp the concepts being taught. They serve as one-on-one tutors with their subordinates, sharing information that will ultimately impact employee growth and development. Typically, tutoring comes in the form of on-the-job training but can involve formal developmental activities.

In the role of learning facilitator, managers guide and direct employees, helping them acquire new skills, knowledge, and appropriate behaviors. Successful managers utilize the communications process and demonstrate how additional skills, knowledge, and appropriate behaviors will produce desired outcomes. We identified several areas that improved as a result of managers' becoming facilitators of learning: technical competence, interpersonal interactions between managers and employees, problem-solving skills, employee performance and quality, relationships with employees, breadth of technological understanding, managerial competence in technical and interpersonal areas via repetitive instruction, and commitment to continuous growth and development (Gilley and Boughton 1996, 37).

Mentor.   Occasionally, managers find it necessary to be supportive and serve as leaders to their employees in the role of mentor. Mentoring allows employees to benefit from a manager's experience—both successes and failures, thus eliminating employees' fears, concerns, and frustrations while promoting celebrations of success, victories, and job accomplishments. Mentoring helps employees avoid costly mistakes and pitfalls so damaging to careers while enhancing their relationships with managers.

Effective mentors possess essential knowledge of the organization, including an understanding of its vision, strategy, direction, guiding principles, operational structure, history, climate, and culture. Mentors maintain a sufficient network, enabling their mentees to make critical contacts useful in career advancement. Although mentors possess and share critical competence, they absolutely must also maintain credibility within the organization. Effective mentors must be willing to bear responsibility for their employees' growth and development. This ownership lies at the heart of the mentor–mentee relationship and is the reason that these interactions are so successful.

By serving as confidants in times of personal and professional difficulty, mentors enhance employees' problem-solving skills and decision-making abilities. They also provide employees with a sounding board upon which to vent frustration during periods of heightened stress. Several outcomes are realized by mentoring:

- developing employees' political awareness and savvy
- understanding and appreciating the special nature of the organization's culture
- creating a personal network within the organization
- enhancing the relationship between themselves and their employees
- developing commitment to organizational goals, guiding principles, and values
- advancing the career of employees
- increasing involvement in the growth and development of employees' careers

Performance Confronter. Since managers have the unique responsibility of improving employee performance, they must confront performance positively. The role of performance confronter requires a managerial shift in style from authoritative to participatory. By relinquishing control and dominance, a manager allows employees to participate as equal partners in examining their careers, performance problems, or difficulties. With this approach, managers develop positive working relationships with their employees.

The participatory approach is nonthreatening, encouraging employees to share in problem solving and decision making. This approach advocates the free exchange of ideas, opinions, and feelings; consequently, employees benefit from a positive communications climate, feel more secure, and openly express their thoughts and ideas. This climate is comfortable, conducive to sharing, and even nurturing to employee development. We contend that a sharing climate delves deep, exhibiting genuine concern for employee well-being and dedication to the improvement of interpersonal communications.

Career Counselor. The final role assumed by developmental managers is that of career counselor. From a developmental perspective, the role of career counselor might be the most important. Managers actively engaged in this role encourage employees to make independent decisions regarding their future career paths. Career counselors guide employees through a reasonably in-depth review and exploration of their interests, abilities, beliefs, and desires pertaining to their present and future careers. Career counselors assist employees in evaluating alternatives and in making decisions regarding their careers inside or outside the organization. By presenting different points of views, counselors help employees develop a more in-depth analysis of career options.

Career counselors help firms better allocate human resources by providing a direct link between employees and the business when the firm is considering the quality and quantity of workers needed to maintain or enhance its competitive readiness. A primary activity of career counselors is applying developmental evaluations and creating employee growth and development plans. These areas of responsibility are most useful in examining employees' future career opportunities. In an earlier book (Gilley and Boughton 1996, 38), we cited several major outcomes of the career counselor role:

- helping organizations identify performance deficiencies
- improving employees' career insights
- enhancing employees' organizational insight
- helping employees make greater career and organizational commitments
- helping employees change their points of view about their career paths
- helping employees become independent and self-sufficient

Managers are a primary link, then, in the evolution from traditional to learning to developmental organizations. They undertake several critical responsibilities and assume different roles to enhance their employees' growth and development. In doing so, managers provide the foundation for the design and development of the developmental organization. They serve as a conduit for organizational transformation and the ultimate evolution and implementation of the developmental approach to enhancing organizational renewal and improving performance capacity. Managers have always been the center of improving organizational competitive readiness. At no other time in the history of managerial interventions are they needed more desperately than now to provide leadership and direction for tomorrow's organizations.

Managerial Responsibilities

Every manager should be held accountable for six additional responsibilities within developmental organizations:

1. Building synergistic relationships
2. Improving performance
3. Applying developmental evaluations
4. Creating growth and development plans
5. Linking compensation and rewards to growth and development
6. Fostering change

Building Synergistic Relationships.   Traditional organizations devote vast amounts of financial and human resources to recruitment and selection. Often, managers are plucked from the ranks of the most prestigious MBA schools in the world as a result of the mistaken belief that an individual's academic preparation is the most critical component of future success. These graduates possess advanced technical knowledge, educational preparation, and the perceived expertise necessary to ensure their development into future organizational leaders. Typically, little or no attention is paid to the managerial skills and experience necessary to secure results through people. We contend that hiring in this manner discounts the importance of interpersonal skills to achieve desired business results. Thus, employees are subject to inexperienced, ineffective, or incompetent managers. Because organizations fail to focus on the interpersonal skills needed to enhance manager–employee relationships, they miss opportunities to create synergy between the individuals responsible for carrying out change initiatives and job performance activities.

We also believe that managers in developmental organizations are responsible for building synergistic relationships that enhance employee commitment to improving performance and quality, increasing productivity, and overall organizational performance. The primary benefits of these relationships include an increase in productivity, and the enhancement and building of manager and employee self-esteem and of organizational communication, understanding, and commitment.

Improving Performance.   Within the developmental organization, managers continue to be held responsible and accountable for enhancing employee performance. Managers communicate specifically what they want their employees to improve, focus on performance problems as opposed to the person, use confrontation to produce desired change without causing the employee to become defensive, and maintain a positive relationship with employees (Gilley and Boughton 1996).

Unfortunately, many managers have difficulty confronting employees who do not perform adequately. Those uncomfortable with confrontation often avoid these encounters, hoping that somehow the situation will improve on its own without their having to address employees. Too often, managers avoid poor performance until it has diminished so significantly that dramatic action must be taken. Overcoming this dilemma requires managers to know the difference between confrontation and criticism. Confrontation focuses on the performance problem and its consequences; it identifies specific performance shortfalls along with corrective action designed to improve future performance. Concurrently, managers concentrate extensively on building and maintaining relationships with their employees.

Criticism, on the other hand, focuses on the person and his or her faults. Typically, criticism surfaces in the form of general, nonspecific statements that blame someone for performance deficiencies. Finally, criticism is a self-serving, self-centered, counterproductive action that allows managers (critics) to vent anger and frustration toward their employees (Gilley, Boughton, and Maycunich 1999).

Focusing on positive confrontation designed to improve employee performance, managers within the developmental organization can accomplish several positive tasks (Gilley and Boughton 1996, 39):

- Identify performance shortfalls
- Develop strategies for performance improvement
- Obtain commitment for continued improvement
- Communicate performance standards
- Encourage employees to perform increasingly difficult tasks
- Enhance employee growth and development

Applying Developmental Evaluations. Traditional organizations require regularly scheduled performance appraisals with every employee, giving managers opportunities to judge employee performance and attach compensation or reward accordingly. In theory, performance appraisals are an effective developmental activity designed to reward past performance, improve future performance, and encourage career development. In reality, nothing could be further from the truth.

One reason for the disparity between performance appraisal theory and practice is in the execution of the performance appraisal. Many organizations rely on performance appraisal or review forms that allow managers to painlessly evaluate their employees by assigning numbers for every possible performance category. Making the process as simple as possible prevents managers and employees from thinking developmentally. We believe that these forms are more damaging than beneficial, preventing managers from working collaboratively with employees in their development. Overcoming this obstacle requires managers to be given the freedom to work with their employees to identify performance problems, solutions, and developmental opportunities. Eliminating useless, wasteful performance appraisal and review forms and substituting them with an opportunity to conduct developmental evaluations solves this problem.

Developmental evaluations allow managers the opportunity to assess employee strengths and weaknesses; thus, managers analyze worker knowledge, skills, and behaviors to determine areas of excellence and those needing improvement. These evaluations present opportunities for managers and employees to discuss current and future developmental goals and objectives along with plans to achieve them and to review the "fit" between organizational expectations and those of the employee. Later in their discussion, the employee and manager discuss developmental and career planning actions. Most importantly, developmental evaluations are a vehicle for discussing future growth and developmental actions that will enhance employees' abilities and competencies, as well as their careers (Gilley, Boughton, and Maycunich 1999, 91).

Developmental evaluations are an excellent tool for analyzing employee performance and making recommendations for improvement. They help managers isolate obstacles to exemplary performance and identify strategies to overcome them. Thus, development evaluations provide formal, summative evaluations of an employee's current performance, skills, and aptitudes and are designed to help employees adopt corrective actions or to identify activities that will enhance their future potential.

The most common type of developmental evaluation fundamentally shifts the focus from assessment of past performance to discussions regarding developmental aspects of an employee's work life. Gilley and Davidson (1993) identified five additional types of developmental evaluations:

1. Human resource planning (Chapter 7)
2. Work planning and review (Chapter 7)
3. Developmental planning (Chapter 8)
4. Career planning (Chapter 9)
5. Compensation review (Chapter 11)

Creating Growth and Development Plans.   As previously discussed, a crucial focus of developmental evaluations involves manager and employee discussion of how to improve performance results. These interactions include examination of employee strengths, weaknesses, and areas requiring improvement. These become the focus of employee growth and development plans and should be designed as long-term developmental strategies rather than as quick fixes.

We believe that managers and employees should mutually design growth and development plans that are realistic, specific, attainable, and tied to a timetable. These actions are at the heart of the developmental organization as it shifts emphasis from short-term performance results to long-term development strategies that enhance an organization's competitive readiness. Shifting the focus guarantees that organizations prepare employees to build their renewal and performance capacity.

Growth and development plans are enhanced by forging a partnership between managers and employees that helps workers acquire new knowledge and skills and apply them to their jobs. This mutually beneficial partnership allows employees to acquire critical skills and competencies that enhance their performance and career development opportunities, while managers enjoy better business results. Enhancing employee growth and development requires managers to become responsible for motivating their employees, to create a self-esteeming work environment, to delegate tasks and responsibilities, to build on employee strengths while managing their weaknesses, and to design designing learning acquisition and transfer plans (Gilley, Boughton, and Maycunich 1999).

Linking Compensation and Rewards to Growth and Development. Developmental organizations compensate and reward people for their growth, development, and commitment, a philosophy that works wonders in improving employee performance and achieving needed results. Historically, compensation and reward programs have been performance based, with little consideration given to rewarding employees for enhancing their skills or competencies. We contend that worker performance and, hence, employee development increase dramatically when organizations link compensation and rewards to employee growth and development (Gilley, Boughton, and Maycunich, 1999, 139).

Our intent is not to diminish the importance of performance, but to make it clear that performance without growth and development prevents an organization from maintaining the growth phase of the organizational life cycle. Failure to perpetuate the growth phase leads to organizational maturity, stagnation, and eventual decline. Shifting compensation and reward programs to encourage employees' growth and development ensures that their skills and competencies continue to evolve, thus guaranteeing an organization's competitive readiness, renewal, and performance capability.

The shift from rewarding performance to rewarding growth and development involves a remarkable transformation. When growth and development are rewarded and reinforced, they will be repeated. In this way, firms encourage employees to become more competent, so that they are better able to produce desired results. Another outgrowth is enhanced employee commitment and loyalty. We propose that becoming development oriented permits organizations to adopt an approach that systematically responds to the performance challenge.

Managers engage in seven crucial activities to bring about this evolutionary shift:

1. Developing a compensation and reward philosophy
2. Aligning compensation and rewards with guiding principles

3. Selecting compensation and reward strategies
4. Identifying performance growth and development goals
5. Identifying rewards that enhance employee growth and development
6. Integrating components of an effective compensation program
7. Linking compensation and rewards to performance growth and development outcomes

Creating Learning Partnerships.   According to Marquardt (1996, 54), coaches (managers) and employees have the responsibility to develop a learning partnership—one that consists of planning, application, and reflection. When planning, learning coaches and employees must determine the gap between the learner's existing knowledge and skills and those demanded by the learning opportunity. Jointly, the partners develop the learning objectives and a plan to meet those objectives and complete any necessary pretask learning.

During application, some of the coach's main responsibilities include coaching the learner according to his or her learning needs (e.g., job-specific, functional, or adaptive needs) and providing the learner with needed opportunities. The coach must also make certain that the learner has access to appropriate references and tools and provide the learner with guidance and feedback when needed (Marquardt 1996, 54).

Marquardt further states that the learner's primary responsibilities include applying the knowledge and skills acquired, using available resources, reflecting on the current task being learned, and asking for assistance and feedback when it is needed.

The final activity of learning partnerships involves reflection. Employees and coaches need to take the time to reflect on lessons learned and ascertain how these can be applied to the job. Employees provide feedback on how well supervisors performed in regard to coaching and continuous learning. Meanwhile, coaches focus on what can be done better, recognizing and rewarding accomplishments. Finally, employees share what has been learned with others who might find the insight useful.

Fostering Change.   Creating the synergy necessary for the developmental organization mandates significant change in organizational philosophy, operations, and strategy. This monumental effort requires organizational players (managers) to sponsor change. These players, like platoon sergeants, football team captains, and committee chairpersons, are frontline doers responsible for incremental pieces of the giant puzzle known as the developmental organization.

Managers serve as organizational cheerleaders, generating excitement and mobilizing commitment for change, altering systems and structures to better support change initiatives, overseeing progress, and encouraging actions that make change last. To determine a manager's aptitude for being a change catalyst, organizations assess the manager's ability to accomplish several tasks (Ulrich 1997, 160):

- build coalitions of support for change
- recognize others who must be committed to change
- enlist support from key individuals in the organization
- build a responsibility matrix to bring about change

Ulrich contends that managers must also modify systems and structures to keep change alive, which requires them to understand how to link developmental change to other human resource systems such as training, appraisals, compensation and rewards, communication, and so forth. Managers must also recognize the organizational system's implications for change of this type (see Chapter 4).

Monitoring progress and making change permanent requires managers to measure the success of change, identify its results, and recognize benchmarks of progress. Further, managers must identify the important first steps needed to start, and maintain employee interest in change both short and long term. Finally, successful managers have a plan for adapting to developmental change over time (Ulrich 1997, 160).

EMPLOYEES' ROLES AND RESPONSIBILITIES

Employees are ultimately responsible for development, improvement, and change, which therefore become their quintessential responsibilities. Employees in developmental organizations understand the relationship between developing skills, performance improvement, and change. Because they are responsible for career planning and identifying their most appropriate career paths, they become gatekeepers of their own success. Consequently, their principle responsibility is to identify the skills, knowledge, and competencies needed for current and future job assignments.

Employee Roles

The principle employee role in the developmental organization is that of *doer*—for today as well as tomorrow. *Doing* is simply "making it happen" by utilizing available personal and organizational resources to the best of one's ability. The success with which one secures these results lies with one's ability to function as a personal change agent, individual career advocate, and career planner (see Chapter 9).

Personal Change Agent.   Change agents take advantage of opportunities to improve their organizations. These employees make the most of opportune moments to positively impact their lives within the organization—from improving relationships with co-workers and supervisors to positioning themselves for promotions due to exemplary performance over time. Change agents recognize and cultivate significant transformation points, namely, instances that provide opportunities for personal breakthroughs that will influence their organization's success and, as a result, their own.

For example, in the movie *Working Girl*, Melanie Griffith portrayed a secretary who, because of her awareness of market conditions, undertakes a challenging new role (unauthorized) within her company and seizes the chance to present a business proposal to a potential client. After the rudimentary trials and tribulations, Griffith's character was rewarded for her efforts with a job offer (and acceptance) that represented quite a promotion with another company.

Career Advocate and Planner.   Employees often fail to accept the responsibility for their own careers, which leads to disappointment when they do not receive desired recognition or rewards (e.g., more responsibility, authority, raises, and promotions) or when they feel taken advantage of by management. Career advocates are self-promoters, taking the initiative to inform management of their talents, interests, and career desires. Advocates clearly articulate their wishes and back them up with solid evidence (work samples, special projects, portfolios, and the like) indicative of their knowledge and skills. Further, advocates routinely share their career desires with managers, maximizing one-on-one meetings (formal or informal), performance evaluations, feedback opportunities, and so forth, to make their point. For example, one of us (Maycunich) worked with a talented individual who advanced from mail clerk to marketing district manager by continually expressing his interests and showcasing his talents to management; dedication, tenacity, and genuine talent pay off.

As career planners, employees proactively strategize to maximize their full potential, plotting a course that incorporates additional training, education, and experience to gain the knowledge, skills, and attitudes necessary to achieve their personal career goals. Career planners constantly assess and renew themselves throughout their careers, understanding the impact of personal growth and development on their professional lives. In this role, employees devise long-term, achievable plans in support of their strategic career goals.

Employee Responsibilities

Employees bear the responsibility for *making it happen* within businesses—via a skillful implementation of organizational policies and procedures. Doing so requires employees to be continuous advocates of change.

Fostering Change.   Essentially, employees are responsible for implementing change, bringing leaders' visions to life via managers' policies and procedures. Employees are often overlooked as an essential element in bringing about lasting change in spite of their usefulness in helping create the conditions that encourage developmental organizations. Because employees are contributors to and benefactors of developmental organizations, it is important that they understand the following points (Ulrich 1997, 160):

- the reason for the implementation of change
- why it is important
- how it benefits them
- how it benefits the organization
- how it benefits customers and other stakeholders

Developmental leaders and managers allow employees to shape the organization's vision by encouraging their involvement and soliciting their ideas. Employees who understand the benefits of a developmental organization must be encouraged to advocate and secure other employee support; in this way, *employees support what they create.* Effective leaders and managers can excite employees about the great potential of a developmental organization, revealing how such a change will improve organizational competitive readiness and renewal.

Leaders (executives), managers, and employees can use a checklist to assess their roles and responsibilities (Figure 5.2). To get maximum benefit from the checklist, respondents should assess themselves honestly. They should mark only the statements that they follow consistently. Unchecked statements require action on the respondent's part.

Conclusion

Organizations cannot make the transition to the developmental level unless their key members—executives, managers, and employees—accept new roles and responsibilities. By doing so, organizations prepare for the tremendous changes required of them when evolving to the developmental level. To ensure a successful transformation, leaders must guide the change effort; managers must mobilize commitment, modify systems and structures, monitor progress, and make change permanent; while employees help shape the vision for change and share in the need for change.

FIGURE 5.2   Checklists of roles and responsibilities for executives, managers, and employees

The following checklist/inventory should be answered honestly. Mark only hose statements that reflect your consistent behavior. Unchecked staements require action on your part:

Executive Roles and Responsibilities Checklist

Within my organization I ...

__ serve as a champion for change by
    __ leading change initiatives
    __ creating a shared need
    __ shaping a vision
    __ mobilizing commitment
    __ modifying systems and structures to support change
    __ monitoring progress of change actions
    __ ensuring that change lasts

__ advocate development of
    __ individual employees, regardless of level or rank
    __ the entire organization

__ initiate and maintain organizational transformation by
    __ shifting HR efforts to outcome-based instead of activity-based solutions
    __ communicating the importance of change to business success
    __ explicitly defining HR professionals' deliverables and holding them accountable for results
    __ investing in innovative, developmental HR practices
    __ improving the professionalism of HR practitioners

__ foster change by
    __ owning and championing change
    __ publicly committing to making change happen
    __ obtaining the resources necessary to sustain change
    __ making a personal commitment to following through with change

Manager Roles and Responsibilities Checklist

Within my organization I ...

— function as a performance coach when I
  — facilitate employee learning by partnering, guiding, and tutoring my employees
  — mentor my employees, serving as confidant, role model, and feedback provider
  — confront performance in a timely, nonthreatening, constructive, participatory manner
  — career counsel my employees, offering guidance and analysis encouraging employee exploration and maximization of career potential

— build synergistic relationships based on trust

— enhance employee performance by
  — expressing my responsibility and accountability for their actions
  — communicating specific needed improvements in employee behavior of performance
  — focusing on performance problems, not the person
  — using confrontation positively
  — maintaining a positive, healthy relationship with my employees

— conduct developmental evaluations with my employees

— create individualized growth and development plans with each employee

— link compensation and rewards to employee growth and development

— create learning partnerships with my employees

— foster change by
  — being a change advocate
  — building coalitions of support for change within the organization
  — recognizing others who must be committed to change
  — building a responsibility matrix to bring about change

Employee Roles and Responsibilities Checklist

Within my organization I ...

__ am a personal change agent because I
  __ recognize the importance of change to myself and my
    organization
  __ recognize and cultivate opportunities for personal breakthroughs
    that will influence my success and that of my organization

__ am my own career advocate because I
  __ take responsibility for my career, and ultimately my own success
  __ am self-promoting, making certain that management knows of my
    talents and career interests
  __ take advantage of developmental opportunites, both within my
    organization and outside it to gain or improve upon my
    knowledge, skills, and attitudes

__ am my own career planner because I
  __ understand the impact of growth and development on my career
  __ proactively strategize to maximize my career potential
  __ constantly review, assess, reflect, and renew myself throughout
    my career
  __ create long-term, actionable plans to support my career goals

__ foster change by
  __ being a change advocate
  __ understanding and communicating the importance of change to
    my success and that of my organization

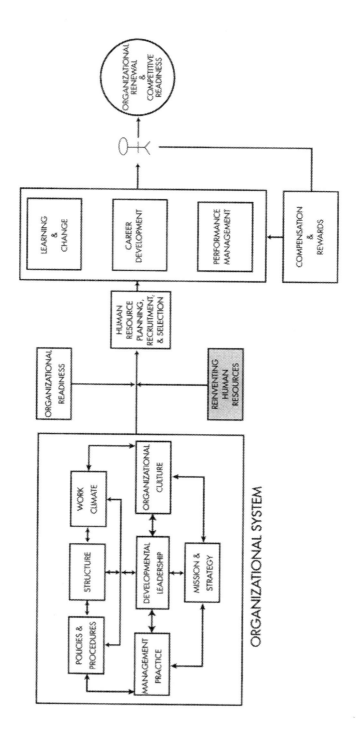

ORGANIZATIONAL SYSTEM

CHAPTER 6

The Human Resource Department for the Twenty-First Century

According to Flannery, Hofrichter, and Platten (1996), the major barrier to the development of new processes and procedures designed to improve an organization's efficiency is the traditional human resource department. Therefore, as organizations consider strategies for improving their performance capacity and renewal (i.e., creating the developmental organization), one important department, human resources (HR), must be examined closely to determine its roles and responsibilities.

REENGINEERING HUMAN RESOURCES

It is no surprise that many HR departments suffer from an image problem. As Rodney Dangerfield might say, "They ain't gettin' no respect." This lack of respect has caused many human resource professionals to suffer from low self-esteem and a persecution complex. As a result, many HR professionals find themselves in a quandary. Do they maintain their narrowly specialized focus, or do they become strategic business partners, strategists, change agents within the organization, or all of the above?

To counter this dilemma, human resource professionals must discover new ways to establish credibility. Without credibility, they cannot solve client problems or satisfy their customers' business and performance needs. We contend that to improve credibility, HR professionals must be willing to leave the "mother ship," the highly centralized administrative unit, and become fully integrated into the broader business operations. They must relinquish most training and development responsibilities (formerly assigned to HR professionals) to managers and supervisors. Human resource professionals must encourage organizational managers and supervisors to become more actively involved in selection, recruiting, hiring, and training practices, while surrendering much of their responsibility for compensation and rewards. Flannery, Hofrichter, and Platten (1996, 208) contend that if HR professionals refuse to budge, and cling tenaciously to traditional structures and strategies, they will be seen as part of the problem and will be indeed left out of the process.

As expected, many HR professionals become quite defensive when they first hear about giving up responsibility, believing that they will lose position power when many of their duties are delegated or shared with managers and supervisors. Consequently, HR people spend much time and energy attempting to block this evolution. Functioning as organizational housekeepers and bit players fails to fully utilize the talents of HR professionals and prohibits them from becoming integral players in the organization's evolution.

Human resource professionals in developmental organizations demonstrate courage as they make fundamental changes and accept new structure, activities, roles, and responsibilities. Although these adjustments may be painful, gone are the days of human resources for human resource's sake, or unprofessional HR practitioners performing administrative duties that add limited value or utility to the firm. In their place is a dynamic HR function and qualified professionals focused on improving organizational performance and efficiency via growth and development.

The Structure of the Human Resource Function

Many believe that the structure of the human resource function must change drastically to facilitate evolution to the developmental organization (Gilley and Maycunich 1998a; Fiorelli, Longpre, and Zimmer 1996; Galbraith and Lawler 1993). The most common suggestions for creating and enhancing a new structure for HR functions include the following:

- decentralization of the HR function
- integrating HR activities with the management process
- making HR part of the management team
- outsourcing services to facilitate higher levels of efficiency and quality
- establishing a customer-service orientation
- establishing a cross-functional career approach whereby HR professionals and managers reverse roles periodically

Each of these activities is designed to bring about economies within the HR function while establishing better relationships between HR professionals and management, thus enhancing the credibility of human resource professionals within the firm.

Activities and Expanded Services of the Human Resource Function

Traditionally, the HR function has been responsible for providing services such as compensation and benefits management, administration of personnel records and activities, employee compliance and outplacement services, employee relations, training and development, staffing and recruiting, and payroll management. These traditional services continue to be vitally important to organizations. Human resources must expand its services to meet the constantly growing needs of the organization and its employees. Expanded service offerings enable HR professionals to build the foundation necessary to bring about the evolution to the developmental organization.

According to Fiorelli, Longpre, and Zimmer (1996), HR functions must provide performance consulting, employee communications, employee feedback, change management, and organizational redesign to serve the needs of tomorrow's businesses. Within firms, these actions lead to change, state-of-the-art communications, employee growth and development, and performance management. Expanded HR services focus on satisfying the needs and wants of both internal and external customers by providing added value as a result of interaction and facilitation of desired business goals and objectives. These activities champion diversity within organizations and provide an environment that empowers employees, encouraging their personal growth while recognizing, rewarding, and holding them accountable for their performance contributions.

Fiorelli, Longpre, and Zimmer also believe that HR functions must adhere to a set of guiding principles to better serve the organization and bring about the change necessary to breed continuous employee growth and development. The guiding principles include the following:

- focusing on business processes such as marketing, manufacturing, and accounting
- learning through collaboration and teamwork
- global orientation with local implementation
- enhanced commitment to people while meeting business needs
- measuring value of every HR activity

Such a set of guiding principles provide direction and focus for human resource professionals while establishing a value based approached critical to creating developmental culture and work climate within the firm.

IMPROVING CREDIBILITY THROUGH PARTNERSHIPS

Another major focus of tomorrow's HR department is the creation of strategic business partnerships. In traditional organizations, few HR professionals successfully forge alliances with clients within their firms. As a result, these professionals often lack credibility as they are not viewed by organizational leaders, managers, or employees as vital, contributing members capable of improving the firm's performance quality, efficiency, or productivity. To overcome this dilemma, HR professionals must develop business partnerships that enhance their credibility and influence within the organization.

Business partnerships in developmental organizations are long-term oriented, are synergistic by design, and focus on relationships that help the firm successfully achieve its goals and objectives. These relationships enable HR professionals to acquire the responsive attitude they need to become more customer-service oriented and to better understand and anticipate client needs.

Human resource professionals establish credibility within developmental organizations in one of four ways. First, they demonstrate the ability to solve complex problems and consequently satisfy client needs and expectations. Second, HR professionals demonstrate their professional expertise and understanding of organizational operations and culture. Third, credibility can be transferred, most commonly by third-party referrals. The transferal is often called a network, that is, a collection of individuals who can introduce HR professionals to key organizational decision makers while keeping them informed (Gilley and Maycunich 1998a, 139–140). Fourth, credibility can be developed via reputation, commonly by delivering results. In essence, credibility must be earned.

According to Ulrich (1997, 253–254), several behaviors enhance credibility:

- being accurate in all HR practices
- being predictable and consistent
- meeting commitments
- establishing collaborative client relationships
- expressing opinions, ideas, strategies, and activities appropriately
- behaving in an ethical manner that demonstrates integrity
- demonstrating creativity and innovation
- maintaining confidentiality
- listening to and focusing on executive problems in a manner that brings about mutual respect

We contend that three types of partnerships enhance HR professionals' credibility within organizations: strategic business partnerships, management development partnerships, and organizational development partnerships.

Strategic Business Partnerships

The most common type of partnership within organizations is the strategic business partnership. In these partnerships, HR professionals align themselves with organizational leaders, managers, supervisors, and employees for the purpose of helping the organization achieve its strategic business goals and objectives. Strategic business partnerships satisfy the needs of internal and external clients alike, while positioning HR professionals in a more positive light within the organization. We propose that strategic business partnerships are important in that they help HR professionals accomplish the following:

1. Develop mutually beneficial, empathetic relationships with clients, resulting in client satisfaction and achievement of objectives.
2. Break down the walls between themselves and their clients, resulting in lasting commitments, investments in growth and development, and innovations that permeate the clients' departments.
3. Understand fully their customers' contributions to an interaction.
4. Develop personal relationships that foster trust and honesty.
5. Demonstrate their willingness to intimately know who they serve and demonstrate their ability to learn from their customers.
6. Direct all their efforts at satisfying their customers, from designing and developing interventions in accordance with clients' expressed interests to providing consulting activities that improve the organization's performance management system and competitive readiness.
7. Establish credibility within the organization.
8. Address various demand states facing their programs, activities, and interventions.
9. Better manage limited financial and human resources.

Furthermore, strategic business partnerships produce economic utility measured in terms of increased organizational performance, profitability, revenue, quality, and efficiency.

Management Development Partnerships

In a previous work (Gilley and Maycunich 1998a, 143), we contend that businesses establish management development partnerships to overcome managerial malpractice. These joint ventures between HR professionals and the organization are designed to improve managers' competencies and skills. Management development partnerships increase the quality and professionalism of managers. The result is improved problem solving, employee performance and quality, and business results.

A critical question that HR professionals must address is: Why create management development partnerships? Four reasons suffice. First, organizations are unable to enhance their competitive readiness or improve their performance capacity until they improve the quality of managers at their respective practices. Second, managers are the lifeblood of a firm—interpreting its vision and executing strategies, mitigating and translating organizational policies and procedures for employees while developing work climates conducive to improving work performance. In essence, managers lead the organization on an everyday basis. Third, managers are responsible for developing employees' performance capacity. Thus, they are the gatekeepers and overlords of quality and performance improvement. Without enhancing employees' skills and abilities, organizational performance will fail to improve. Fourth, managers are the principle enhancers of employee motivation and satisfaction, responsible for improving employee self-esteem and loyalty. In the final analysis, managers are truly the only persons in the organization capable of demonstrating appreciation and concern for employee well-being. Without enhancing their skills and abilities, organizations will struggle in their attempt to energize the workforce.

Organizational Development Partnerships

Establishing credibility and influence within one's organization requires HR professionals to adopt long-term, strategic solutions to problems facing the firm by employing proven organizational development interventions and techniques. Organizational development partnerships, therefore, are aimed at improving organizational renewal, performance capacity, growth, and competitiveness. These long-term-oriented partnerships require the involvement of all organizational members. According to Gilley and Eggland (1989), organizational development partnerships are not part of a "fix-it" strategy but rather a continual way of managing organizational change that eventually becomes a way of organizational life. Thus, organizational development partnerships can be considered a planned, data-based approach to change, involving goal-setting, action planning, monitoring, feedback, and evaluating results.

Organizational development partnerships involve a systems approach that closely links human resources to technology, business processes, and change. These partnerships result from employee demands for better work environments and participation in decision making, ever-changing economic conditions, and market competitiveness that force organizations to adjust to constantly mobile marketplaces.

A business benefits from organizational development partnerships because they represent collaborative forums for employees to function as human beings instead of resources in the productivity process. These partnerships also provide opportunities for each organizational member, and the firm itself, to develop its full potential. Organizational effectiveness is increased as the partnerships help firms achieve their strategic business goals and objectives. Organizational partnerships create an environment where employees find exciting, challenging work. Workers have opportunities to influence how they relate to work, the work environment, and the organization. Ultimately, organizational development partnerships enable employees to be treated as valuable human beings with a complex set of needs and values, all of which are important in their work and life (Gilley and Eggland 1989).

STRATEGIES FOR EFFECTIVE HUMAN RESOURCE PRACTICE

The human resource function within developmental organizations faces numerous new challenges while continuing to fulfill its traditional responsibilities. Human resource professionals adopt several new strategies to meet these challenges, five of which have been identified by Galbraith and Lawler (1993):

1. To support teams and other lateral forms of organization
2. To support employee involvement
3. To foster leadership necessary in the organization of the future
4. To support the strategy-setting process and provide services for the line organization
5. To orchestrate organizational change and facilitate organizational learning

Each strategy requires HR professionals to embrace new roles and responsibilities within the organization.

Human Resource Professionals' Roles and Responsibilities

Traditionally, HR professionals have been responsible for six activities: staffing, development, appraisal, rewards, organizational design, and communications (Ulrich and Lake 1990). Each activity tends to restrict the influence of HR professionals within the organization; consequently, HR activities have less impact on organizational performance, competitive readiness, and renewal. Figure 6.1 (page 159) demonstrates that traditional HR practices have low organizational impact and influence. Therefore, it is essential for HR professionals to assume additional roles as they help the organization evolve.

Human Resource Professionals' Roles

To make the transformation from the traditional to the developmental organization, HR professionals must assume additional roles. We have identified five such roles that offer HR professionals opportunities to enhance their organizational impact and influence. The first two roles are most commonly found in learning organizations, whereas the remaining three are exclusively prevalent in developmental organizations (Figure 6.1).

1. Partnership builder
2. Organizational expert
3. Employee champion
4. Performance consultant
5. Organizational development change agent

Partnership Builder.   Forging partnerships within the organization increases HR professionals' credibility within the firm and helps ensure their livelihood. Assuming the formal role of partnership builder allows these professionals to improve customer-service-oriented relationships that help break down the walls between them and their clients. As a result, lasting commitments are forged, investments are made in learning, and discoveries are made in everything pertaining to their clients' departments, activities, and goals. HR professionals become immersed in their clients' problems, needs, concerns, and expectations. Consequently, their organizational influence increases, which in turn improves their overall organizational impact (Figure 6.1).

The partnership-building role enables HR professionals to develop trust and honest communication with their clients, allowing for the sharing of ideas, perspectives, and vision for the organization's future. Partnerships help HR professionals develop a responsive attitude necessary for them to become customer-service oriented. We believe that HR professionals engage in five interdependent activities to develop the partnership-builder role, each of which enhances their credibility within the organization while helping meet clients' business and performance needs (Gilley and Maycunich 1998b). Thus, the organization benefits via achievement of its strategic business goals and objectives. Partnership-builder activities include the following:

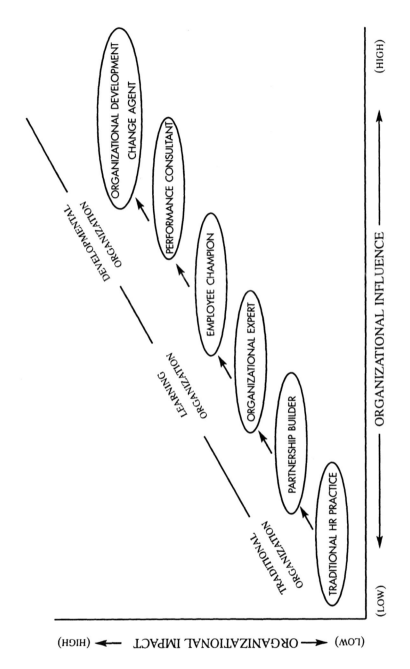

FIGURE 6.1 Evolution of HR professional's poles, organizational impact, and influence

1. Embracing a customer-service strategy committed to helping clients achieve their business goals and objectives
2. Creating a positive customer-service environment that enables HR professionals to respond quickly to the business and professional needs of the client via the development of interventions and services that improve performance and enhance organizational effectiveness
3. Examining human resource interventions and services to determine their respective values and benefits, allowing HR professionals to make critical decisions about the interventions and services that best serve the organization
4. Helping clients make positive decisions about performance improvement and organizational development to shape the firm's direction and ensure future viability
5. Identifying why clients participate in HR interventions and services, enabling HR professionals to understand clients' motives and how to adjust accordingly

Becoming partnership builders better positions HR professionals to understand and deal with resistance within the organization. Block (1981, 113) believes that resistance is predictable and a natural part of the learning process. Therefore, it comes as no surprise when clients resist change or innovative ways of achieving business results. Effectively handling resistance involves comprehending its underlying causes and addressing them accordingly.

Client resistance may usually be traced to the client's difficulties in handling unpleasant or challenging situations. The predicament is exacerbated when decisions are forced upon clients without their input or approval. Some of the most common reasons for resistance include the following:

- the purpose for change is not made clear
- employees affected by change are not involved in planning
- poor communications regarding change
- fear of failure

- cost is too high or rewards are inadequate
- perceived loss of control
- anxiety over job security
- lack of respect or trust in the change agent
- past experience with change is negative
- lack of management support for change

Generally speaking, the root cause of resistance is fear—people fear losing control, power, status, authority, and position. Fortunately, partnership building creates synergistic relationships that nourish trust and honesty, diminishing if not eliminating client resistance to organizational change or innovations.

Organizational Expert.   Human resource professionals can improve their organizational impact by demonstrating their insight into the business's operational aspects, that is, what we call their business acumen. A person's insight, including his or her knowledge of business fundamentals, systems theory, organizational culture, and politics, reveals an understanding of organizational philosophy that guides business action. Hence, it is critical for HR professionals to think like their clients and understand how things get done inside the organization and how and why decisions are made.

Business acumen permits HR professionals to be members of the organizational family responsible for its improvement. By understanding business operations, HR professionals promote business initiatives that help the organization improve its competitive readiness, performance capacity, and renewal capabilities. They adopt developmental programs that motivate employees to increase their personal productivity and performance, which leads to overall organizational improvement (Figure 6.1).

Human resource professionals also demonstrate business acumen through their understanding of stockholder needs and expectations. Effective professionals adapt their practices, procedures, products, innovations, and services based upon this knowledge, which allows them to better service their clients.

Ulrich (1997) contends that HR professionals add value to the organization by understanding business operations. In doing so, human resource personnel are no longer working in a professional void; their expertise takes on a valuable, practical aspect. Thus, HR professionals need to gain operational experience in functional areas such as marketing, finance, operations, and sales. Ulrich further believes that HR professionals must understand business conditions to generate pertinent, practical solutions for their clients.

Understanding client needs and expectations, being aware of the financial and business issues facing the organization, and creating long-term solutions to difficult problems provide excellent opportunities to improve the organization's strength and viability. Keen insights and operational understanding of the business maximize an HR professional's knowledge and expertise to improve the firm's performance. Three subroles exhibit business understanding: roles that we call the scout, the strategic partner, and the systems linker (Figure 6.2).

As scouts, HR professionals operate as visionaries within the organization. Scouts maneuver through the trees, avoid obvious obstacles, and guide the organization through uncharted territory in the quest for change. In short, these professionals lead the organization into areas where it has not gone before. HR professionals in the scout role generate innovative solutions to complex problems, set priorities, integrate client input, translate these into action plans, and direct the organization toward achieving its business goals.

As strategic partners, HR professionals understand the critical factors affecting organizational competitiveness and communicate benefits that change strategies and interventions provide to the firm. Strategic partners thoroughly understand business fundamentals, core processes, operations, and procedures.

Most organizations comprise a myriad of divisions, departments, units, and functions that work in harmony to achieve efficient, effective business results. Human resource professionals in the role of systems linker unify these groups via the alignment of a common set of guiding principles that help define the organization's direction and provide its purpose and focus. Hence, the systems linker helps members of the organization

FIGURE 6.2   Pyramid of HR roles, subroles, and competencies

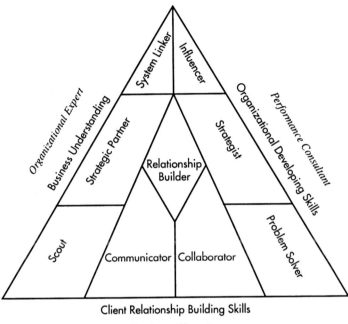

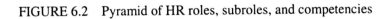

pull in the same direction to achieve a common set of business results. Effective HR professionals then establish connections between departments by communicating the value and importance of teamwork. When cooperation such as this is present, the affected parts of the organization work together in harmony.

Employee Champion.   Human resource professionals are in a unique position to serve as employee champions (Ulrich 1997). As such, they reveal the correct balance between work demands and resources, identifying legitimate demands on employees and helping these workers focus by setting priorities. Employee champions also distinguish creative ways of leveraging resources so that employees do not feel overwhelmed by what is expected of them.

When work demands cannot be diminished, employees should respond appropriately by allocating resources efficiently. Ulrich (1997, 135) believes that ten questions help determine whether employees and organizations are responding appropriately to demand situations:

1. Do employees control key decision-making processes that determine how work is done? (control)
2. Do employees have a vision and direction that commits them to working hard? (commitment)
3. Are employees given challenging work assignments that provide opportunities to learn new skills? (challenging work)
4. Do employees work in teams to accomplish goals? (collaboration, teamwork)
5. Does the work environment provide opportunities for celebration, fun, excitement, and openness? (culture)
6. Are employees compensated and rewarded for work accomplishments? (compensation)
7. Do employees enjoy open, candid, and frequent information sharing with management? (communication)
8. Are employees treated with dignity while differences are openly shared and respected? (concern for due process)
9. Do employees have access to and use of technology that makes their work easier? (computers and technology)
10. Do employees have the skills necessary to do their work well? (competence)

Ulrich further contends that positive answers to these questions enable an organization to determine the adequacy of employee control, the commitment to the organization, the type of challenging work provided to employees, the degree to which collaboration and teamwork are employed, the adequacy of organizational culture, the quality of the compensation and reward system used, the quality and quantity of organizational communications, the concern for due process, the adequacy of technology, and employee competence. Human resource professionals devote a majority of their time to guarantee that the organization positively answers each of the preceding ten questions. Doing so allows HR professionals to continually enhance their organizational impact and influence (Figure 6.1).

To be effective employee champions, HR professionals develop client relationship skills such as listening, reflecting, questioning, and summarizing to build mutual acceptance and positive regard with their clients. These skills help clients develop a sense of trust when implementing change for the first time. These skills also promote rapport and enhance credibility so that clients will be willing to accept HR's recommendations. Human resource professionals assume three subroles to build client relationships: relationship builder, collaborator, and communicator (Figure 6.2).

According to Gilley and Coffern (1994), several activities help HR professionals become competent relationship builders. These include turning assertions into questions, giving clients options, making meetings and reports meaningful, helping clients implement solutions and interventions, being accessible, and—always, always—adding value. We believe that one good way to improve client relationships is to help them learn new skills and competencies. Learning enhances client self-esteem, which in turn improves the HR professional–client relationship. Human resource professionals enhance customer relationships by encouraging the development of critical thinking skills that improve clients' professional practices and result in better approaches to accomplishing work.

As collaborators, HR professionals establish credibility and gain employee confidence to implement change. Collaborators tailor communications to their audience, listen and ask appropriate questions, present ideas clearly and concisely via well-organized written and interpersonal communications, and engage in informal communications that build support and identify commonalties among their various client groups to determine shared interests.

An important subrole is that of communicator. Important skills of the communicator include active listening, using silence, demonstrating understanding, establishing rapport, communicating empathy, clarifying statements, and appropriately employing summarization techniques.

Performance Consultant.   An effective way for an HR professional to improve his or her influence and simultaneously enhance organizational impact is to accept the role of performance consultant (Figure 6.1). Unfortunately, many HR professionals cannot make the transition to performance consultant, because they are not prepared for the complexity, ambiguity, and uncertainty common in consulting. According to Robinson and Robinson (1996), to make the transition HR professionals must develop and apply specialized consulting competencies and skills, and apply the role of performance consulting to improve organizational effectiveness. They also must appreciate and understand the performance consulting process.

Effective performance consultants remain impartial, regardless of their values and biases, and in spite of an organization's culture, traditions, and vested interests. Their impartiality is often referred to as objectivity.

Human resource professionals know where to go for information, insight, recommendations, or coaching in order to avoid pitfalls common in organizational life. They must be operationally smart, possessing organizational awareness that helps them better understand the political structure, decision making, or procedures, all of which are essential in rallying the support needed to implement meaningful change.

Additional organization development competencies and skills are necessary for the performance consulting role. These abilities include interpersonal, conceptual, technical, integrative, analytical, political awareness, and conflict resolution skills.

As performance consultants, HR professionals engage in three subroles in which they respond to unforeseen contingencies; provide appropriate solutions to complex, sensitive issues; and conduct a wide range of activities designed to modify or enhance results. We call these subroles the influencer, the strategist, and the problem solver (Figure 6.2).

Performance consultants, as influencers, are very directive in their attempt to influence client thinking, initiate change, or provide specific recommendations that address difficult organizational problems. To succeed as an influencer, HR professionals guard against their own personal biases and overpowering opinions, remaining receptive to others' views and recommendations while encouraging organizational members to take risks to achieve their goals and objectives.

As strategists, HR professionals are competent in assessing organizational needs using quantifiable and qualifiable methodologies, developing and executing business initiatives, and evaluating the effectiveness of learning interventions and other drives. Strategists incorporate the ideas of others into directive action plans.

Problem solvers take an active role in the decision-making and change-management process, spending a majority of their time helping clients make decisions beneficial to achieving desired results. Problem solvers strive to guarantee that the perceived problem is indeed the one critical to the organization.

Finally, performance consultants must become experts in applying the consulting process, which serves as a guide in establishing client relationships, identifying organizational performance problems and developmental needs, revealing client resistance to change, conducting diagnosis, providing clients with feedback, selecting and implementing appropriate change interventions, and evaluating results. Each of these steps represents the components of the performance consulting process. When applied, this process ensures that root causes of problems have been identified and appropriate solutions have been selected and implemented, resulting in suitable outcomes.

Organizational Development Change Agent.   In the role of organizational development change agent, HR professionals wield the greatest organizational impact and influence (Figure 6.1). This role requires knowledge of HR practices, partnering and negotiating skills, business acumen, client relationships, and organizational development. In other words, the role is a microcosm as well as an aggregate of all roles previously discussed. It is in this role that true organizational change occurs. When HR professionals act as change agents, they establish high credibility within the organization and great influence with key decision makers, line managers, and employees. This role is not unlike that of performance consulting, except that the interventions by change agents can include those that directly impact the organizational system, such as an examination of organizational culture, work climate, mission, strategy, structure, policies, procedures, managerial practices, and leadership.

Performance consulting, as discussed previously, focuses on interventions designed to improve employee performance and productivity (see Chapters 5 and 10).

The organizational development change agent role requires HR professionals to work with all levels and types of individuals within the firm while treating each in the same respectful, valued way. After all, certain clients have the power to make decisions and to provide the financial and human resources needed to implement and support change. Some clients can derail an intervention prior to its execution, whereas others affect the outcome by manipulating individuals' perceptions. Client groups may provide technical advice and the support needed to ensure change. Additionally, they may assume all or some of the responsibility for implementing interventions or solutions for change, and they may guide the interaction between other client groups.

In most situations, four types of clients prevail: decision makers, stakeholders, influencers, and advocates (Gilley 1998). Decision makers are most commonly senior executives and managers who have the authority to secure final approval for change. They have direct access to financial and human resources and are primarily interested in the bottom line and the impact that an intervention will have upon an organization.

Stakeholders, on the other hand, have the most to gain or lose as a result of change because they must implement, supervise, and asses the intervention's results. We assert that stakeholders have to live with the intervention; hence, change becomes a very personal decision for which they are held accountable.

Influencers screen solutions to difficult, complex situations, deeming their appropriateness and practicality for the organization. As a result, they serve as gatekeepers by changing the perceptions of decision makers and stakeholders regarding selected interventions. Although they typically lack the authority to approve the selection of an intervention, they can greatly influence the selection process. Therefore, it is important that human resource professionals not discount or minimize influencers' impact. Effectively dealing with influencers involves soliciting their opinions, ideas, perceptions, and assistance—in short, validation.

Advocates seek to discover ways of implementing change. They often work behind the scenes and historically have not been visible unless HR professionals solicited their advice. If they possess credibility with decision makers, stakeholders, and influencers, then advocates can be a vitally important resource for HR professionals, providing and interpreting information about problems, potential causes, types of clients involved, client expectations, and the way to proceed. Advocates may be found throughout the organization, including the HR department, the stakeholder division, or other operational units.

Human Resource Professionals' Responsibilities

Every organizational system consists of departments, units, and divisions, which collectively produce products and services purchased by customers. Traditionally, these organizations are broken down into three separate levels. The first level is organizational, at which decision making, policies, procedures, firm structure, job design, and other organizational decisions are made. The second level is the business process level, where various departments within the business interface. The third level is the performer level, at which most work is accomplished (Figure 6.2).

Figure 6.3 (page 170) illustrates the responsibilities of the HR professional. At the organizational level, HR professionals engage in human resource planning, recruitment and selection, redesigning the organizational system (culture, structure, managerial practices, and work climate), and compensation and reward program. Historically, these responsibilities constituted *human resource management,* whose activities traditionally provided organization-wide and strategic thrust. At the business process (departmental) level, HR professionals hold one primary responsibility—performance management. This responsibility is ultimately used to improve current and future performance. At the performer (employee) level, HR professionals design and refine career development and planning to enhance employee career options, while managers facilitate learning and change activities. The activities at the business process and performer lev-

FIGURE 6.3 Organizational Levels and HR Professional Responsibilities

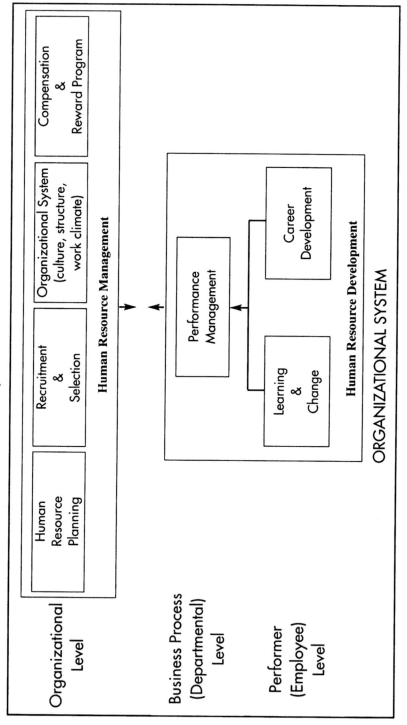

els are known as *human resource development*. The combination of human resource management and human resource development activities make up what has been traditionally considered the field of human resources.

In many organizations, HR management and HR development responsibilities are separated into two distinct operational departments. HR professionals of the organization of the future (developmental organizations) hold management *and* development responsibilities along with their corresponding competencies.

Each of the seven separate HR practice areas previously discussed can be used in combination to facilitate transformation from the traditional to developmental organization. In Figure 6.3, HR management activities work in combination with those of human resource development. For example, human resource planning ultimately impacts the selection and recruiting process, which in turn is affected by the organizational system (culture, structure, managerial practices, and work climate). Consequently, recruiting and selection policies and procedures are influenced by these two activities. Employees recruited and selected by an organization will eventually be required to engage in learning and change actions to advance or improve their knowledge, skills, and behaviors, for either their current or future jobs. This is further influenced by an organization's performance management process, which, over time, impacts the career development and planning activities of employees as they advance their careers.

Finally, the firm's compensation and reward strategies affect individual employee performance, management, and career development. In short, HR professionals must understand their individual responsibilities and must interface with one another to enhance employee and organizational growth and development. Each of these human resource practices will be discussed in greater detail in Chapters 7 through 11. We will also discuss state-of-the-art HR practices instrumental in building the developmental organization.

We see several new responsibilities for the HR professional, including helping managers and supervisors with the following tasks (Gilley, Boughton, and Maycunich 1999, 193–194) :

- designing jobs and work flow
- selecting and recruiting employees
- developing employees
- measuring and managing performance
- making the transition to performance coaching
- transforming performance appraisals into developmental evaluations
- creating growth and development plans
- linking compensation and rewards to growth and development

A summary of these activities reveals that a HR professional's primary responsibility is to help organizations become developmentally focused, transforming employees into the organization's greatest asset.

OUTCOMES OF THE HUMAN RESOURCES FUNCTION

A primary benefit of HR functions operating developmentally involves having the right people in the right place at the right time interacting with the right leadership. Consequently, it is important to select and develop human resources necessary to meet present and future business goals and objectives. Specific strategies that will bring about desired results include, first, creating competitive advantage through people and processes and, second, building competencies in people and the organization (Fiorelli, Longpre, and Zimmer 1996).

To create competitive advantage through people and processes, growth-oriented firms adopt the principles and practices of the developmental organization. In this way, organizations treat their employees as their most valuable component in achieving global competitiveness, organizational renewal, and enhanced performance capacity and capability. We also suggest that firms adopt the principles of developmental leadership (Chapter 3); sculpt an organizational system that encourages development (Chapter 4); build organizational capacity and capability through human resource planning, recruiting, and selection (Chapter 7); enhance organizational renewal via learning and change (Chapter 8); implement career development strategies (Chapter 9); apply the performance alignment process

(Chapter 10); and encourage development through effective compensation and reward strategies (Chapter 11). Each approach nourishes an organization's capability through state-of-the-art human resource practices.

When organizations adopt the principles, practices, and ideas of the developmental organization, they will indeed improve their competitive readiness, enhance organizational renewal, and increase their overall performance capacity and capability.

CONCLUSION

Human resource professionals are important players in the evolution of the developmental organization, adopting a multitude of new roles and responsibilities to help the firm move beyond the mere learning organization. Developmental HR professionals reinvent their function by identifying the strategies necessary to bring about effective HR practices, restructuring the HR function, identifying the actions and guiding principles necessary to enhance employee growth and development, identifying specific outcomes that serve as targets for both the HR function and the organization, and creating partnerships throughout the organization.

Human resource professionals in developmental organizations accept their responsibilities for HR management and development actions within the organization, participating in the ever-demanding roles of organizational champions, performance consultants, and organizational development change agents.

174

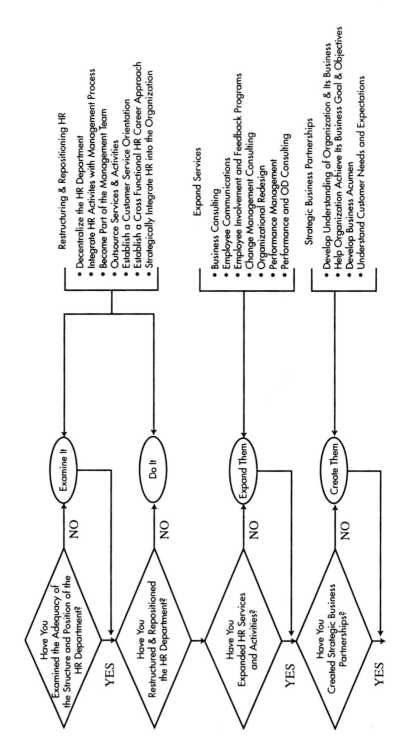

FIGURE 6.4 Steps and ingredients required for creating the HR department for the twenty-first century

Restructuring & Repositioning HR
- Decentralize the HR Department
- Integrate HR Activites with Management Process
- Become Part of the Management Team
- Outsource Services & Activities
- Establish a Customer Service Orientation
- Establish a Cross Functional HR Career Approach
- Strategically Integrate HR into the Organization

Expand Services
- Business Consulting
- Employee Communications
- Employee Involvement and Feedback Programs
- Change Management Consulting
- Organizational Redesign
- Performance Management
- Performance and OD Consulting

Strategic Business Partnerships
- Develop Understanding of Organization & Its Business
- Help Organization Achieve Its Business Goal & Objectives
- Develop Business Acumen
- Understand Customer Needs and Expectations

Have You Examined the Adequacy of the Structure and Position of the HR Department?

NO → Examine It

YES

Have You Restructured & Repositioned the HR Department?

NO → Do It

Have You Expanded HR Services and Activities?

NO → Expand Them

YES

Have You Created Strategic Business Partnerships?

NO → Create Them

YES

(continues)

(continued)

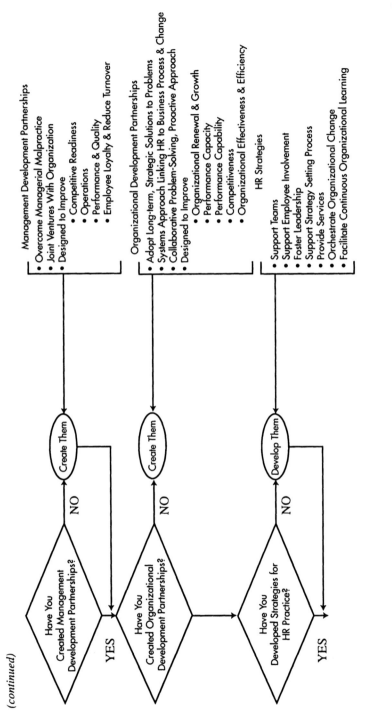

Management Development Partnerships
- Overcome Managerial Malpractice
- Joint Ventures With Organization
- Designed to Improve
  - Competitive Readiness
  - Operations
  - Performance & Quality
  - Employee Loyalty & Reduce Turnover

Organizational Development Partnerships
- Adopt Long-term, Strategic Solutions to Problems
- Systems Approach Linking HR to Business Process & Change
- Collaborative Problem-Solving, Proactive Approach
- Designed to Improve
  - Organizational Renewal & Growth
  - Performance Capacity
  - Performance Capability
  - Competitiveness
  - Organizational Effectiveness & Efficiency

HR Strategies
- Support Teams
- Support Employee Involvement
- Foster Leadership
- Support Strategy Setting Process
- Provide Services
- Orchestrate Organizational Change
- Facilitate Continuous Organizational Learning

Create Them

Create Them

Develop Them

NO

NO

NO

YES

YES

Have You Created Management Development Partnerships?

Have You Created Organizational Development Partnerships?

Have You Developed Strategies for HR Practice?

176

(continued)

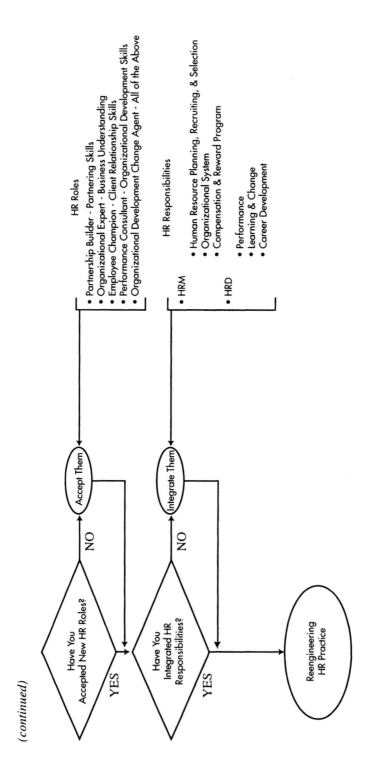

PART THREE

Human Resources Practices

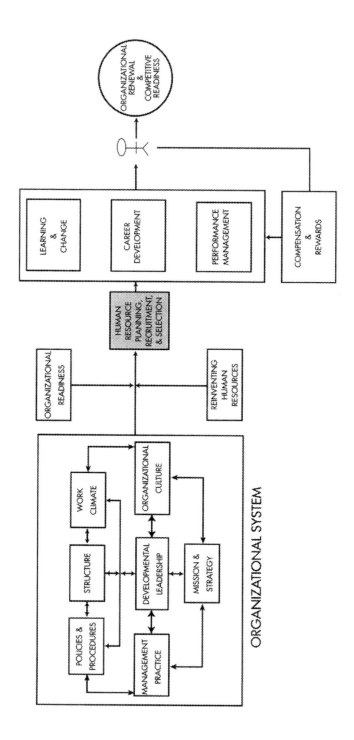

ORGANIZATIONAL SYSTEM

CHAPTER 7

Human Resource Planning, Recruiting, and Selection

Over the past fifty years, we have witnessed the importance of human resource planning, recruiting, and selection in every professional and collegiate sport. During the 1940s and 1950s, the New York Yankees dominated professional baseball, whereas the Cincinnati Reds ruled in the 1970s, and the Atlanta Braves in the 1990s. In the 1950s and 1960s, the Boston Celtics were without match in the National Basketball Association, winning championship title after championship title. Finally, in 1999, the Denver Broncos won their second consecutive Super Bowl, nearly impossible in today's era of free agency.

How did these teams produce such successful results? Simple. They understood the relationship between human resource planning, recruiting, selection, performance, and growth and development (Figure 7.1). In essence, they had a plan for getting the right people—including players (employees) and coaches (organizational leaders and managers)—at the right place at the right time.

At the heart of human resource planning, recruiting, and selection is enhancing an organization's competitive readiness and renewal capabilities, motivating factors to a developmental organization. Without human

FIGURE 7.1 Human resource planning, recruitment, selection, and growth and development

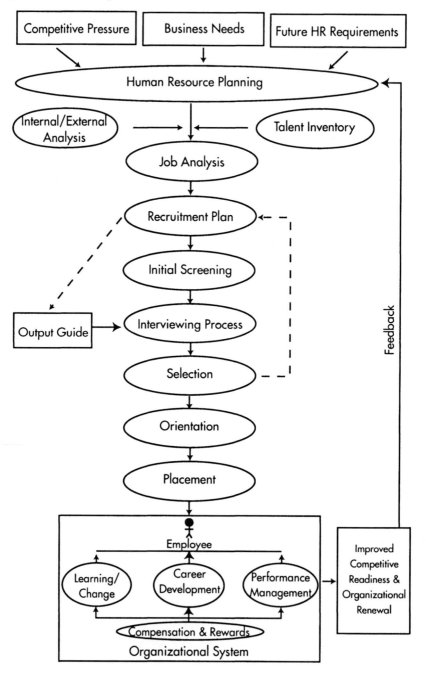

resource planning, an organization is steering blind on a dense, foggy night, certain to run aground and seriously jeopardize its crew, cargo, and anything or anybody else having the misfortune of getting in its path.

Traditional organizations seldom cite organizational renewal or competitive readiness as reasons for conducting human resource planning. Some learning organizations, however, do mention these factors as reasons that human resource planning is important. Developmental organizations absolutely believe in planning for future human resource needs and possibilities. They do so to improve business results and to remain at full alert, poised to do battle at a moment's notice.

In developmental organizations, human resource planning, recruiting, and selection determines the quantity and quality of human resources needed to foster organizational renewal and enhance competitive readiness. Thus, human resource professionals and organizational leaders engage in a series of related steps to guarantee that appropriate human resources are identified, recruited, selected, and developed. The process begins by analyzing what influences human resource planning, factors such as the business needs of the organization, competitive pressures, and future human resource requirements. Once these factors are identified, HR professionals and leaders analyze the conditions impacting current and future organizational success through internal and external environmental analysis, which reveals the firm's strengths, weaknesses, opportunities, and threats. Next, a talent inventory reveals employees' skills, knowledge, abilities, and potential, and how they are currently being used. Job analysis follows; it identifies the performance outputs, standards, and activities required of each job and the competencies needed by employees to execute them. These criteria serve as job requirement data, for which recruiting plans are designed, as measurement criteria useful in the initial screening and interviewing of available candidates, and as the final determinant in selecting new employees. Another important criterion, an employee's growth and developmental readiness, is a critical attitudinal element that must be identified during the screening, interviewing, and selection processes. Once selected, employees participate in orientation programs designed to socialize them within the organization and help them with placement on the job. Finally, developmental organizations link the human resource planning, recruiting, and selection process with the organization's employee growth and enhancement activities (i.e., learning and change, career development, performance management, and compensation and rewards). In this way, each process impacts the others, providing continuous feedback that fosters organizational renewal and enhances competitive readiness. Each step, its corresponding activities, and outcomes will be examined throughout this chapter (Figure 7.2).

Human Resource Planning

Cascio (1995, 142) defines human resource planning as an effort to anticipate future business and environmental demands on an organization and to provide qualified people to fulfill business needs and satisfy demands. Human resource planning is viewed as a process, not merely a component of an HR professional's job description. As a process, human resource planning focuses on identifying an organization's human resource needs under changing conditions and developing the interventions and initiatives necessary to satisfy those needs.

A developmental organization's long-term success depends on its employees' competencies, which can be either developed internally or acquired on the open market. Planning for long-term use and development of human resources proves to be a complex activity that requires careful analysis and forecasting skill. To complicate the process, human resource planning pervades the entire organization because it is not the sole domain of HR professionals, instead requiring input, involvement, and action from organizational leaders, managers, and employees.

Human resource planning is a process of systematically organizing the future, of putting into place a plan designed to address upcoming performance problems or productivity and quality requirements. By addressing unknown variables, developmental organizations align and structure their future to guarantee specific and certain outcomes. Failing to do so would be like starting a vacation without any idea of your destination or what you're going to do. Hence, the probability of having a relaxing, comfortable, fun-filled vacation is in serious peril. In the same way, failing to conduct human resource planning jeopardizes the organization's future success.

FIGURE 7.2   From human resource planning to growth and development: the steps, activities, and outcomes

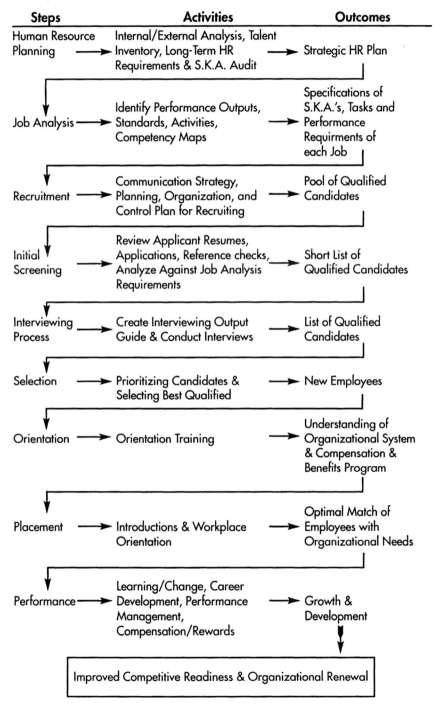

Steps	Activities	Outcomes
Human Resource Planning	Internal/External Analysis, Talent Inventory, Long-Term HR Requirements & S.K.A. Audit	Strategic HR Plan
Job Analysis	Identify Performance Outputs, Standards, Activities, Competency Maps	Specifications of S.K.A.'s, Tasks and Performance Requirments of each Job
Recruitment	Communication Strategy, Planning, Organization, and Control Plan for Recruiting	Pool of Qualified Candidates
Initial Screening	Review Applicant Resumes, Applications, Reference checks, Analyze Against Job Analysis Requirements	Short List of Qualified Candidates
Interviewing Process	Create Interviewing Output Guide & Conduct Interviews	List of Qualified Candidates
Selection	Prioritizing Candidates & Selecting Best Qualified	New Employees
Orientation	Orientation Training	Understanding of Organizational System & Compensation & Benefits Program
Placement	Introductions & Workplace Orientation	Optimal Match of Employees with Organizational Needs
Performance	Learning/Change, Career Development, Performance Management, Compensation/Rewards	Growth & Development

Improved Competitive Readiness & Organizational Renewal

Human resource planning is integrated with the developmental organization's strategic plan and other organization-wide initiatives, revealing a strong interdependency among HR activities such as recruitment, selection, orientation, placement, performance management, the learning and change process, career development, and compensation and rewards (Figure 7.1). Absent an integrative approach, human resource planning cannot positively impact the type and quality of employees needed to ensure developmental organizational renewal and competitive readiness.

Influences on Human Resource Planning

Influences of human resource planning include the business needs of the organization, competitive pressure, and future HR requirements. An understanding of each influence assists organizations in preparation for their future success.

Business Needs.   Every organization has needs that must be satisfied. Examples are increased business revenue, profitability, quality, effectiveness, efficiency, safety, and customer satisfaction. These needs place tremendous pressure on organizations and their human resources. Such pressure requires "smart organizations" (developmental organizations) to anticipate how the quality and quantity of their human resources can be employed to adequately address needs. In fact, this is one reason why developmental organizations are motivated to grow and develop their employees. A tenet of the developmental organization is to meet or exceed business needs through the continuous growth and development of employees.

Competitive Pressures.   Every organization must respond to competitive pressure or be crushed by it. Therefore, developmental organizations are continuously examining themselves to determine whether they can adequately respond to their competitors. One of the best ways to appropriately respond to outside competitive pressure is a sufficient supply of human resources. This can be best facilitated by aggressively employing the growth and development enhancement activities outlined in Chapters 8 through 11 and utilizing the steps and recommendations in Chapter 12.

Future Human Resource Requirements.   The necessity to forecast the number and type of employees required in the future exemplifies the importance of human resource planning to developmental organizations. In the same way, a professional baseball, football, or basketball franchise anticipates its future human resource needs to remain competitive. The franchise must forecast the future strengths and weaknesses of the team; anticipate retirements; project the departures of key players; assess its bench; determine when certain players can be used; identify which players have developed well enough to play every day; blend the team with a mix of veterans, young players, and rookies; and have key backups in vital positions. In short, human resource planning is greatly influenced by future HR requirements of the organization, prompting HR professionals and leaders to analyze their situation carefully and make projections accordingly.

The purpose of human resource forecasting is to estimate labor requirements at some future date (Cascio 1995). Forecasting includes looking at (1) the external and internal supply of labor and (2) the aggregate external and internal demand for labor.

"Internal" refers to the conditions inside an organization, whereas "external" refers to the labor market as a whole. Each of these four components must be carefully examined by HR professionals and developmental organization leaders to accurately project the quantity and quality of future human resources.

IDENTIFYING HUMAN RESOURCE AND ORGANIZATIONAL NEEDS

Internal and external environmental analysis and talent inventories are two human resource planning activities that enable HR professionals and leaders to identify human resource needs and those of the organization. Both analyses provide a wealth of information useful in forecasting human resource requirements and matching them with human resource strategies.

Internal and External Environmental Analysis

An important human resource planning activity conducted in developmental organizations is an internal and external environmental analysis (Figure 7.1). Upon completion, HR professionals and organizational leaders have identified the strengths and weaknesses (the internal environment) and the opportunities and threats (the external environment) facing the firm—a process called a SWOT analysis.

SWOT analysis information is useful in adjusting human resource forecasts and in taking corrective actions necessary to overcome weaknesses and address threats. This information also helps developmental organizations build on strengths and capitalize on opportunities.

In a previous book (Gilley and Maycunich 1998a, 98–99), we identified several questions and statements useful for conducting an internal environmental analysis. Once these questions and statements are addressed, HR professionals and leaders are able to describe its relative strengths, weaknesses, and impact on long-term human resource planning (Figure 7.2).

1. What is the financial condition of the organization?
2. What are the aptitudes and abilities of managers and employees?
3. What is the current condition of facilities?
4. What is the current state and quality of technology?
5. How much technology, and what kind, does the organization employ to achieve business results?
6. What is the quality and quantity of internal human and material resources?
7. How is the organization structured?
8. Describe the organizational culture.
9. Describe the work climate within the organization.
10. Describe the managerial practices within the organization.

11. Identify the policies and procedures that enhance or impede organizational performance, effectiveness, and development.
12. Describe the organization's leadership.
13. Identify the organization's mission and strategy.
14. Describe the organizational learning system.
15. Describe the compensation and reward system.
16. Describe the performance appraisal and coaching process.
17. Does the organization advocate employee growth and development?
18. Is organizational renewal and competitive readiness important to the organization?
19. What performance gaps exist within the organization?
20. What organizational effectiveness gaps exist?
21. What is the current state of human resource practice within the organization?

External Environmental Analysis.   External environmental analysis reveals the health of an organization, its values, political climate, its use of technology and resources, its competitive rank within the industry, its overall image, and the areas requiring improvement (Gilley 1992). Such information will be invaluable to HR professionals and developmental organization leaders when they are making decisions regarding the allocation of human resources.

We have identified several questions that will assist in the examination of the external environment:

1. What are the economic conditions of the nation, region, and local community?
2. What social and cultural values predominate within the industry and its geographic region?
3. What external human resources are available?
4. What is the quantity and quality of external human resources?
5. What is the organization's image in the marketplace?
6. What is the company's competitive rank within the industry?

Identifying the opportunities and threats facing an organization allows HR professionals and leaders to avoid costly mistakes common when inappropriate growth and development activities are encouraged. Instead, they implement growth and development strategies that maximize performance output and employee proficiency. This is extremely important to the long-term competitiveness of developmental organizations and, ultimately, their success.

Talent Inventory.   Identifying the skills, knowledge, and abilities of an organization's current employees is known as a *talent inventory* (Figure 7.1). Talent inventories enable HR professionals and organizational leaders to identify employee proficiencies and establish a reliable baseline of human capital. Once this baseline has been established, growth and development decisions can be made regarding the competencies of employees as a group and on an individual basis. In addition, decisions can be made about future external recruiting efforts necessary to improve skill and knowledge gaps.

Talent inventories reveal employees' specialized training; current employment information; significant work experiences; educational background (including degrees, licenses, certifications); language skills; growth and development plans (past and present); professional association leadership; and awards received (Cascio 1995). Information such as this assists organizations in developing profiles of their employees' capacity and capabilities.

JOB ANALYSIS

Once human resource planning efforts have been identified, HR professionals and organizational leaders conduct job analysis activities to identify requirements for each job within the organization (Figure 7.1). These analyses also create a solid basis on which to make job-related employment decisions (Schneider and Konz 1989), helping organizations establish interviewing criteria, performance appraisal systems, and selection requirements, upon which hiring and promotional decisions are made. Job analysis also helps with the following tasks:

- clarifying job requirements and the relationships among jobs
- forecasting human resource needs
- identifying training, transfer, and promotion requirements
- evaluating employee performance and conduct
- compensation reviews
- recruiting future employees
- improving labor relations
- enhancing career planning
- improving job design
- developing job classifications
- improving career counseling activities
- resolving grievances and jurisdictional disputes
- improving working methods
- identifying job classifications useful in developing selection, training, and compensation systems (Cascio 1995).

Job analysis is a process consisting of five separate but interrelated components (Figure 7.2). At the heart of job analysis are the organization's strategic business goals and objectives that focus employees' efforts. Jobs that fail to support organizational achievement of its strategic goals and objectives cease to be valuable (Gilley 1998). Thus it is critical to link job analysis to these outcomes.

Business Process

Every job within an organization is housed within a business process—a subpart of an organizational function (department or business unit) in which various departments interact with one another. Part of the job analysis process involves identifying these interfaces to eliminate breakdowns or to isolate areas of improvement that ultimately impact organizational performance capacity. Hence, job analysis uncovers opportunities for performance improvement and employee growth and development.

The interfaces within a business process include four interrelated components: performance outputs, performance activities, performance standards, and competency maps.

Examination of these four components and their relationships allows developmental organizations to assess how well work has been designed and the organizational system's impact on performance.

Performance Outputs.   Performance outputs are the tangibles and intangibles that employees are paid to produce. These outputs define an employee's job. Performance outputs can be the number of successful sales calls made by telemarketing representatives, the number of sales made per month by sales personnel, the service claims satisfied by customer service representatives, the number of proposals written each month, the number of packages delivered per day by postal workers, and so on. Outputs represent the hourly, daily, weekly, monthly, quarterly, and/or yearly expectations of employees in a specific job classification (Gilley 1998, 91).

Internally, one employee's outputs become another employee's inputs that he or she uses in the execution of the job. Externally, performance outputs are the products and services produced for customers outside the organization. Whether internal or external, outputs are the tangible outcomes of employee performance that defines one's contribution within the organization.

Performance Activities.   Once business processes and outputs are identified, HR professionals and developmental organization leaders identify performance activities required by employees to generate performance outputs. In short, performance activities are the steps that employees take to create performance outputs. Each performance activity consists of microtasks, which collectively form the steps of an employee's job.

When analyzing a job, developmental HR professionals and organizational leaders examine performance activities to determine possible breakdowns as well as tasks that contribute to the successful completion of products and services. If a problem is identified, a growth and development intervention is designed to help employees perform acceptably.

Job descriptions demonstrate the relationship between performance outputs and activities. They should be written to clearly identify performance outputs for each job, performance activities required by employees to produce these deliverables, and the relationship between activities and outputs. Moreover, each performance action or collection of activities produces one or more performance outputs. Consequently, a job description is simply a written document that describes an employee's performance activities and deliverables (Gilley 1998).

Performance Standards.   Performance standards represent excellence criteria used to measure product and service quality and worker efficiency. Employees can compare their actions and output against performance standards to determine whether they are performing at acceptable levels.

Identifying performance standards permits developmental employees to regulate the quality of their productivity, which aids them at higher levels, prevents needless mistakes, and maintains consistency—which ultimately leads to better organizational results. Performance standards help managers determine acceptable performance and measure the quality of performance outputs. Without these standards, managers and employees lack the ability to ascertain whether they have created performance outputs or executed performance activities acceptable to internal and external stakeholders.

According to Berke (1990), performance standards are based on performance outputs rather than on the way employees do their jobs. He adds that the standards must be achievable, easily understood by managers and employees, specific and measurable, time-based, written, and subject to change.

Standards allow employees to monitor and correct their performance because they can determine for themselves how well they are performing and whether they are producing satisfactory performance outputs. Performance standards encourage employees to continue to produce at an acceptable level. Consequently, they will do their jobs and know when they are doing them well.

Competency Maps.   Once performance outputs, activities, and standards are identified, HR professionals and leaders isolate the competencies (e.g., skills, knowledge, and attitudes) that employees need to accomplish their performance activities. HR personnel and leaders often use competency maps—comprehensive lists of all competencies needed for a specific job charted against each employee—to determine individual and overall gaps. Competency maps, which may be quite complex, are useful in recruiting and selecting employees for given job classifications. Organizations also use competency maps to determine the growth and development activities in which employees must participate to master performance. Finally, competency maps reveal employee strengths and weaknesses, thereby guiding career development as well as performance growth and development plans (Gilley, Boughton, and Maycunich 1999, 45).

Recruitment

After a job has been profiled and its required competencies have been identified, recruitment can begin (Figure 7.1). In developmental organizations, recruitment means finding employees with the skills, knowledge, and attitudes appropriate for the job along with the desire and ability to grow and develop continuously. Developmental employees are hungry to learn and develop throughout their personal and professional lives.

Recruitment involves developing a grand plan for communicating developmental organization opportunities to both the internal and the external labor markets. Opportunities can be disclosed in several ways, including position announcements in trade and professional journals, job postings within the firm, solicitations and recommendations from key organizational members, employee referrals, executive search firms, and temporary worker pools (Figure 7.2). Whatever form the activities take, the purpose is to "get the word out" about the company's employment opportunities.

In developmental organizations, recruiting is more than institutional advertising. Rather, it exemplifies a long-term strategy intended to attract and retain the types of individuals who will enhance an organization's competitive readiness and renewal capabilities. Developmental organizations seek *lifelong learners* who want to continuously grow and develop. This single characteristic—the pursuit of lifelong learners—separates developmental organizations from other types of firms (traditional and learning).

FIGURE 7.3   Coachability index

	Never	Frequently	Sometimes	Frequently	Always
1. Desires performance feedback	1	2	3	4	5
2. Solicits suggestions for improvement	1	2	3	4	5
3. Listens to another's point of view	1	2	3	4	5
4. Receptive to constructive feedback	1	2	3	4	5
5. Supportive of others' successes	1	2	3	4	5
6. Willing to acquire new knowledge, skills, and competencies	1	2	3	4	5
7. Receptive to new technology and improvement techniques	1	2	3	4	5
8. Willing to participate in growth and development plans	1	2	3	4	5
9. Willing to compare oneself with high achievers	1	2	3	4	5
10. Willing to develop critical reflective thinking skills to improve one's performance	1	2	3	4	5

High coachability: 45–50
Moderate coachability: 40–44
Low coachability: below 39

Recruitment in developmental organizations includes strategies for identifying and evaluating a potential employee's aptitude and desire for growth and development. One indicator of an individual's predisposition for personal growth and development is his or her *coachability index* (Figure 7.3). The index reflects a person's receptivity to constructive criticism and to suggestions for improvement, and his or her willingness to learn, discover, and accept new ways of performing. A low coachability index (below 39) is common in employees who are contrary and resist new and better ways of performing. They resist suggestions for improvement, are unwilling to listen to another's point of view, and feel that they are always right. Although these employees are critical of others' success, they are unwilling to adopt new approaches themselves, resisting growth and development planning and activities.

In contrast, a high coachability index (45–50) is characterized by enthusiasm for learning and development, heightened interest in new and better ways of performing, willingness to solicit and receive performance feedback, desire to compare oneself with high achievers, impatient enthusiasm to be the best one can be, career-focused ambitions, and developed reflective and critical thinking skills. By seeking out these types of individuals, developmental organizations establish a strategy for long-term success.

Initial Screening

One way of ensuring the selection of appropriate employees involves developing effective initial screening procedures (Figure 7.1). Screening includes the following steps: First, obtain the job requirements identified during the job analysis process. Second, focus on the skills, knowledge, and attitudes identified when examining candidates' applications, resumes, or both. Third, screen applications and resumes by focusing on (1) key words that match the job requirements, (2) quantifiers and qualifiers that indicate whether candidates meet these requirements, and (3) skills they might transfer from previous jobs to the new job. Fourth, identify the candidates who meet or exceed job requirements. Fifth, develop a short list of qualified candidates (Cascio 1995).

Interviewing

In developmental organizations, the interview is a formal, in-depth conversation conducted to evaluate a candidate's qualifications, acceptability, match with job requirements, and aptitude and desire for continuous growth and development (Figure 7.1). Developmental interviews seek to answer six broad questions:

1. Is the candidate qualified to do the job?
2. Will the candidate do the job?
3. How does the candidate compare with others being considered for the job?
4. Will the candidate continue to grow and develop?
5. Does the candidate have the desire, ability, and aptitude to grow and develop?
6. What is the candidate's coachability index?

Developmental organizations capitalize on two components of the interviewing process: creating an interviewing output guide, and conducting the interview. These steps are critical in answering the previous six questions.

An interviewing output guide focuses and directs the actual interview, providing structure and purpose to each step while linking job requirements to the interviewing process (Figure 7.4). The guide is a simple, straightforward planning document that identifies the purpose, expectations, and outcomes of each step of the interview. The "purpose" section of the guide should be linked to job requirements in order to solicit accurate information useful in evaluating each candidate. The "expectations" section identifies the type of exchange that will occur during the interview. This section is also useful in helping an interviewer create an effective, developmental approach to the interviewing process. Finally, the "outcomes" section helps interviewers identify the results of each step of the interview.

Interviews typically consist of five steps: interview preparation, creation of rapport with candidates, information exchange, interview termination, and evaluation of the interview (Werther and Davis 1996). Although these steps are not new, developmental organizations use them to create long-term relationships with potential candidates by demonstrating their pro-employee philosophy and their dedication to continuous employee growth and development. As a result, all potential candidates view the organization more positively, regardless of whether or not they are se-

FIGURE 7.4   Interviewing output guide

Interviewing Step	Purpose	Expectations	Outcomes

lected. The organization's image is thus enhanced in the marketplace, which helps during future recruiting efforts.

Werther and Davis (1996, 227) identified five types of interviews used to evaluate candidates:

- Unstructured interviewing: unplanned and spontaneous, used to help interviewees solve problems
- Structured interviewing: relies on predetermined checklists of questions usually asked of all candidates, used to validate results
- Mixed interviewing: combination of unstructured and structured questions, used to model realistic practice that yields comparable answers plus in-depth insight
- Behavioral interviewing: questions limited to hypothetical situations to evaluate the solutions and approaches of candidates, used to understand applicants' reasoning and analytical abilities under modest pressure
- Stress interviewing: a series of harsh, rapid-fire questions intended to upset the candidate, used for stressful jobs, such as handling complaints

A sixth type of interviewing, called developmental interviewing, incorporates unstructured, structured and behavioral interview techniques. This interviewing technique uses specific and random questions to determine the developmental readiness of candidates. Developmental interviewing ascertains applicants' long-term development plans by providing them with various employment situations and determining the type of growth and development strategy each would employ. Thus, this technique reveals the depth and breadth of their understanding of continuous renewal. Furthermore, developmental interviewing seeks to match the candidate's desire, ability, and aptitude for continuous growth and development with the position being considered. Finally, developmental interviewing is based on a fifty-fifty philosophy—that interviewing is a two-way street whereby organizations and candidates simultaneously evaluate and determine the goodness of fit between them. When both parties have reached consensus, a positive, long-term relationship begins.

Psychological Principles for Interpreting Interviews

Interpreting interviewing data can sometimes be hopelessly complex (Smart 1983, 121–131). Some candidates mask, distort, or whitewash information to project a better image. They may deliberately shade the truth about their work experience or educational background to improve their opportunities. Consequently, interviewers must interpret biased interviewee expressions. Smart identified nine principles that can be used to interpret interviewing data:

1. People's strengths become overused and at times are shortcomings.
2. Recent past behavior is the best predictor of near-future behavior.
3. Nature and nurture are equally irrelevant and relevant.
4. All behavior is motivated.
5. Red flags demand interpretation.
6. People may or may not change.
7. Evaluative judgments of personal characteristics and experiences may not be accurate.
8. One's attributions of success and failure may reveal underlying needs.
9. At the highest levels in organizations, people succeed not so much because of their outstanding strengths, but because of a lack of understanding of their liabilities and weaknesses.

SELECTION

The completion of candidate interviews leads to the next step, selection of the most qualified candidate(s). If the previous steps have been handled thoroughly and correctly, selection can be straightforward, consisting of prioritizing and selecting the best candidate(s) (Figure 7.2). However, one further consideration should be addressed before a job offer is extended: The interviewers must determine how well the candidate's personality, career objectives, values, beliefs, and attitudes align with those of the organization. According to Cascio (1995, 195), "culture is the pattern of basic assumptions a given group has invested, discovered, or developed in learning to adapt to its external and internal environments." Thus, patterns of assumptions are deeply embedded and transmitted through mechanisms like these:

- formal statements of organizational philosophy
- material used during recruiting, selection, and socialization of new employees
- promotion criteria
- stories, legends, and myths about key people and events
- what leaders pay attention to, measure, evaluate, control, and reward

Determining the cultural match between candidate(s) and the firm is critical because the culture of developmental organizations differs radically from that of traditional and learning organizations. Furthermore, new employees must possess the values, beliefs, and attitudes necessary to engage in continuous growth and development. If these are absent, the resulting mismatch between employee and organization can ultimately hurt both.

ORIENTATION

Failing to prepare new employees for the organization and their co-workers will bring on *employment shock,* the psychological gap between what a new employee expects and what he or she finds. To avoid this unfortunate condition, developmental organizations religiously use orientation training programs. In developmental organizations, Werther and Davis (1996) assert, orientation programs familiarize new employees with their roles and responsibilities, the organizational system and its expectations, performance standards, performance output requirements, reporting relationships, growth and development requirements, and growth and enhancement practices used to ensure organizational renewal and competitive readiness. When such programs are used, employee turnover and the cognitive dissonance associated with unresolved expectations can be greatly reduced.

SOCIALIZATION

Considering organizational culture from a developmental perspective, it makes a great deal of sense to look at socialization. Gibson, Ivancevich, and Donnelly (1997) define socialization as a process by which organizations bring new people into the culture. Developmental organizations practice more effective techniques of socialization than do traditional firms (in which, all too often, employees are left on their own to sink or swim within the muck of organizational culture).

Three phases of socialization predominate within organizations: anticipatory, accommodation, and role management (Feldman 1967). Each phase requires different undertakings to increase an employee's chances of enjoying a successful career within a developmental organization.

Anticipatory Socialization

When employees first consider working for an organization, they typically pose two questions. First, what will it be like to work for the firm? Second, are they suited to the jobs available within the firm? Each question should be addressed by the organization before it hires the individual—after all, first impressions are typically lasting ones. If questions are addressed correctly, employees will feel a heightened sense of satisfaction and loyalty.

Accommodation Socialization

The second phase of socialization, accommodation socialization, occurs after an employee becomes a member of the organization. During this phase, employees discover the organization and its jobs as they really are. Over time, employees become competent performers on the job and active participants within the firm. This so-called break-in period can be very stressful for most individuals. Four common activities constitute the accommodation phase of socialization:

- establishing new interpersonal relations with both co-workers and managers
- learning the tasks required to perform the job
- clarifying one's role within the organization via formal and informal groups
- evaluating one's progress toward satisfying demands of the job and the role (Gibson, Ivancevich, and Donnelly 1997, 38)

If all goes well during this phase, employees will feel a sense of accomplishment and acceptance by co-workers and superiors while gaining confidence in performing their jobs.

Role Management

Role management refers to the conflicts that occur once an individual has been fully integrated into the organization. Conflict may involve job performance, interpersonal relationships with co-workers or managers, inadequate development opportunities, insufficient job assignments, misinterpretation of rules or regulations, and so on. Regardless of the root of the conflict, role management socialization refers to the organization's ability to address and resolve conflicts between employees and the firm. Successful resolution results in reinforcement of positive organizational perceptions while unresolved or poor resolution may cause resentment, poor attitudes, or lukewarm cooperation on the part of personnel. Developmental firms focus on resolving conflict in a positive way to enhance relationships and build organizational esprit de corps.

Characteristics of Effective Socialization

Developmental organizations are more effective in socializing employees into their culture than are traditional or learning organizations. Developmental organizations understand the importance of recruiting employees with effective job interviewing techniques followed by selection and placement using realistic career path projections. In this way, organizations address and resolve the issues most concerning employees before they join the organization.

202

FIGURE 7.5 Human resource planning, recruitment, and selection

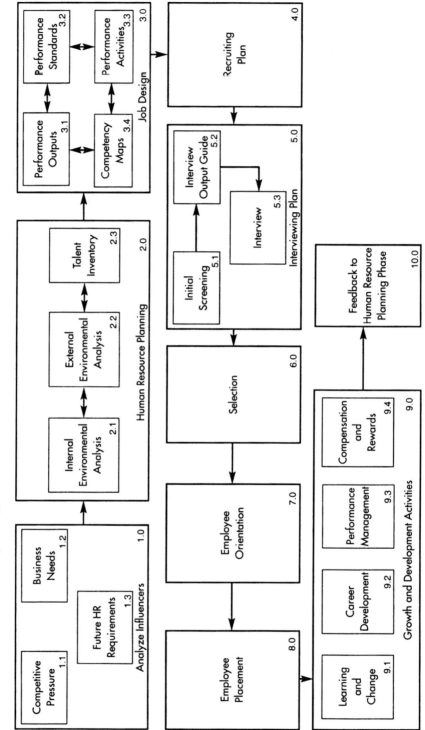

Developmental organizations focus on enhancing employee socialization through five efficacious activities:

1. Individualized orientation programs
2. Social and technical skills training
3. Performance evaluations designed to provide supportive and accurate performance feedback
4. Challenging work assignments that stretch an employee's abilities and talents
5. Demanding but fair managers who practice effective performance coaching techniques (Gibson, Ivancevich, and Donnelly 1997)

Each activity retains and develops new employees while reducing tension and conflict within the organization.

Developmental organizations understand fully the damage caused by conflict within the firm. As a result, agents are commissioned to provide professional counseling opportunities when conflict arises. Developmental organizations encourage managers to accept roles as career counselors and performance confronters so that employees have a forum and people with whom to discuss career opportunities as well as difficulties on the job.

PLACEMENT

Placement is the process of introducing new employees to their co-workers, supervisor, and managers. Placement is sometimes referred to as the career path identified by the employee, the organization, or both. Regardless of definition of "placement," the first few days on a new job can be very difficult. Developmental organizations understand the difficulty of personal integration on the job and provide "shadow" employees to make introductions and provide overviews of the workplace, special procedures, the locations of materials and equipment, and so forth. In some situations, mentors are provided to help with long-term indoctrination and growth and development activities.

LINKAGE

The final phase of human resource planning, recruiting, and selection involves integration with the achievement phase and the performance improvement process, which we call linkage. The purpose of the linkage process is to guarantee a connection between performance, employee growth and development, and the actual acquisition of human resources. In this way, acquisition of quality human resources and their placement, performance, and growth and development are forever united.

Performance output and growth and development activities (learning and change, career development, performance management, and compensation and rewards) directly influence future human resource planning efforts (Figure 7.1). Hence, the developmental organization blueprint reflects total integration of human resource practices and their effectiveness in transforming firms.

CONCLUSION

The human resource planning, recruiting, and selection process ensures that organizations have the right people in the right place at the right time. When working effectively, this process improves the quality and quantity of human resources, guaranteeing selection of employees who possess the aptitude and appetite for continuous growth and development—the cornerstone of the developmental organization.

Organizational renewal capacity and competitive readiness are determined by human resource supply, quality (skill, experience, education, knowledge), and propensity for personal growth and development. Supply and quality are obvious aims of organizational human resource planning; however, developmental organizations take the process a step further by emphasizing employee predisposition to renewal (which is the result of reflection and change). Those individuals possessing personal renewal capacity transfer that to the firm.

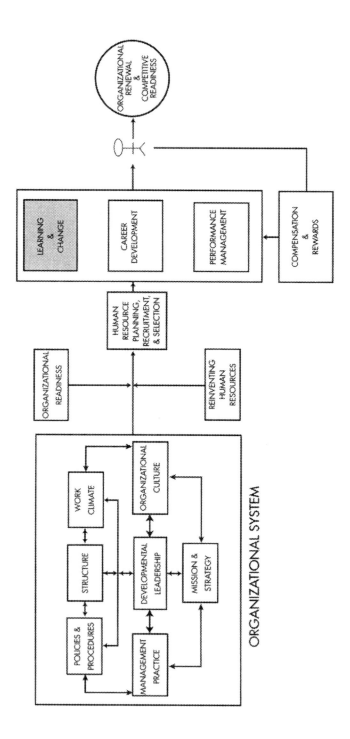

ORGANIZATIONAL SYSTEM

CHAPTER 8

The Learning and Change Process

The learning and change process is the key to transforming traditional organizations into developmental organizations. This fundamental process brings about opportunities essential to continuous organizational renewal and improved performance capacity. In fact, absent learning and change, development *cannot* occur and organizations will not enhance their competitive readiness.

While the learning and change process is essential to the creation of the developmental organization, it is only one of many elements of the developmental organization framework.

Before embracing learning and change, organizations must accept a viable definition of the terms. Learning can be defined as knowledge obtained by self-directed study, experience, or both; the art of acquiring knowledge, skills, competencies, attitudes, and ideas retained and used; or a change of behavior through experience (Gilley and Eggland 1989, 120–121). The latter implies that learning includes change. Although many could argue about the different levels of learning (e.g., knowledge, comprehension, application, analysis, synthesis, and evaluation), most agree that true learning occurs when an overt action results. That is, learning is demonstrated when behaviors change. Consequently, we believe that the learning and change process internalizes information through practice and review activities that ensure transfer and integration on the job. From this definition we conclude that learning affects change that, over time, enhances an individual's performance capability.

Senge (1990) believes that learning has little to do with taking in information; rather, it is a process that enhances capacity. "Learning is about building the capacity to create that which you previously could not create. It ultimately relates to action, which information is not" (191). These definitions parallel ours in their focus on individual developmental capacity such that employees are able to produce outcomes previously foreign to them. In a developmental organization, the learning and change process improves the individual capacity and capability of employees so that the firm will be in position to continuously grow and develop.

To capture the essence of learning and change, three critical questions must be answered. First, who is responsible for learning and change? Second, what phases and laws of the learning and change process must be addressed to enhance individual employee capability and performance capacity? Third, how can the phases and laws of the learning and change process explain the types of learning engagements occurring within organizations that create truly developmental learning opportunities? Three approaches effectively address these questions:

- creating learning-and-change partnerships
- identifying the various phases and concepts of the learning and change process (discussed below)
- applying the learning and change process model

CREATING LEARNING-AND-CHANGE PARTNERSHIPS

One of the age-old questions facing every organization is: Who should be responsible for learning and change? In many organizations this responsibility has fallen at the feet of a specialized group known as training and development practitioners. These individuals are typically experts in the design, development, and presentation of training programs. Most possess excellent communications skills, relate well to others, have outgoing and enthusiastic personalities, can engage people for long periods, and employ a solid foundation in adult learning, theory, and practice. The majority of these attributes are dedicated to employee well-being, learning, and change opportunities. Although all are positive attributes of this group of highly talented professionals, they have a limited impact on improving organizational performance. Few, if any, training and development practitioners are held accountable for employee growth and development. Further, rarely are these professionals required to conduct performance appraisals for the individuals they are responsible for training. In essence, training and development practitioners are neither responsible nor accountable for employee utilization of knowledge, skills, or competencies on the job.

Why are training and development practitioners allowed to be responsible for the growth and development of the organization's most important asset—its employees? One reason lies with organizations' systematic elimination of managers' responsibility for the development of their employees. Managers have been co-conspirators of this process by failing to insist on developing their people.

Another explanation surrounds the myth that the learning and change process requires specialized talent that most managers lack, such as interpersonal and communications skills. The primary skills that most managers deploy to secure results through people are, simply, interpersonal and communications expertise. Managers must possess these critical skills to be effective and influential with employees and in the learning and change process. Managers without these skills or unable to acquire them should not be managers at all. Washing one's hands of employee development because one lacks sufficient interpersonal or communications skills only exacerbates an organization's inability to improve its performance and renewal capacity.

We believe that organizations should hold managers accountable for employee performance and productivity. Managers should be ultimately responsible for implementing learning and change, conducting employee performance reviews, and confronting poor performance. They should be held accountable when employee productivity declines or the organization fails to meet its goals and objectives. Since managers are responsible and accountable for these actions, we contend that they should be primarily responsible for the growth and development of employees via the learning and change process.

If managers are responsible for training, what should training and development practitioners do for the organization? In some situations, organizations attempt to eliminate this valuable asset by absorbing their roles and responsibilities within the firm. One solution advocates that training and development practitioners evolve into employee champions, performance consultants, or change agents (Chapter 5). When training and development professionals accept these types of responsibilities and roles, a learning-and-change partnership can be forged that improves employee performance and organizational productivity through developmental engagements. This partnership requires training managers to function as facilitators of learning and change, designing and implementing activities that catalyze real change while forging a team with managers.

Training and development practitioners should be responsible for teaching managers how to facilitate the learning and change process. This important activity helps managers become more competent as training and development specialists, which positively impacts their credibility with employees.

Training and development practitioners should also be responsible for designing and implementing developmental activities. In most circumstances, managers are not qualified to function as instructional designers; they need professional help to build and implement developmental activities that improve employee performance and organizational productivity.

When organizations engage in advanced developmental activities, it may be appropriate for training and development practitioners to work side by side with managers to foster specialized knowledge, skills, or competencies. Innovation, technology, and complex skills often require the help and expertise of a professional trainer. Further, developmental activities can occur in formal or informal settings, depending on time, staff availability, planning requirements, and so forth.

The learning and change process consists of both the dissemination of information and the facilitation of learning. Occasionally, managers will be responsible for providing new information to improve individual employee performance or enhance their skills. It is equally important to encourage employees to initiate self-directed learning activities designed to deepen their experiences and understandings.

One need not look any further than the definition of the word "education" to find a basis for the dissemination of information and the facilitation of learning. The etymology of the word has two distinct meanings. The Latin roots for education *(educere)* refer to infilling and *(educare)* drawing out of information. The infilling process includes the inculcation and formation of ideas, whereas drawing out involves activities and experiences (Chadwick 1982).

Managers involved in the infilling process present information utilizing methods that minimize interaction between themselves and employees. The primary goal of this approach is to increase the employee's reservoir of knowledge. The drawing out process, on the other hand, refers to the application of ideas, facts, concepts, theories, and data, relying upon employees' experiences and background. This process emphasizes the interaction between manager and employee. Occasionally, the use of activities, games, or group discussions requiring application and input by employees increases their ability to exercise newly acquired knowledge, skills, and competencies. Any learning-and-change partnership must be founded on these two critical approaches, thus maximizing the effects of developmental activities.

IDENTIFYING THE PHASES AND CONCEPTS OF LEARNING AND CHANGE

To understand the five phases and various laws of learning and change, consider the following analogy. When a farmer decides to plant a crop, what does he or she do? Simple observation enables us to identify five critical steps in this process.

- First, farmers prepare the soil for planting via tilling, weed removal, and fertilization.
- Second, the seeds are planted deep into the earth at the most opportune time in spring.

- Third, the seeds are allowed ample time for germination in the warm, rich earth; they are allowed to take root and begin the process of growth and development.
- Fourth, farmers irrigate if mother nature does not cooperate, continuing to weed and water during the long, hot summer months.
- Fifth, the crop is harvested–either shipped to market or stored for later use. The soil is then reworked, which begins the process anew.

This analogy is comparable to the five phases and numerous concepts of the learning and change process (Figure 8.1).

Phase 1: Preparations for learning and change
Phase 2: Information exchange
Phase 3: Knowledge acquisition and practice
Phase 4: Transfer and integration
Phase 5: Accountability and recognition

The first step in the learning and change process is preparation, similar to preparing soil for planting. The second step involves information and content exchange between managers and employees (facilitator and learner), akin to the farmer's planting a crop. Third, germination parallels the knowledge acquisition and practice process, with which employees acquire new knowledge, skills, and competencies, and practice their application during simulations or on the job. The fourth step involves transfer and integration. Employees apply and integrate new knowledge, skills, and competencies on the job; are given reinforcement and feedback; and are provided opportunities to reflect upon what they have learned. As in farming (watering, fertilizing), this is the most difficult, complicated process, but if executed correctly yields the greatest bounty. The fifth and last step is the accountability and recognition of new knowledge, skills, and competencies. Similarly at harvest, farmers collect and sell their crops or store them for future use. Of course, as with the farming analogy, the learning and change process begins anew as employees prepare for

FIGURE 8.1   Five Phases of the Learning and Change Process and Its Impact

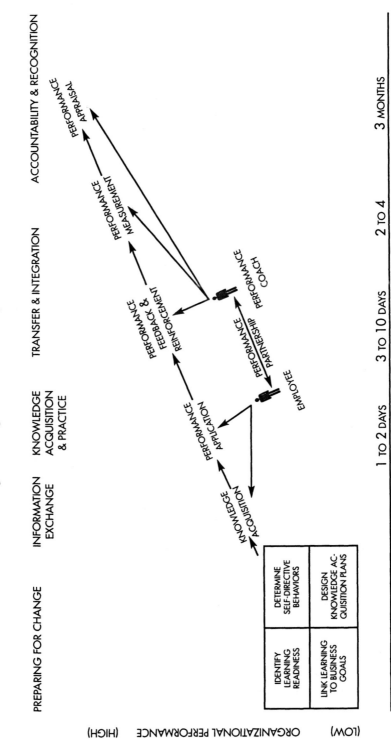

new and challenging learning and change opportunities—repeating the cycle over and over again.

Another reason this analogy works relates to the importance of farmers, the backbone of the world's viability. Without them, famine reigns, societies will crumble. Similarly in the business world, absent learning and change, organizations will never create the performance capacity and capability necessary to perpetuate the growth and development cycle so critical for organizational competitiveness.

The analogy also applies because farmers are often taken for granted by the economic community. Most consumers assume that crops will show up at the market at fair, reasonable prices. In the same way, learning and change is taken for granted in most organizations. Consequently, organizations fail to prepare adequately for the future. As we explained in a previous book, "organizations must adopt a strategic approach . . . in preparing for their future. However, the seeds of their effort are not better products and more capital, but their human resources. People are the organizational asset least developed and cared for—but they are the heart of every organization. Without their people, organizations would not be able to operate. They would not be able to service their customers. They would not be able to produce products or provide services" (Gilley and Boughton 1996, 47–48).

Applying the phases and concepts (described below) of the learning and change process readies organizations for future challenges, and avoids impending disaster. Firms will accumulate a storehouse of intellectual capital, skills, and competencies to be drawn upon whenever necessary to achieve desired business goals and objectives. We will now examine each phase of the learning and change process more closely and will outline the various concepts that govern the process. Each of these elements is critical to enhancing organizational renewal through learning and change.

At no time do we address group or team learning. Quite simply, groups do not learn, people do. Although self-directed work and project teams provide excellent opportunities for growth and development, and team members may learn from one another, the learning and change process remains an individual activity. Thus, we focus on the individual learner, whose aggregate improvement enhances organizational performance capacity.

PREPARING FOR LEARNING AND CHANGE

Most of us experience the phenomenon of the weekend warrior—when we attempt to recapture our youth by engaging in activities such as softball, tennis, skiing, yard work, home repair, and the like. We approach the weekend with all the gusto and enthusiasm of our adolescent years, only to discover that we are masses of sore muscles, painful blisters, and swollen appendages. This phenomenon exists because many of us fail to prepare for such strenuous activities. The same can be said about learning and change. For learning and change to be effective, meaningful, and enjoyable, organizations must adequately prepare for the acquisition of new information so that it will have significance and utility (Figure 8.1). Four concepts must be applied to adequately prepare for learning and change:

1. Learning readiness
2. Self-direction
3. Linkage
4. Designing knowledge acquisition plans

Learning Readiness

Employees must be ready, willing, and able to learn before they can hope to acquire knowledge and skills. If organizations fail to acknowledge employee readiness or accept their innate motivation for learning, subsequent facilitation and developmental activities will fall short of achieving desired ends.

Employees neglect to acquire and transfer knowledge and skills to the job for many reasons; the most egregious of which is their failure to adequately prepare for the exchange of new information. Possessing an attitude receptive of learning and change allows employees to acquire the skills and knowledge necessary to improve performance on the job.

Zemke and Zemke (1995) contend that employees seek learning experiences to cope with specific life-changing events, which can lead to promotional opportunities and improved job performance. Thus, the more practical the learning and change process becomes, the more prepared employees are to participate in it.

A large part of learning readiness is affected by how employees focus their attention on learning and change. Attention is defined as directing one's mind on an internal or external object. When employees observe formal procedures or the execution of a specific skill, they are focusing their attention externally. When reflecting on the meaning of some idea or recalling a past experience, they engage in internal attention. According to Gilley and Eggland (1989), three types of attention are present in learning and change situations: passive, active, and secondary passive. Each is critical to understanding learning readiness.

When employees simply follow the strongest stimulus present instead of genuinely concentrating, they are passively attentive, exerting little or no effort—an instinctive, reactionary response basic in human beings. An example is when people drive their cars with the radio on. In most cases, the radio is simply background noise to which the driver pays little or no attention; commercials and songs played generally are not recalled by the listener.

Managers (facilitators of learning and change) must guard against passive attention, which may hinder learning. If employees have little or no interest in remembering the information being shared or are not concentrating effectively, instructions can be either misinterpreted or misapplied. When passive attention prevails, employees fail to remember most, if not all, of the information shared with them.

Active attention involves distinguishing between stimuli and consciously selecting the appropriate one. Active attention occurs when an employee chooses between two stimuli, for example, either reading at one's desk or answering a ringing telephone. Employees react to the strongest or most appropriate stimuli, becoming actively involved and fixing their concentration accordingly.

To ensure active attention during developmental activities, managers may exercise a variety of methods such as role-playing, group discussions, simulations, or demonstrations designed to focus employees' concentration. Employees will master skills easier and retain more information when they pay active attention. As a drawback, however, tremendous dedication and energy are required with active attention. Although employees very appropriately use active attention when critical information or complex skills are being taught (Gilley and Boughton 1996), they may experience mental overload if required to pay active attention for long periods.

Secondary passive attention mirrors passive attention in that little or no employee effort is required; topics or skills are usually attractive and interesting in and of themselves. Secondary passive attention differs from passive attention in that the learner focuses on the material, persistent in his or her effort to comprehend it. Typically, employees learn best and most easily when absorbed in their work. Learning becomes so fascinating and exciting that it simply carries the employee with it.

Secondary passive attention enables employees to have a pleasant learning experience while improving their knowledge, skills, and competencies. Therefore, managers should adapt the length of developmental activities so as not to completely exhaust employee attention, appealing whenever possible to a worker's personal interests. Managers utilize a variety of presentation methods to arouse employee attention, reduce sources of distraction, and encourage active participation in the design, development, and implementation of learning and change activities. Since most people enjoy interaction, the presentation of new information via third-party stories, dialogue, and analogies for illustration draws them in to the story line as points are made along the way. Managers can enhance secondary passive attention by maintaining and exhibiting genuine interest in the subject at hand and by preparing thought-provoking questions prior to each interaction with employees. Finally, effective managers pause whenever attention is interrupted or lost, waiting until it is completely regained before resuming discussion.

The two primary enemies of attention are apathy and distraction. Each must be identified and confronted to minimize their effects. Apathy is the lack of interest in a subject or skill, whereas distraction refers to outside stimuli that divide or detract one's attention.

To illustrate the damage of distraction on the learning and change process, consider the following. Several years ago we were providing management development training for a large consulting firm in Southern California that chose the Long Beach Yacht Club's conference room as a training site. We agreed to the site, as the firm wanted to provide a comfortable, status-oriented environment for their senior consultants. Upon arrival we discovered that the selected glass-enclosed room magnificently overlooked the harbor. Needless to say, the attention of most participants was everywhere but on the discussion. At least thirty times over a two-day period, we had to stop and refocus the participants' attention as they, undoubtedly, daydreamed endlessly about sun, sailing, and Catalina Island. Considering their lack of attention, we might as well have started before the participants entered the room or continued after they left. Consequently, we were as exhausted as the learning participants.

Self-Direction

To facilitate learning and change, employees must become self-directed learners. The first tenet of self-directed learning involves self-teaching, whereby individuals take on the controls and techniques of teaching themselves about a particular subject. The second tenet is that of personal autonomy. According to Knowles, Holton, and Swanson (1998, 135), autonomy is "taking control of the goals and purposes of learning, and assuring ownership of learning—leading to an internal change of consciousness in which the learner views knowledge as contextual, and fully questions what is learned." Combining these two tenets directs the learning and change activities that employees should be prepared to engage in, ones in which they possess personal autonomy and the ability to learn by themselves.

Employees desire responsibility for their own developmental activities and involvement in the design and implementation of same. They have a strong need to take responsibility for their own lives. Fortunately, self-directed learning does not mean learning without assistance. Self-directed learners use networks, resources, and other effective strategies to maximize growth and development. Consequently, employees must be competent in self-directed learning. They should be able to:

- differentiate assumptions about learners and the skills required in teacher-directed learning versus self-directed learning
- view themselves as independent, autonomous, and self-directing
- relate to peers collaboratively, seeing them as resources for diagnosing needs, planning learning and change activities, and providing feedback or constructive criticism when necessary
- diagnose their own learning needs realistically with the assistance of peers and other resources
- translate learning needs into performance objectives via formats that ensure their accomplishment
- relate to managers as facilitators, helpers, and change agents, taking the initiative to utilize them as resources
- identify human and material resources appropriate for different types of performance objectives
- identify and select effective strategies for utilizing learning resources, and implement these tactics skillfully and with initiative
- collect and validate evidence that demonstrates accomplishment of their performance objectives (Knowles 1975)

Linkage

To become developmental, organizational leaders, managers, human resource professionals, and employees must link all learning and change activities to the firm's strategic business goals and objectives. Learning and change actions that fail to help an organization achieve its goals and objectives cease to be of value. Communicating the organization's goals and objectives to every employee creates an educated workforce that understands its impact on improving business results. Further, knowledgeable workers are fundamental in driving organizational success—a pillar in the foundation of the developmental organization.

Developmental organizations openly discuss business plans, including each employee's impact on the firm's ability to achieve desired goals and objectives. This approach should be initiated at the highest levels of the organization, filtering down to all business participants. Next, each business unit, department, and division must guarantee that its team goals are linked to the organization's strategic business goals and objectives. In this way, every manager and employee understands how achieving his or her personal performance goals and objectives will ultimately drive the organization's successful completion of its aims. From a developmental perspective, linking learning and change activities to these same strategic goals and objectives ensures that all employees focus on developmental results critical to the firm's success. Thus, focusing on business results permits employees to feel more like owners and participate accordingly.

Designing Plans for Knowledge Acquisition

Organizations prepare their workers for learning and change by collaboratively planning for knowledge acquisition to help employees attain performance results that enable them to accomplish their career goals and objectives. The first step involves the identification of employees' current performance baselines, then comparing their accomplishments with standards to isolate performance gaps. These become an employee's "performance benchmark," revealing areas requiring performance improvement (Gilley, Boughton, and Maycunich 1999).

Next, managers and employees isolate competencies that need improving. Competency areas critical to organizational initiatives should be part of employees' knowledge acquisition plans, along with areas of strength and weakness. Thus, employees acquire and transfer learning that helps them overcome performance gaps or capitalize on strengths. Once performance baselines and areas of focus (strengths or weaknesses) have been identified, employees should answer the following questions to design learning and acquisition plans:

1. What do I need to learn or do differently to improve my performance?

2. What resources (human and material) are needed to achieve my performance objectives?

3. When will I complete my learning and acquisition plan?

4. How will I apply what I have learned on the job?

5. How will I know when I have successfully achieved my performance objectives?

6. What criteria or means will I use to validate the measurement indicators?

7. How will I celebrate my new learning, increased skills, or improved attitudes?

8. Once performance objectives have been achieved, what rewards and recognition will be appropriate (Gilley and Maycunich 1998a)?

The answers to each of these questions guide employees in the successful design of learning and acquisition plans. Let us consider each in greater detail.

Employees must identify what they intend to learn. This activity translates identified performance needs into performance objectives. As we explained in a previous book, "a well-written performance objective should be clear and understandable, identify what the employee will learn, describe the observable behavior that will demonstrate that learning occurred, identify the acceptable level of performance for the learned behavior, describe the conditions under which performance will be measured, and be stated in such a way that the degree to which it is accomplished can be estimated or measured" (Gilley and Maycunich 1998a, 251).

Next, employees must identify resources they will use to achieve their performance objectives. These may include human and material resources such as peers, superiors, books, journal articles, handouts, newspapers, suggested readings, videotapes, cassette tapes, and the like.

Once resources have been identified, employees determine when each performance objective will be completed. Establishing a date provides employees with planning parameters that force appropriate time management techniques.

Implementing knowledge and acquisition plans poses the next challenge. Execution forces an individual to develop an approach to the plan, including assembling resources and engaging selected learning and change activities designed to invoke developmental outcomes.

After knowledge acquisition, it is appropriate for employees to identify how they will apply what they have learned on the job. Learners then turn their attention to learning measurement, ensuring that they have achieved their performance objectives; thus improving their performance behavior and enhancing organizational renewal and performance capacity. Measuring performance improvement requires employees to clearly identify the indicators of accomplishment—the criteria and means of validating gauges. The process involves gathering performance improvement data, comparing this data with performance standards and baselines, and determining the degree of improvement (Gilley, Boughton, and Maycunich 1999). The following questions will help managers and employees identify the indicators of accomplishment:

1. How will employees know when they have achieved their performance objectives?
2. Who will employees rely on to determine that they have completed their performance objectives?
3. How will employees measure what has been learned and what they are able to do differently?
4. How will employees measure the performance produced by their new knowledge, skills, or behavior?

Indicators of accomplishment also require criteria for validation. Once validated, employees gather performance data illustrating growth and development, comparing it to performance standards and their performance baselines to reveal the amount of improvement. This analysis determines whether individual performance objectives have been achieved.

Finally, success should be celebrated with employee rewards and recognition for continuous development. Developmental organizations reward employees for improving their performance via developmental activities. In this way, they create an environment where development is perceived as an important ingredient to organizational success.

INFORMATION EXCHANGE

Once an organization has successfully prepared for learning and change through the implementation of the concepts of learning readiness, self-direction, linkage, and designing knowledge acquisition plans, it is then ready for the information exchange process. The exchange is defined as the period in which "truth" is taught or acquired by learners. Truth refers to any information relevant to enhancing an employee's performance capacity or capability (Figure 8.1). The exchange process provides employees with opportunities to obtain the information necessary to improve knowledge, skills, or behaviors. It follows five interrelated concepts:

1. The learning and change environment
2. The learning and change agent
3. Adult learners
4. Communications
5. Instruction

The Learning and Change Environment

A learning and change environment supportive of the free exchange of ideas and feelings, in which learners feel secure and participate in open, two-way communications, facilitates development. This nonthreatening, comfortable environment nurtures employee growth and development. We further contend that this environment transcends the superficial, demonstrating a deep concern for employee well-being and a dedication to improving interpersonal relationships.

In creating learning and change environments that foster innovation and participation, developmental managers strive to maintain an attitude of empathy, acceptance, and understanding—accepting employees' points of view with respect and dignity. Developmental managers build lasting relationships between themselves and their subordinates and a deepening understanding of their employees' developmental needs and aspirations, thus creating trusting bonds that bring about honesty and candor.

A dynamic learning and change environment exudes physical and psychological comfort. In talking with employees, managers carefully protect employees' self-esteem and ego, understanding the risks associated with acquiring new knowledge and skills. Simultaneously, managers understand that adult employees bring a great deal of life experience into a learning situation, an invaluable asset in and of itself. Thus, adults can learn much through dialogue with respected peers (Zemke and Zemke 1995).

The Learning and Change Agent

An important player in the information exchange process is the learning and change agent—the individual responsible for presenting information to employees in an understandable, meaningful, and manageable way. These individuals possess knowledge of the subject matter along with job experience necessary to assist employees in the application of new information.

A manager's knowledge and experience are the materials with which he or she works—without either, no learning or change occurs. A serious mistake is to allow inexperienced managers to act as learning and change agents—similar to the blind leading the blind. Competent, experienced managers give their employees needed confidence and reassurance. Simultaneously, well-prepared, qualified managers awaken in their employees the desire to learn, change, grow, and develop.

Learning and change agents delve deeper. A manager with limited knowledge of the subject, task, skill, or competency is likely to be ineffective and unenthusiastic. One who fully understands and has passion for the subject is fueled by enthusiasm and excitement. Enthusiasm, combined with knowledge, subconsciously inspires employees' interest and curiosity, and can be quite contagious.

Undoubtedly, expertise and passion are two important prerequisites to becoming an effective learning and change agent. Another characteristic is an agent's ability to inspire in employees a love of learning that fuels their own passion for growth and development. The result is the employees' ability to renew themselves over and over again as their journey of evolution progresses.

Effective learning and change agents also relate materials to their employees' lives. Illustrating new ideas and facts in terms of everyday experiences allows employees to develop a familiar frame of reference that fosters understanding.

Learning and change agents comprehend the natural order of information to be presented. Every learning and change activity has a logical path—from the simplest ideas and steps to the most complex. Managers identify a starting point upon discovery of what their employees already know about the subject. Presenting information and concepts by relating them to things already known by the employee allows the learner to understand the unknown via the known.

To enhance their skills and abilities, learning and change agents should set aside definite times of study for each learning and change session, in advance of the activity. This helps them gather fresh perspectives, insights, and illustrations before the actual engagement with employees. Finally, learning and change agents identify the most important, valuable human resources to be used during learning and change actions. These people are invaluable allies in motivating employees to acquire developmental perspectives throughout their careers.

Many managers fail to adequately develop learning and change agent competencies. One reason is their belief that employees are responsible for their own growth and development and that management has no role in their subordinates' matriculation. These managers are often indifferent and ill prepared to share with employees new and innovative ways of performing tasks or activities—often severely hampering current job performance and retarding worker developmental potential.

Some managers possess poor organization skills and fail to sufficiently plan initial learning and change activities—believing that random talk and an occasional war story suffices for a well-planned learning session.

This may be an attempt to hide their own lack of knowledge or preparation. Regardless of the reason, this behavior demonstrates a managerial lack of respect for the development of their people.

Finally, the very ignorance of employees regarding knowledge, skills, or competencies tempts some managers to neglect preparation and study. Anything they say will be sufficient, as employees cannot ascertain whether the information is factually correct. This lack of preparation is certainly one of the easiest ways for managers to destroy their own credibility.

Adult Learners

Much has been written in the past several decades about adult learners. The most noteworthy research was conducted by Malcolm Knowles in the early 1960s and 1970s. He coined the term "andragogy," which refers to the art and science of helping adults learn. Distinct assumptions must be made to effectively work with adults. First, Knowles contended, adult learners need to know why learning a new skill, acquiring new knowledge, or changing their behavior is important. It is simply not enough to ask adults to engage in learning and change activities without providing thorough, thoughtful explanations as to why these competencies are necessary on the job.

Second, adult learners' self-concepts require them to be self-respecting and responsible for their own actions and activities. Thus, learning and change must be presented in a way that adults can control and influence the outcomes.

Third, andragogy is based on the belief that learners' experiences are invaluable resources to be tapped and utilized during learning and change events. As a result, adult learners benefit by learning from each other.

Knowles (1975) believes that adults are pragmatic, ready to learn what they need to know in order to cope with real-life situations. Thus, most adults facing life-centered situations are highly motivated to utilize the knowledge and skills they obtain. Knowles contrasts adult learners with children and adolescents by advocating that adults are life-centered (task- or problem-centered) in their orientation to learning, whereas children and adolescents are subject-centered. That is, adults are motivated to learn because they perceive that learning will help them perform tasks or deal with problematic, real-life situations (Knowles, Holton, and Swanson 1998).

Without a doubt, adults are very responsive to external motivation such as promotions, advancements, increased compensation, recognition, and other rewards. Knowles, Holton, and Swanson (1998) believe that the most potent motivators are intrinsic, enabling adult learners to increase their job satisfaction, self-esteem, and quality of life while acting on and demonstrating their values and beliefs. This has serious implications when organizations consider the types of recognition and rewards presented to employees for engaging in developmental activities. We believe that a combination of intrinsic and extrinsic motivators enhance the developmental perspective exponentially—which will be discussed in more detail later in this chapter.

Adult learners possess a great deal of firsthand experience that can be transferred to the job and at the same bring a great deal of pride to learning situations. In most cases, adult learners have established habits and strong opinions regarding learning, which can have both positive and negative impacts.

Although most adult learners react positively to authority and demonstrate respect, learning and change agents will sometimes be tested until they are able to establish credibility with the audience. Adult learners abide by a set of guiding principles, attitudes, and beliefs that affect their behaviors. Thus, contrary learning and change activities are often challenged vehemently. Although adult learners are quite capable of change, they need a purpose for existence or a meaning in life, which effective learning and change activities reinforce.

Adult learners respond favorably to positive reinforcement, embracing honest, factual, constructive feedback designed to improve their skills, abilities, and competencies. Finally, the experiences, interactions, and assumptions of adult learners can either interfere with or accelerate their learning and change propensity. Occasionally these experiences prevent positive predisposition to development, necessitating problem isolation and correction so that the experience, interaction, or assumption can be changed. Otherwise, developmental opportunities may be severely miti-gated throughout the life of the employee.

Communications

An important part of the information exchange process involves the medium of communications used by managers and employees to enhance learning and change. Two persons engage in intellectual communica-tion—defining innermost thoughts and feelings using symbols, signs, and words.

Language functions as the instrument of thought. Words are tools by which managers shape their employees' minds. Because ideas become in-culcated in words, they take the form of language and stand ready to be studied and known, marshaled into the mechanism of intelligible thought (Gregory 1884). Thus, as surgeons use their instruments to save lives, managers use language to bring about comprehension and enlightenment.

Language consists of words and symbols whose meanings are based on common experiences and understandings. Learning will be incomplete unless the language used is plain, understood, and common to the learner.

Learning and change intervention symbolism often represents highly technical information that is a language unto itself. Thus, managers must frequently test their employees' understanding of words to guarantee their correct usage. Constant study of employee language helps managers un-derstand the meaning behind employees' words and symbols. If the learner fails to comprehend, the manager should repeat the idea using other words or give an analogy as an example. Using the simplest and fewest words possible to express meaning decreases confusion and the possibility of misunderstanding. In essence, short sentences simply con-structed are preferable to long, unnecessarily confusing diatribes.

Language has still another use; it is the storehouse of knowledge. All that we know about civilizations, theories, and other phenomenon has been conveyed via the written or spoken word. Thus, words are not only the signs of our ideas, but the clues by which we construct themes and ex-plain what we believe to be true—we master truth by expressing it.

The conversion of talking into thinking requires an independent, original effort by the learner—not mere repetition or memorization of words. Employees are encouraged to communicate (talk) during learning and change activities, thus expressing their level of understanding via specific language, words, or symbols used.

Many managers mask their own inadequacies by using verbiage that employees do not grasp. Obviously, misunderstandings and confusion result. Other common problems with communication include the misuse of language by both managers and employees, and taking language for granted.

Many managers and employees have no appreciation for the character and complexity of language; thus, they use it haphazardly in an attempt to convey their superior knowledge. The opposite is often the case. Occasionally, managers mistake an employee's interested look as a sign of comprehension when, in fact, some workers will falsely acknowledge an understanding of an idea in an attempt to protect their own egos. Further, employees may fail to ask for explanations or examples when confused, causing managers to assume that employees understand them. Managers sometimes view silence as permission to proceed forward, only to discover that learning cognition did not take place. Finally, on occasion the information being shared with learners falls outside their experiences and interactions. In this instance, managers are responsible for identifying the terms, symbols, and words that employees are familiar with before the learning and change intervention.

Instruction

Much has been debated regarding the role of instruction in the learning and change process. Should managers disseminate information or facilitate learning? Should instruction be the cornerstone of learning and change or an instrument by which content and information are shared? Many believe that learning cannot take place without an instructor. Research demonstrates otherwise—employees can and do learn without instructors. In fact, most long-term change occurs within individuals when they actively participate in the learning and change process. Those who teach best teach least.

The principle aim of learning and change is to acquire information or content to develop skills or competencies. However, employees who are taught without having to study for themselves are like those who are fed without being given any exercise—they will lose their strength (Gregory, 1884). Thus, the responsibility for learning and change should shift from manager (instructor) to employee if growth and development are to occur.

Effective managers present information in a way that motivates employees to become absorbed by it (secondary passive attention). Absent this stimulation, employee growth and development falter as they become disenchanted with a learning and change process that fails to help them reach their professional and personal goals.

Managers are responsible for knowing their employees' reservoir of knowledge regarding the content and information being shared, which becomes the starting point of instruction. They then utilize learner knowledge and experience to solve problems and make applications during formal practice activities, relating material to previous instruction as well as currently held skills.

Information is arranged so that each step leads easily and naturally to the next. One idea should be presented at a time, allowing employees ample opportunity to integrate it with their existing knowledge. Instruction is most effective when presenting meaningful, practical information in a problem-centered approach. The more practical it is, the better. Further, information should be presented in a manner permitting mastery.

Although people maintain the ability to learn throughout their lives, special consideration should be given to employees who cannot obtain or retain information as quickly as others. Using illustrations, examples, and stories while encouraging employees to share their own experiences with their peers provides a common framework on which to base the learning and change activity. Pictures give people a visual anchor for the new information they are learning.

Finally, managers encourage employees to incorporate their knowledge during formal learning and change activities as well as on the job. Manager support and encouragement are vital if learning is to be transferred to the job.

A common mistake in the learning and exchange process involves information overload, whereby too much material is presented in too little time. Information overload causes employees to become confused, feel overwhelmed, or unmotivated. It inhibits their ability to comprehend and apply knowledge and skills. Consequently, employee performance on the job fails to improve.

Overcoming information overload requires managers to forgo the traditional instructional approach to training sessions in favor of a more effective methodology. We call such a methodology the concept-unit approach (Gilley 1998). It allows learners to absorb and apply new skills and knowledge more efficiently—by breaking down interventions into smaller units around a single idea or concept group. Each session lasts approximately two to three hours, with the entire program spread over several weeks. Although the same amount of information is covered as would be in a traditional approach, the amount of time to do so is greatly expanded.

Other common errors of the instruction process include failure to relate the material to previous data; management's negligence in motivating employees by neglecting to heighten their interest and enthusiasm for learning; managers' inappropriate attitudes toward employees regarding their abilities, skills, or level of comprehension; criticism of workers' lack of learning acceleration or memory; and the failure to familiarize employees with elementary facts or definitions before presenting reams of new information or content.

When mistakes such as these are made, learning and change fails to occur. Overcoming these errors requires management's adherence to several practical rules for instruction:

1. Ask thought-provoking questions to excite employee interest in the topic.
2. Place yourselves in your employees' position, joining their search for additional information and knowledge.

3. Give employees the time to sort out material and gain insight and understanding.
4. Repress the desire to tell all you know about a subject or lesson.
5. Encourage employees to ask questions when they are confused or do not understand.
6. Give employees the time to answer questions or complete exercises on their own.
7. Accept the responsibility to awaken your employees' minds, to not rest until each employee demonstrates his or her mental activity and involvement.
8. Adapt learning and change activities to the experience, preparation, and skill of employees.
9. Be dedicated to begin each learning session in a manner that stirs the learners' interest and enthusiasm.
10. Teach your employees to ask Who, What, How, Where, and When questions so they better understand information.
11. Avoid answering your own questions; allow employees to struggle with thought-provoking questions (which will enhance their learning).
12. Avoid information overload.
13. Repress your impatience with the learners' inability to grasp ideas or to master skills.
14. Consider carefully the material to be presented, identifying points of contact with the lives, interests, and experiences of employees (Gilley and Eggland, 1989).

KNOWLEDGE ACQUISITION AND PRACTICE

At some point, learning and change activities cause an employee to transpose information into new awareness that ultimately alters behavior. This is typically known as learning. According to Gibbons (1990), three kinds of learning are most common: natural, formal, and personal. Natural learning occurs when individuals interact spontaneously with the environment. Formal learning results when content or information is chosen by others and presented to the learner. Personal learning is when an individual designs self-directed, intentional learning activities to enhance knowledge, skills, and behaviors on the job. With personal learning, an individual decides what to learn, how to manage the process, how to learn from experience, how to identify and select learning resources, and how to take learning action. We believe there is a fourth type of learning, developmental learning, which is a combination of formal and personal learning (Figure 8.1). Three fundamental concepts support knowledge acquisition and practice: enlightenment, repetition, and review.

Enlightenment

John Milton Gregory, in his 1884 classic *Seven Laws of Teaching*, pointed out that

> learning is not memorization and repetition of words and ideas of the instructor. . . . contrary to common understanding this is much more the work of the learner than the instructor. . . . learning comes by progressions of interpretation which may be easy and rapid. . . . no real learning is wholly a repetition of the thoughts of another. The discoverer borrows largely on facts known to others, and the learner must add to what he or she studies from his or her own experience. His or her aim should be to become an independent searcher in the fields of knowledge, not merely a passive learner at the hands of others. (Pp. 106–107).

Gregory contends that "the practical relationship of truth and the forces which lie behind all facts are never really understood until we apply our knowledge to some of the practical purposes of life and of thought. . . . thus, what was idle knowledge becomes practical wisdom" (p. 109). In more conventional language, learning is simply the process of internalizing in one's own mind the truth to be learned and applying it in some form or fashion. We refer to this as the law of enlightenment.

Enlightenment requires learners to internalize information and to apply it in some way. We believe that learning and change is not complete until this last stage has been reached. To ensure that this occurs, managers (learning and change agents) should help employees form a clear idea of the work to be done; ask employees to express in their own words or in writing the meaning of the information or content as they understand it; ask questions of learners in a nonthreatening manner, encouraging them to embellish and share their point of view; and help employees become self-directed, independent investigators responsible for their own learning, growth, and development. "Instructors (managers) should constantly seek to develop in employees a profound regard for truth as something noble and enduring" (Gregory 1884, 112). Finally, developmental managers challenge their employees' conceptions regarding reproduction of information in a correct, acceptable form and provide assistance whenever workers are unable to grasp concepts and ideas quickly.

Some of the most common violations and mistakes made during the enlightenment period are as follows:

- failing to insist on original thinking by employees
- consistently neglecting practical application of information
- providing inadequate instructions or assistance in the application of information or content
- blindly assuming that employees' failure to ask questions implies understanding of material

Whole-part-whole learning, according to Knowles, Holton, and Swanson (1998), avoids these common mistakes. The learner is first presented with a complete model or description of the full complexity of an object, an abstraction, or a job. Instruction is then organized around parts of the whole. Finally, a summary is provided to help learners retain information. Using this whole-part-whole process, managers provide a comprehensive "big picture" of an employee's entire job. A thorough job overview ensures complete understanding as managers break down tasks into component parts, demonstrating how each piece fits in the puzzle. Individual job segments are explained in detail only after employees understand the overall job. After each part of the job is understood, managers summarize by explaining the job again to reinforce or review. Using this approach, managers show employees where their responsibilities lie in the overall organizational picture, allowing workers a greater appreciation of their value to the organization.

Repetition

Observing skilled athletes' performance leads many of us to conclude that it looks easy. For example, both of us have attempted to learn to ski, having observed the free-flowing skills of an experienced skier and foolishly believing these abilities were simple to acquire. Such was not the case, and we both quickly realized that gravity remains a powerful force with which to be reckoned. Similarly, most people have failed to perform effectively the first time out. Over time, through a process known as repetition, we grasp the skills and master the techniques. Baseball players are a prime example. Hitting a baseball appears easy until one begins trying to do so. With proper instruction and practice most individuals learn to adequately strike a ball with a wooden stick. Why is this phenomenon so important? Because this is the first time learning moves from a theoretical to a practical act. It is at this point that new awareness and insights prevail. Repetition is also an important step in learning and change when we have to "unlearn" an improper method or incorrect technique. Until these obstacles are removed, learning will be severely retarded, with little progress toward growth and development. Therefore, repetition should continue until learners overcome prior improper learning or replicate skills, techniques, or behaviors in a safe environment.

We differentiate repetition from application in a simple way. Repetition occurs during formal learning and change activities conducted in safe environments where failure is common and often encouraged. Although repetition should be as realistic as possible, failures will not endanger others, diminish self-esteem, or reduce productivity. Repetition need not be a concluding action during the learning and change process but can occur throughout learning and change activities as new tasks and steps are introduced.

Review

Learning and change are greatly enhanced by rethinking, reviewing, re-producing, or applying the material communicated. That is, managers should use feedback and frequent summarization to enhance retention and recall (Gilley and Eggland 1989). In our haste to complete the learning and change process, unfortunately, this step is often overlooked or greatly de-emphasized. Failure to incorporate feedback and review into learning and change activities could result in incorrect application of material or failure to apply it altogether.

Review aids our understanding that knowledge, skills, competencies, and behaviors are best developed when employees have opportunities to rethink, reproduce, and apply each. However, review is more than repetition. A machine can complete a process, but only intelligent human beings can review and assess it. Review implies the rethinking of a task, skill, or competency to deepen one's understanding of how to perform it correctly, including making new associations and conceptualizations (Gilley and Boughton 1996, 113).

Review is not a separate act added to an instructional event, but an important part of the process itself. Thus, neglecting the review phase leaves work unfinished. Any exercise or activity using previously presented information or content is considered a review. Effective reviews propose practical problems or circumstances, providing employees with opportunities to apply new skills or competencies accordingly. These controlled situations are safer and more secure than actual job situations, allowing for mistakes that otherwise might cost the organization thousands of dollars.

Developmental managers embrace review, realizing that reviews are part of learning and change and an excellent way to integrate new material with old. Managers establish an appropriate time for review, often at the completion of each learning session or the close of the learning and change activity. Finally, effective managers never omit a final review, as it may be their last opportunity to challenge employees to incorporate material and information into personal understandings and orientations.

TRANSFER AND INTEGRATION

Before learning can be translated into value for the organization it must be applied to the job (Figure 8.1). Unfortunately, many employees are left on their own immediately after participating in a learning and change intervention. Management fails to assist in integrating change, skills, or knowledge on the job, causing confusion and frustration on both sides. Consequently, much of the change is lost.

Because employees are frequently on their own after the learning and change event, the newly acquired change, knowledge, and skills never transfer to the job. Employees take the path of least resistance, often reverting back to their old habits as opposed to struggling with integration of new skills and knowledge. They neglect to transfer learning to the job for many reasons, including fear of change, delayed application, lack of confidence, no perceived payoff for trying new skills or knowledge, on-the-job failure when applying new skills, and peer pressure.

Some employees require a great deal of support or encouragement when using new skills or applying new knowledge, whereas others must relearn skills in a safe environment. Developmental managers engage in several actions before, during, and after learning and change activities to ensure learning transfer. Prior to learning and change, effective managers develop performance standards, show their support for learning and change as well as its importance, identify rewards, and sharpen their performance coaching skills. While conducting learning and change activities, managers foster a positive learning environment, initiate employee learning readiness, encourage participation, employ practical learning exercises, give positive feedback, and reward and recognize learners. After completion of learning and change activities, developmental managers facilitate additional training to boost employee confidence and encourage their discussion of how their new skills have been incorporated on the job. Further, developmental managers aid learning transfer by offering refresher courses, job aids, follow-up activities, mentoring, and daily logs or journals to track improvement (Gilley and Coffern 1994).

A profound reason for employee failure to transfer learning to the job lies with management's lack of support or involvement. Sadly, many managers fail to coach their employees, reinforce worker behavior, communicate expectations (thus setting the stage for poor performance), confront poor performance, provide reinforcement on the job, be positive role models, establish adequate performance standards, or create work environments conducive to learning.

Organizations contribute to the lack of learning transfer by establishing policies, procedures, work environments, and managerial practices inappropriate or not conducive to creating a developmental organization. Many organizational leaders believe that employees are easily replaced, hence reinforcing the notion that learning and change wastes time.

Human resource professionals present their own barriers to learning transfer. They may fail to: realize that the learning and change process is the responsibility of everyone within the organization; involve stakeholders in the learning and change process; relinquish learning and change activities to managers and supervisors, and; link learning and change activities to strategic business goals and objectives (Gilley, Boughton, and Maycunich 1999, 250).

The following questions assist organizations, human resource professionals, managers, and employees in improving learning transfer:

- How are knowledge, skills, and attitudes being used on the job?
- What barriers prevent learning from being transferred?
- What role do managers and supervisors play in transferring and reinforcing learning on the job?
- What should be done before, during, and after implementing the knowledge acquisition plan to enhance learning transfer?
- What role do employees play in learning transfer?
- What role does the organization play in learning transfer?
- What activities should be used to improve learning transfer?
- What can be done to increase learning effectiveness and efficiency?

Each of these questions frames the learning and change process, focusing on employee application of learning to the job.

Application

Managers greatly enhance learning transfer by adhering to one simple principle—people learn by doing. Actually completing a task or an assignment involves learners to the fullest, allowing them to improve a skill, apply new knowledge, or change a behavior. Learning by doing is simply a process of making application through knowledge and skill on the job. Research has shown that the most effective learning and change results when application on the job immediately follows initial training.

Because new knowledge and skills may interfere with current employee performance, it is critical for managers to analyze the long-term effects of such conflict to determine their impact on overall productivity—a process known as failure analysis (Gilley and Boughton 1996). Failure analysis allows managers and employees to identify possible conflict so they can better integrate learning in the future.

According to Gilley (1998, 83), "one of the best ways of improving learning transfer is by allowing employees to fail in safe environments such as work simulations and case studies. Employees allowed to fail in comfortable, supportive settings will learn a great deal about what skill levels will or will not work on the job." This approach is useful when employees attempt to apply new skills and knowledge on the job.

Developmental managers resist demanding perfection the first time an employee attempts to utilize new learning. They know that learning failure often allows for a quicker, more accurate application of new skills and knowledge. By allowing learning failure, managers encourage long-term success rather than short-term performance improvement. Learning failure helps employees increase their long-term productivity and improve their overall performance (Gilley 1998, 83). Thus, the law of application is simple: Allow employees opportunities to use what they have learned or the behaviors they desire to change; encourage failure and protect self-esteem.

Reinforcement and Feedback

Simply stated, reinforcement and feedback enhance learning and change since employees are more likely to repeat activities when positive reinforcement and feedback occur. This principle provides rich incentives for learning transfer by enhancing employee self-esteem and encouraging positive performance patterns. Reinforcement and feedback can be as simple as a nod of the head, a verbal pat on the back for a job well done, or a formal conversation between managers and employees.

We believe that one of management's best reinforcement tools is the performance review, which allows managers the opportunity to measure employee application of new skills and knowledge on the job. Incorporating evaluation of learning and change into the performance review and appraisal process communicates to employees the value and importance of learning transfer. If new skills and knowledge are being evaluated, they must be worth obtaining (Gilley 1998).

Managers fail to reinforce learning and change when they believe that employees know when they are performing their jobs correctly, perhaps as a result of divine inspiration or the ability to read minds. On the contrary, most workers desire reinforcement and feedback as reassurance that they are performing adequately. Developmental managers follow several guidelines when providing reinforcement and feedback to employees, including the following:

- being specific so that employees know what they did correctly
- being sincere so that employees accept feedback without manipulation
- delivering feedback immediately after employees perform tasks correctly
- giving specific, individualized feedback
- giving feedback frequently but randomly to strengthen performance behavior

- conveying feedback clearly and concisely so that employees understand it (Gilley and Coffern 1994)

Reflection

Reflection proves a powerful activity. With reflection, employees can enhance the transfer and integration of new knowledge, skills, or behaviors. As previously discussed, a variety of reflection activities are available. According to Peterson and Hicks (1996), the goals of reflection are several:

- to solidify one's insight and to guarantee that mistakes and successes just learned are remembered
- to identify themes and patterns of performance
- to challenge one's assumptions to ensure that one learns appropriately
- to remain open to new learning and change opportunities

They further contend that employees should reflect on a daily basis after major events such as crises, the completion of big assignments, and major milestones in a project. Reflections should occur monthly or quarterly to summarize one's progress and at the completion of every major job assignment or project. Thus, employees will have ample opportunity to examine the application and results of new skills, knowledge, and behaviors on the job.

Reflection provides employees with occasions to consider their next opportunities to apply new knowledge and skills. Reflection also allows employees to consider different situations in which their learning may be applied, as well as what they might do differently under current circumstances. Finally, employees consider what performance components can be improved the next time they are able to apply the skills and knowledge being reflected upon. Reflection enables employees to learn from their mistakes, to listen to their own thoughts and feelings, to cope with barriers within the organization, and to plot strategies for future use and application of skills and knowledge.

ACCOUNTABILITY AND RECOGNITION

There comes a point when employees must be held accountable for learning and change, *and* be recognized for their efforts and improvements (Figure 8.1). This is analogous to harvesting one's crops after a long, hot summer. It is a time to take into account successes as well as failures, and what might be done to improve future performance.

Expectation and Inspection

After employees have had an opportunity to integrate new learning on the job, developmental managers assess whether the subsequent changes improved performance enough to enhance business results. Developmental managers often discuss these expectations with employees prior to engaging in learning and change activities. According to Gilley and Boughton (1996), a two-way technique known as expectation and inspection allows managers to guarantee that what they receive is what they expect while concurrently communicating to employees their accountability for improved skills and knowledge. Developmental managers share with employees what and how they are expected to perform as a result of new learning and change, including the quantity and quality of their performance outcomes.

Expectation and inspection requires managerial scrutiny of employee performance to determine whether established performance standards have been met and how learning and change activities helped facilitate improvements. In this way, expectations are linked with accountability, which ultimately enhances learning transfer. This is especially true when new skills and knowledge are involved. In other words, the transfer of learning will only take place when managers combine expectation and inspection into one activity. Employees know what they are being asked to do and how they will be held accountable.

Recognition and Reward

When employees engage in learning to improve their knowledge, skills, attitudes, values, and understanding, they should be rewarded and recognized for their achievements. Thus, learning plans are not complete until the identification of rewards and recognition improve performance, growth, and development. Bestowing appropriate rewards and recognition encourages employees to continuously grow and develop via knowledge acquisition.

Most employees want to be rewarded and recognized for improving their performance. When this does not occur, employees often avoid transferring new skills and knowledge to the workplace. Failure to reward performance improvement (i.e., growth and development) prevents learning transfer from occurring and organizations from achieving desired outcomes.

Establishing a connection between performance growth and development and organizational rewards is the single greatest factor in improving individual achievements. Rewarding people for improved performance encourages them to transfer learning. According to LeBoeuf (1995, 9), "the things that get rewarded get done." Learning transfer, therefore, must be rewarded if an organization wishes to ensure its success.

Before distributing rewards and recognition for enhanced learning and change, managers should consider how they will celebrate employees' new learning, increased skills, and improved attitudes. Management's active participation in the celebration reinforces the importance of learning and change.

APPLYING THE LEARNING AND CHANGE PROCESS MODEL

The phases and laws of the learning and change process can be integrated into a three-dimensional model (Figure 8.2). The first and last phases (i.e., preparing for learning and change, and the accountability and recognition process) are viewed as inputs to the three-dimensional model, which depicts the relationship between the information exchange process (vertical component), the knowledge acquisition and practice process (diagonal component), and the transfer and integration process (horizontal component).

The learning and change model reflects the operational relationship of each of the three components. Each type of learning is portrayed by a se-

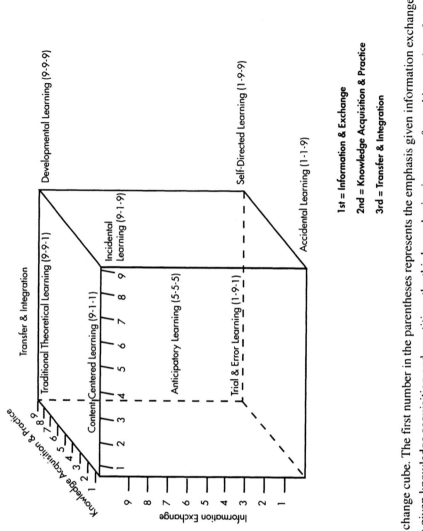

FIGURE 8.2 Learning and change cube. The first number in the parentheses represents the emphasis given information exchange; the second number, emphasis given knowledge acquisition and repetition; the third, emphasis given transfer and integration of learning

ries of numbers, the first of which depicts the information exchange process along with its emphasis on the importance in learning. The second number represents knowledge acquisition and practice and its utilization during learning. The third number symbolizes the transfer and integration process, revealing the degree of transfer and integration that occur as a result of learning. When applying a numerical value to each dimension, eight different types of learning are characterized (see the following).

Content-Centered Learning. Content-centered learning (9–1–1) presumes that instructors are primarily disseminators of information via lecture or direct instruction. The major emphasis is on information, with little focus on learning transfer, practice, or integration.

Trial-and-Error Learning. Trial-and-error learning (1–9–1) occurs when employees are on their own with little or no instruction provided regarding job duties or responsibilities. Nevertheless, they are responsible for acquiring the knowledge and skills necessary to be effective in spite of the lack of feedback or reinforcement. Learning occurs sometimes, but not always. If employees are lucky, they acquire the necessary skills and knowledge to be successful; if not, they will be organizational casualties.

Accidental Learning. Accidental learning (1–1–9) occurs when little emphasis is placed upon sharing information, helping employees acquire knowledge, or practice new skills. Somehow, somewhere, employees transfer and integrate appropriate skills for the job. In many cases they learn by accident, having survived organizational witch-hunts designed to eliminate poor performers. These learners demonstrate adequate, acceptable performance, but nowhere it is near the level of mastery necessary for organizations of the next century.

Anticipatory Learning. Anticipatory learning (5–5–5) is a process by which information exchange, knowledge acquisition and practice, and transfer and integration are equal partners in the learning and change process. While typically acceptable, anticipatory learning fails to reach its potential because it usually occurs at a lower level of intensity.

Incidental Learning. Incidental learning (9–1–9) occurs most often when employees are given the information to do their jobs. Resources are made available through handbooks and job-flow analysis; however, employees are on their own to practice, on or off the job. Employees able to grasp the plethora of data available to them and transfer it to the job survive.

Traditional Theoretical Learning. Traditional theoretical learning (9–9–1) is the most common category of training and development activities. Information is presented as employees participate in formal training activities designed to enhance knowledge acquisition and transfer. The only downside of this approach is that most organizations have not yet grasped the importance of transfer and integration on the job, nor have they provided policies and procedures enabling it to occur. Thus, learning transfer via learning and change never materializes.

Self-Directed Learning. Self-directed learning (1–9–9) is perhaps one of the most important and powerful types of learning. This occurs when employees become responsible for knowledge acquisition and practice, and the transfer and integration thereof. The downside is that employees are on their own in determining the information appropriate to acquire the skills and knowledge necessary to be successful. While very bright, capable employees are able to make this determination, learning is left to chance.

Developmental Learning. Developmental learning (9–9–9) occurs with an equal emphasis on information exchange, knowledge acquisition and practice, and transfer and integration at a high level. This kind of learning takes into account the importance of preparation, accountability, and recognition for learning and change. Representing the pinnacle of individual and organizational learning, developmental learning allows an organization to combine the strengths of traditional theoretical and self-directed learning into a process whereby managers forge a learning and change partnership with employees.

CONCLUSION

At the heart of the developmental organization lies the learning and change process. In this chapter we discussed managers' and human resource professionals' roles. We also identified the phases and concepts necessary to enhance learning and change. Finally, we reviewed the application of these phases by constructing an interactive, three-dimensional model representing eight different types of organizational learning. The pinnacle of our model is developmental learning, whereby information, content, knowledge acquisition and practice, and transfer and integration work in harmony to improve employee skill and knowledge. Developmental learning perpetuates employee growth and development, thus enhancing organizational renewal and increasing organizational performance capacity.

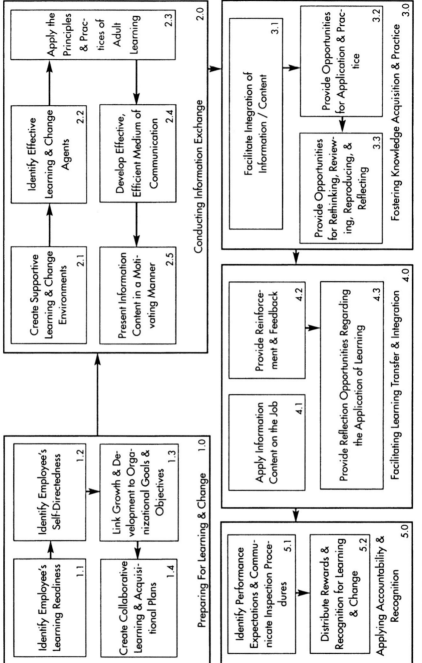

FIGURE 8.3 Applying the road map for the learning and change process

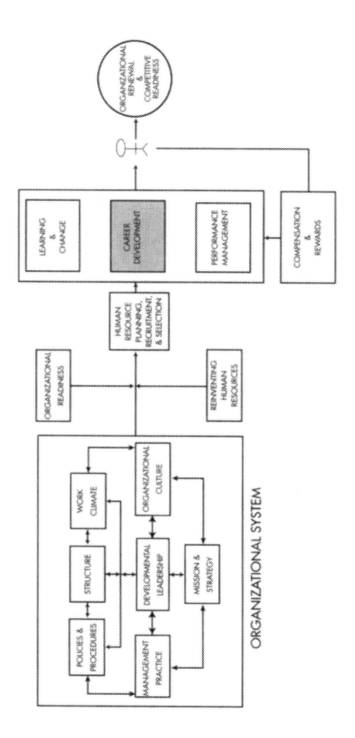

ORGANIZATIONAL SYSTEM

CHAPTER 9

Career Development Strategies

Organizations can enhance their renewal and performance capacity only if their employees have developed the skills, competencies, knowledge, and aptitudes at the highest possible levels. Learning and change activities contribute to a limited degree by focusing on current job efficiencies (see Chapter 8); hence, the organization is only indirectly impacted. This is the individual perspective of enhanced organizational renewal and improved performance capacity.

Organizational renewal and improved performance capacity are the result of organizational development activities—referred to as the systems approach. Unfortunately, individual employees are often overlooked during this process. Without employee commitment to growth and development, results will be minimized or short-lived. Both the individual and the systems approaches to enhancing organizational readiness and improved performance capacity have their weaknesses, thus necessitating the accommodation of the two processes. Career development provides that linkage.

THE RELATIONSHIP BETWEEN INDIVIDUAL AND SYSTEMS APPROACHES TO ORGANIZATIONAL RENEWAL

Career development is a process designed to enhance organizational readiness and improve performance capacity via individual employee

251

growth and development. Through career development, employees grow and develop beyond the fundamental skills, knowledge, competencies, and aptitudes used in their current job assignments. Organizations can provide learning and change activities that improve employees' abilities by viewing enhanced organizational readiness and improved performance capacity from an individual perspective while remaining dedicated to overall organizational enhancement (systems approach).

Many organizations fail to understand the connection between learning and change and overall organizational development. These terms are often used interchangeably, which leads to increased confusion and the misapplication of each process. We will attempt to clearly define the two processes.

What is growth and development? For purposes of our discussion, growth and development refer to enhancing human resources within an organization. However, the nature of growth and development proves difficult to define because the field of human resources is evolving at a rapid pace. Therefore, to characterize growth and development properly, a closer examination of the terms "human resources" and "development" follows.

WHAT ARE HUMAN RESOURCES?

Organizations employ three types of resources: physical, financial, and human. Physical resources comprise facilities, equipment, materials, and the like, used in the manufacture or production of goods and services. Impressive physical resources such as corporate offices or state-of-the-art manufacturing facilities provide a measure of tangible success observable by the public, investors, competitors, and employees.

Financial resources refer to the organization's liquid assets, such as cash, bonds, stocks, investments, and operating capital, and reflect a firm's overall financial stability and strength. Financial health is determined by comparing assets (physical and financial) with liabilities (debt) of the firm to determine net worth (which is one figure that banks, investors, and the public use to determine a firm's financial viability and investment potential). Financial resource availability proves crucial to an organization's ability to seize opportunities for expansion and growth (Gilley 1989).

Human resources are the people employed by an organization. Determining the value of human resources proves far more difficult than gauging the worth of financial and physical resources because of a lack of standard or traditional measures for personal value. As a result, human resources are not appreciated like physical resources, nor do they reflect organizational worth as do financial resources.

A firm's human resources are more important than physical and financial resources; unfortunately, organizational leaders often ignore this fact because employee value is not used to reflect business prosperity. One measure available to leaders in determining the importance of human resources involves the substantial costs incurred to replace valuable employees: recruiting, hiring, relocating, training, orientation, and lost production, to name a few.

The value that firms place on knowledge, skills, and competencies is another measure of the importance of human resources to organizations. Obviously, well-trained, highly skilled, knowledgeable employees are more valuable to the firm than uneducated, unskilled workers. This worth, also called "intellectual capital," is reflected in increased productivity, efficiency, and employee attitudes toward their jobs, management, and the organization.

Many firms fail to recognize the importance of human resources, as evidenced by their failure to include their workers in organizational asset portfolios. Consequently, many organizations and their managers fail to comprehend the need for, or importance of, performance improvement or learning and change activities. They further overlook the need for improving employees' knowledge, skills, competencies, and attitudes that improve overall organizational efficiency and effectiveness—which in return impact organizational readiness, renewal, and performance capacity.

What Is Development?

Examining development raises two questions: (1) What is meant by the development of human resources, and (2) what type of development occurs within an organization? The development of human resources concerns the advancement of knowledge, skills, competencies, and improved behaviors for both personal and professional use—reflecting individual *and* organizational focus (resulting from a philosophical commitment to human resources). As individuals improve, the organization benefits.

Some managers, unfortunately, stubbornly refuse to accept the obvious. For example, a very talented former co-worker of one of us is a sales and marketing representative for a large company. "Lauren," the department's star salesperson, enjoys a challenge; exudes organization, dedication, and multitask orientation to the extreme; and is one of those rare individuals who exceeds expectations with regularity. Her career interests lie in the area of project management, for which she is superbly skilled, given her aptitude for detail; her knowledge of company products, policies, procedures, and players; and her ability to manage competing demands. After three years in her current position Lauren has made it clear to the two levels of management above her (manager and vice president) that she is ready, willing, and able to handle additional responsibility and authority. While supported wholeheartedly by her manager, Lauren's vice president, Bill, refuses to allow her to transfer out of his department (and cultivate her talents, grow and develop professionally) because she is "the star," and he wants her sales performance reflected in his division's numbers. Bill fails to realize that Lauren's unhappiness is growing exponentially; she plans to leave the organization (soon) if unable to advance. Given Lauren's sales expertise and knowledge of the competition, industry, and products, she is a powerful ally who would be a formidable adversary if recruited by a rival company. Bill's refusal to accept that an individual's growth fuels organizational growth and his selfish, shortsighted behavior may well harm his organization.

Traditional organizations focus development on individual performance, typically neglecting organizational issues and opportunities. Development, whether individual or organizational, will not occur unless people participate in activities that introduce new knowledge and skills or improved behavior. Traditional organizations often rely on daily work experiences—a hit-or-miss approach—which usually prove ineffective in bringing about true growth and development. In fact, routine work may actually lead to acquisition of inadequate or inappropriate competencies. Improvement is best facilitated via organized activities, away from the job, that foster increased knowledge, skills, and competencies and improved behaviors. Quite simply, intentional learning and change actions bring about desired performance results.

From an organizational perspective, simple improvements in knowledge, skills, competencies, or behaviors fail to yield sufficient business results. Improvements must lead to increased productivity, efficiency, and quality to be useful, to further enhance an organization's competitive readiness, and to increase its performance capacity. Thus, the goal of developmental learning and change activities is to ultimately enhance performance (Gilley 1989). Therefore, performance improvement can be defined as organized learning and change activities within an organization that increase performance while enhancing the growth and development of employees to improve the job, the individual, the firm, or both (Gilley and Eggland 1989).

As discussed previously, the focus of traditional organizations remains the same in that individual employees engage in development activities designed to improve their job performance on present or future assignments. Individual development emphasizes the importance of personal growth and development through learning and change activities, enabling employees to develop their knowledge, skills, competencies, and behaviors. Individual development occurs in formal or informal settings. Formal learning and change actions address specific competencies, whereas informal learning, often called "incidental learning," is less focused and produces fewer tangible results.

During the past decade, organizations have begun examining in greater earnest the purpose and results of performance improvement and learning and change events. As a result, organizations better understand that these actions must be based upon the needs of learners as well as those of the organization. Today, more and more performance improvement and learning and change activities are focused on needs-oriented programs that benefit learners while also benefiting the organization.

In developmental organizations, individual growth and development have evolved to encompass far more than skill enhancement that can be transferred to one's current job or future assignments. Developmental organizations live and breathe a culture and philosophy of continuous growth, development, and renewal—whose supporting activities are implemented at all employee levels, utilizing several different delivery systems.

Thus, individual focus is as much about personal and professional growth and development as performance improvement. The organization is ultimately the benefactor of both activities. This also implies an individual perspective of organizational development in that each employee contributes to the overall efficiency of the firm while increasing his or her competencies that enhance productivity and improve business results.

WHAT IS ORGANIZATIONAL DEVELOPMENT?

Organizational development, the focus of this book, aims to improve a firm's performance capacity, growth, and renewal capability by enhancing these same characteristics in its employees. Organizational development challenges management on both the internal and the external organizational fronts. Internally, leaders and managers are forced to assess and refine all organizational systems while facing employee demands for rehumanization of the workplace, greater participation in decision making, and more control of their work lives. Firms desirous of evolving from the traditional to the learning to the developmental levels have enacted measures to improve the quality of work life, organizational culture, structure, and work climate (see Chapter 4).

Externally, competitive pressures and economic changes (cycles) have forced organizations to adjust to an ever-changing marketplace. Firms have been required to implement changes and take risks instead of tolerating the status quo or organizational equilibrium. The success of managerial efforts to bring about positive change rests in large part with their proficiency in organizational development (Gilley and Maycunich 1998a). Human resource professionals have been primarily responsible for enhancing management's awareness of, and skills in, organizational development.

We contend that organizational development focuses on personal, professional, and organizational growth, confidence, dignity, and freedom in a process that occurs over an extended period. Organizational development is guided by change agents whose primary responsibility is to act as catalysts in this dynamic process.

Successful organizational development initiatives must be inclusive, mobilizing all firm members in a planned, ongoing process. This process includes action research and application of the scientific method to organizational problems aimed at improving the problem-solving capacities of leaders, managers, and employees.

According to Gilley and Eggland (1989, 75), "organizational development is often viewed as a planned, data-based approach to change involving goal setting, action planning, implementing, monitoring, and taking corrective action when necessary." Organizational development also involves a systems approach—both systematic and systemic, which closely links human resources, structure, and management processes. Organizational development is a continuous method of managing organizational change that, over time, becomes a way of organizational life (Gilley 1989, 47). Hence, Beer (1985) defines organizational development as a systemwide process of data collection, diagnosis, action planning, intervention, and evaluation aimed at the following goals:

- enhancing congruence between organizational structure, processes, strategies, people, and culture
- developing new and creative organizational solutions
- developing an organizational self-renewing capacity

Organizational development occurs via the collaboration of individual members working with a change agent (human resource professional) who uses behavioral science techniques, research, and technology to focus on the following:

- overall organizational effectiveness
- development of innovative problem-solving approaches

- establishment of a survivalist attitude toward ever-changing environments, technological advancement, and cultural change (Gilley and Eggland 1989, 76; Gilley 1989)

Organizational development is concerned with long-term, planned change in the organization's culture, structure, work climate, and management system (see Chapter 6). We consider organizational development both a philosophy and a collection of methods for organizational improvement, characterized by emphasis on collaborative participation and data collection, diagnosis, planning, intervention, and evaluation in order to improve the entire firm.

We further contend that organizations also rely on learning as a means to bring about desired change. Here, the emphasis is on the overall human system within the organization rather than on individual members within the system. Thus, organizational development can again be viewed as a systems approach to enhancing organizational renewal and improved performance capacity in that the organizational development process assumes that the principle benefactor of any developmental activity, attitudinal enhancement, cultural improvement, or operational or structural change is the organization itself. Employees are the secondary benefactors.

This largely held view of organizational development fails to account for the myriad of individuals working within firms who must implement organizational changes and interventions. A systems approach to organizational renewal takes into consideration that change cannot occur nor performance improve without each employee improving his or her respective skills, competencies, knowledge, and attitudes.

Organizations do not exist unto themselves, but instead are made up of people who accept and act upon a common set of organizational goals and objectives. After all, organizations do not run organizations, people do. In exchange for their efforts, employees receive compensation and rewards both intrinsic and extrinsic. Individual employees release their personal power and control to organizational leaders so that the organization runs more efficiently. Without this compliance, organizations could not maintain control or operate effectively (Gilley 1989, 48–49).

We also point to the importance of employees in an organization. Although organizations consist of physical, financial, and human resources, people (human resources) control the other resources. Within an organization, certain people are considered more important than others. Despite the value ascribed to these people, organizational leaders would be at a loss without their support staffs. Administrative and support professionals are critical to today's organization; without them, the organization would quickly cease operation (Gilley 1989, 49).

Remarkably, some organizations believe that they would indeed survive if their employees elected to leave. As a result, organizations often operate with a revolving-door philosophy based on supply-side economics whereby the supply of qualified personnel exceeds the organization's demands (Gilley and Eggland 1989, 77). This philosophy is common in traditional organizations that desire improved performance as a means by which to enhance their operations. Employee growth and development are nonissues.

The revolving-door philosophy also exemplifies the attitude that employees exist *for* the organization, which has control over their movement, distribution, and development. Fortunately, many organizations have recognized the error of this practice, which is not necessarily the most efficient approach to the human resource management.

Given the acceptance of individual and systems perspectives toward enhanced organizational renewal and improved performance capacity, firms often maintain both a learning and change process and an organizational development process—a counterproductive activity as the two processes compete for limited resources. An unhealthy environment prevails because the same goals and objectives are being attempted from two completely opposite positions. The result is ambiguity and confusion regarding the importance of employee development and the lack of a strategic approach by organizational leaders for the enhancement of organizational renewal and improved performance capacity (Gilley 1989).

The solution lies in exploiting commonalities in the individual and systems perspectives. The primary similarities involve improved performance and employee growth and development, both needed to enhance the organization's competitive readiness. Taking advantage of these commonalities requires organizational commitment to maximizing employees' career potentials.

Organizations do not improve; their employees do—whether in productivity, knowledge, or skills. When individuals improve their proficiencies, organizations may be perceived as more efficient. Operational changes (i.e., changes in policies and procedures) can improve organizational efficiency; however, since employees implement these policies and procedures, a firm's success is directly proportionate to the effectiveness of its employees.

Since organizational members are usually an eclectic group, improvement must be uniquely tailored to each member of the firm. Then and only then will the organization gain additional renewal capacity.

What Is Career Development?

The individual and systems perspectives of enhanced organizational renewal and performance capacity share a critical commonality—individual employees within the firm and their respective development, a commonality best understood from the perspective of career development. Many managers and HR professionals treat career development as a separate process from learning-and-change activities and organizational development. The linkage between them becomes clear upon closer examination of the purpose of career development.

Purpose of Career Development

Career development helps employees analyze their abilities and interests to better match human resource needs for growth and development with the organization's needs. A working definition of career development is an organized, planned effort including structured activities or processes that result in practical career-management actions between employees and the organization (Gilley and Eggland 1989). Career development, then, involves learning and change activities such as those instrumental in the individual development process. For example, learning and change actions help employees obtain basic knowledge, skills, and competencies to perform effectively in their current jobs. Educational activities provide a means of career advancement and mobility, whereas developmental activities enable employees to reach their full potential.

Within the system of career development, employees are responsible for career planning, whereas the organization is responsible for career management (Gilley and Eggland 1989). Figure 9.1 illustrates this interface. These two separate but related processes combined form organizational career development, a partnership between the firm and its individual employees (Gilley 1989).

Organizations employ developmental planning—the process of assessing appropriate goals and objectives and the proper allocation of physical, financial, and human resources. The allotment includes human resource planning, allocation, and utilization; recruitment and selection; developmental evaluations; and learning and change activities.

Employees in developmental organizations engage in career life planning. Through this process, employees analyze their personal goals and competencies and realistically evaluate their future opportunities. The benefits of career life planning are occupational choice, organizational choice, choice of job assignments, and career self-development.

In developmental organizations, both firms and employees conduct three types of analysis—needs, competency, and development—to assess the match between the employee and the organization. The matching process enables firms to identify human resource needs and develop employees accordingly. This focus allows firms to develop individuals for the purpose of improving organizational performance capacity and renewal. While not viewed as an individual development activity, the matching process illuminates for employees the possible options that may enhance their careers. Matching is also a systems approach in that overall organizational performance capacity improves as a result of aligning employee and organizational needs. Thus, the purposes of the individual and systems perspectives have been met.

Organizations use career development to increase productivity, improve employee attitudes, and promote job satisfaction (Gilley 1989, 52). Thus, when firms implement career development programs, they encourage commitment and loyalty, and improve morale and motivation. The

FIGURE 9.1   Organizational career development

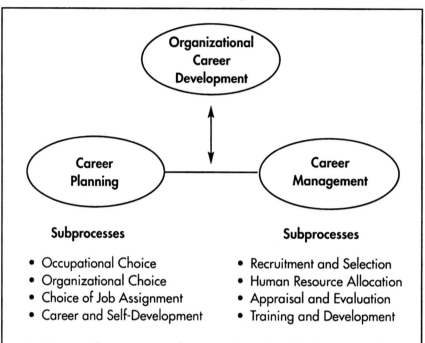

Subprocesses

- Occupational Choice
- Organizational Choice
- Choice of Job Assignment
- Career and Self-Development

Subprocesses

- Recruitment and Selection
- Human Resource Allocation
- Appraisal and Evaluation
- Training and Development

A. Career: The sequence of a person's work-related activities, behaviors and associated attitudes, values and aspirations, career management processes.

B. Organizational Career Development: The outcomes of the interaction between individual career planning and institutional career management processes.

C. Career Planning: A deliberate process for: becoming aware of self, opportunities, constraints, choices, and consequences; identifying career-related goals; and programming work, education, and related development experiences to provide the direction, timing, and sequence of steps to attain a specific career goal.

D. Career Management: An ongoing process of preparing, implementing, and monitoring career plans undertaken by the individual alone or in concert with the organization's career system.

Gilley, J.W. 1989. Career development: The linkage between training and organizational deveopment. *Performance Improvement Quarterly* 2 (1): 6–10.

company consequently enjoys reduced turnover, in direct opposition to the revolving-door philosophy common in businesses today.

Career Development Responsibilities

Employees and organizations working together as a team are necessary to guarantee career development's success (Gilley and Eggland 1989). Leaders, HR professionals, and managers organize and direct the program, including the identification and establishment of career development activities. In meeting their respective responsibilities regarding career development, all the key players (i.e., organizational leaders, HR professionals, managers, and employees) build a stronger link between individual and organizational development.

Developmental organization leaders generate career development program policies, allocate financial resources, and provide opportunities for collaboration and integration. They also advocate the importance of career development to the overall success of both individuals and the firm.

HR professionals provide guidance and information regarding the impact and importance of career development. They exhibit leadership and expertise in creating career development activities and interventions that initiate or improve employee growth and development, and serve as a liaison between employees and the firm.

Managers are the most intricately entwined agents in the career development process, bearing most of the responsibility for its success. Developmental managers provide support and advice to employees whenever possible, and serve as career counselors who share their experiences, insights, and expertise regarding career path decisions. They provide employees with historical context and understanding of how their current jobs and career paths fit into the organization's overall success equation, while projecting trends that may eventually impact career opportunities within the organization. Managers also provide performance feedback aimed at giving employees ample time to correct their performance or acquire new knowledge, skills, and behaviors necessary for career advancement.

Employees, responsible for their own career success, function as career planners and enhancers. As such, they are auditors of their own skills sets, determining gaps in performance proficiency and identifying areas of strength upon which career development actions can be based. Employees in developmental organizations identify their own training and development needs and implement new skills and knowledge on the job to improve their performance.

How Organizations Enhance Career Development

Since organizations reap the benefits of employee career development, firms must relate to staff at all levels (e.g., senior executives, managers, supervisors, and employees) for career development to be successful. Developmental organizations cultivate individuals who are responsible for various career development roles—such as administrators, developers, providers, counselors, and managers of career development functions—so that career development becomes a vital part of individual and organizational enhancement. Simultaneously, these people emphasize the importance of career development to employees, inform and update others within the firm while serving as mentors and career counselors with employees, and maintain a careful balance of facilitating, coordinating, and monitoring of staff career development activities (Gilley 1989).

Absent a clear and separate list of responsibilities, the career development process would fail to bridge individual and organizational development. Employees lacking direction would simply participate in career development activities as a reward or time-wasting action, never accomplishing their personal career goals.

Activities that enhance employee growth and development include the following:

- developing mentoring activities (Chapter 4)
- training managers as career counselors (Chapter 4)
- planning and forecasting human resource needs (Chapter 8)
- developing career path programs (Chapter 8)

- utilizing developmental evaluations and growth and development plans (Chapter 11)
- planning and implementing career development activities designed to improve strengths and manage weaknesses (next section, this chapter)

Human resource professionals, managers, and employees are responsible for the identification, implementation, and management of each of these career development activities. In developmental organizations, everyone accepts his or her respective responsibilities, actively participating in the organization's career management function and in the development of learning systems designed to change behavior. As a result, career development enables organizations to meet the developmental needs of employees, ensuring improved organizational performance capacity and renewal.

THE MYTH OF FIXING EMPLOYEE WEAKNESSES

Organizations often establish training or career development programs to help employees overcome their weaknesses. Many firms mistakenly believe that "fixing" weaknesses will make employees more productive in the short or long term. Most career development activities are based on the prevailing myth that fixing employee weaknesses will improve their performance and enhance the organization's competitive readiness. In practice, unfortunately, fixing employee weaknesses only makes their performance normal or average, not outstanding (Gilley 1998). Excellence is the result of building on employee strengths while managing their weaknesses, not by their elimination (Gilley and Boughton 1996).

As one of us maintained in an earlier book, "one problem with developmental strategies within organizations is that they are in the business of fixing employees rather than discovering their uniqueness and the things they do well. Therefore, career development activities are designed to correct weaknesses" (Gilley 1998, 68). Strategies such as this can sabotage organizational efforts to improve employee performance while communicating that something must be wrong with the firm or its employees.

Organizational managers often contend that employee weaknesses will take care of themselves (through time, experience, or luck)—yet another myth. As with any other problem, weaknesses do not "disappear"; they must be addressed and minimized. Employees build expertise via continual practice and reinforcement; hence, effective career development activities improve their existing competencies rather than fix their deficiencies (Clifton and Nelson 1992).

Another myth involves managers' and employees' belief that anything is possible, regardless of difficulty or obstacles. In reality, certain things are just not feasible, in spite of the effort expended. Phrases such as "If at first you don't succeed, try, try again," "Practice makes perfect," or "If I can do it, you can do it" oversimplify potentially complex organizational issues—frustrating or discouraging those attempting to master an unattainable goal. The belief that anything is possible erroneously assumes that all people are the same, possessing identical talents, abilities, and competencies. As we all know, individuals have a finite and eclectic set of strengths, weaknesses, skills, knowledge, and competencies—they are not clones.

Improving organizational performance capacity and enhancing renewal requires a fundamental shift in philosophy—from fixing weaknesses to building on strengths and managing weaknesses.

IDENTIFYING STRENGTHS

In certain professions, individual expertise is easily demonstrated, measurable, or noticeable by others. Athletes, musicians, surgeons, and the like, come to mind. These individuals have certain strengths on which they capitalize, and organizations usually place persons strategically to take advantage of these skills to the fullest. After all, Mark McGwire plays first base, not short stop; Kenny G plays the saxophone, not the drums; and anesthetists are typically not called upon for intricate brain surgery. Capitalizing on strengths makes sense; asking these professionals to perform outside their arenas of expertise wastes valuable talent. Why, then, do organizations spend millions of dollars every year on career development "fix-it strategies" unrelated to employee strengths? Often, the answer lies in organizational ignorance of the value of focusing on strengths, the inability to identify strengths in employees, or a combination of both.

Identifying strengths challenges leaders, managers, and employees to analyze their behaviors and successes. Clifton and Nelson (1992) identified four characteristics indicative of individual strengths:

- internal burnings
- high satisfaction
- rapid learning
- performance zones

Internal Burnings

According to Clifton and Nelson, strengths form in the mind and can be characterized as an internal, burning desire for something. One of us (J. W. G.), for example, wanted to be a professional baseball player; the other (A. M.) has always wanted to play the piano. Our own "burning desires" aside, we maintain that an individual's internal self-talk fuels the initiative to try new things, creating an attraction to, or curiosity about, a subject or an activity. Curiosity leads to heightened interest, which, if allowed to flourish over time, forms genuine interest. If one participates sufficiently and possesses basic, innate abilities, one often builds proficiencies that eventually become strengths.

Needless to say, desire for something does not necessarily indicate strength on one's part. The world is full of frustrated would-be artists, singers, professional athletes, and managers. Motive is sometimes suspect as well. For example, many salespeople want to become sales managers for the sake of power, control, or career advancement. Often, these individuals demonstrate little concern for the development of people—the primary purpose of management. Gilley and Boughton (1996) describe this as internal dishonesty, which prevents employees from identifying their true strengths and opportunities for mastery. We advocate instead the pursuit of internal honesty during career development activities.

FIGURE 9.2   Steps and components of building career development programs

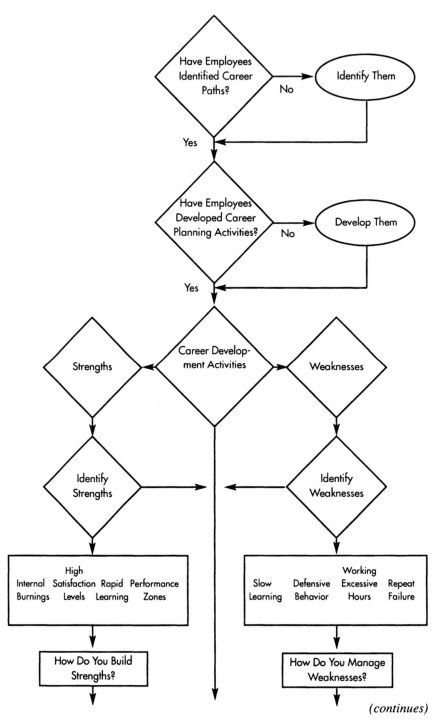

(continues)

(continued)

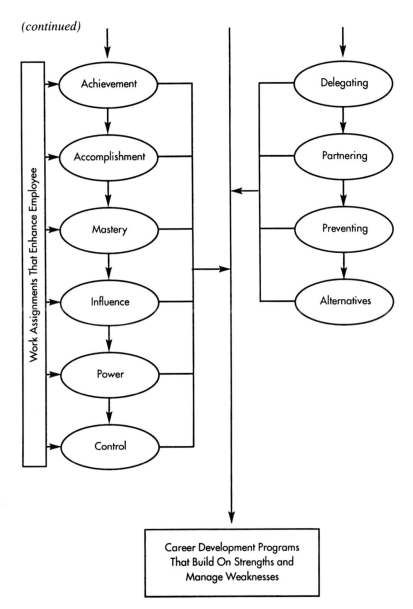

High Satisfaction Levels

Completing tasks or activities that yield high levels of satisfaction are often indicative of a strength. When employees enjoy intrinsic pleasure each time they perform a certain task or activity, the strength becomes a motivator in itself.

Conversely, employees might be very good or even excel at performing a particular activity, but hate doing it. Competence and satisfaction are not always related. For example, an individual may succeed at securing adequate results as a supervisor while disliking close interaction with people. Employees such as this possess competencies in accomplishing tasks but lack critical supervisory skills necessary to build and maintain relationships. As a result, they may lack the ability to be successful supervisors, in spite of their ability to produce desired business results. Over time, they may become dissatisfied or may burn out from a lack of fulfillment in their jobs. The key is "If it doesn't feel good, find something else that does" (Gilley and Boughton 1996, 61).

Rapid Learning

Strength is indicated when something comes easily or is learned very quickly. Computer hackers are an excellent example of people who learn by jumping in and discovering how something is done. For them, learning occurs via interactions and experiences; discovery is part of the process. Clifton and Nelson (1992) call this phenomenon "rapid learning"—when employees catch on quickly and are often good at performing tasks the first time they are tried.

Unfortunately, we are not all experts the first time out. In fact, some employees simply cannot perform certain tasks well, regardless of how hard or often they try. This slow learning depicts "non-strength." For example, one of us (J. W. G.) has been successful in writing a number of books (eight in total). Over the years, however, he has come to the realization that he is unable to comprehensively edit his manuscripts. Numerous attempts to acquire editing skills have proven futile, although he has improved significantly. Frustrated and discouraged, he discussed this dilemma several years ago with an editor of one of his books. Much to his delight, he realized that writing is significantly different from editing, and that his slow learning was simply evidence of "non-strength." Although he may never become an excellent editor, it makes sense for him to manage this weakness by partnering with individuals who possess that skill. In recent years he has worked with excellent coauthors whose strengths include the ability to edit manuscripts. This example illustrates slow learning resulting from a non-strength. We will discuss managing weaknesses later on in this chapter.

The hunger for knowledge and the desire to learn as much as possible is yet another indication of a strength. For continuous, lifelong learners, learning is a delight, not a chore. Individuals reading this book are excellent examples of those trying to develop their strengths in organizational leadership and development. Furthermore, rapid learning indicates whether employees are using their strengths. Of course, learning rates differ from employee to employee; hence, the key involves isolating activities that employees perform well and allowing them to continue.

Performance Zones

When employees or teams perform without any conscious awareness of the steps involved, Clifton and Nelson (1992) refer to this as the "performance zone." These employees unconsciously rely on their strengths and complete tasks with ease, often exceeding their own expectations. One of our favorite examples of performance zones is the 1996 Fiesta Bowl blowout, when the University of Nebraska destroyed the University of Florida 62 to 24. Prior to the game, Nebraska was as much as a twenty-point underdog to the mighty Gators. Before seventy-five thousand screaming fans, the Cornhuskers ran up more than six hundred yards, burying Florida by scoring 26 unanswered points in the second quarter, on their way to winning their second straight NCAA national championship. Nebraska played an almost perfect game, relying on its strengths—the running game and an overwhelming defense. This is what champions and championships are made of.

Employees enjoy supreme satisfaction while in the performance zone, which is the ultimate demonstrator of strength. They feel invincible and powerful, wanting to repeat the performance over and over again. These experiences enhance employees' self-esteem and shape their confidence. Repetition brings improvement, which leads to expertise and mastery—a cycle that developmental organizations employ to enhance organizational renewal and improve performance capacity.

BUILDING ON STRENGTHS

Maximizing strengths requires managers and employees to develop personal master lists of strengths (Clifton and Nelson 1992). The four characteristics previously discussed can be used as a guide. After compiling the personal master list, managers and employees isolate one strength to be developed for a month. Participants should first select a strength they will have an opportunity to employ on a regular basis. Next, they use this strength as often as possible during the month and record *how* it is used and the *outcomes* that result. Meanwhile, developmental managers should informally discuss the employee's efforts throughout the month, providing encouragement and praise when appropriate. At month's end, managers should discuss how many times the strength was used and its results. Finally, they should ask employees how they felt about using the strength and whether performance improved.

Developing personal master lists of strengths and focusing on each improves performance, job satisfaction, work relationships, and employee confidence. This experience emphasizes managers' and employees' special skills and abilities, providing a foundation upon which they may rely in the future. Employees also realize that they enjoy improving their performance when allowed to build on strengths rather than "fix" weaknesses. This process should be repeated until all strengths have been fully developed.

As employees grow and develop, there comes a moment of truth when each must choose a career path that defines him or her within the organization (Gilley and Boughton 1996). Pursuing graduate studies, professional credentials, or advanced development activities encourages employees to discover their own areas of expertise. With strengths in mind, developmental employees strike a direction and "go for it." Managers, at this time, have a particularly opportune occasion to assist employees with this decision by using their career coaching and feedback skills (see Chapter 3).

Developmental managers encourage employees to continually improve their strengths via practice, practice, more practice, and reflection. While mastery is the result of many hours of hard work and dedication, reflection allows employees to uncover new meaning that leads to renewal. And thus the cycle begins anew.

Reliving success permits employees to enjoy the moment over and over again. The more past successes are relived, the more future success is encouraged. Employees, teams, and organizations are strongest when successes are clearly pictured in their minds. Clifton and Nelson (1992) contend that employees build on strengths by visualizing and writing and talking about them.

Visualization is the process of mentally rehearsing a successful event. Again and again, employees picture themselves completing a job assignment, facilitating a training session, giving a speech, or developing a new product—they visualize whatever they have done well. Mental reflection allows employees to relive the emotions and satisfactions of the moment, each time being inspired to further develop their strengths.

Some employees capture the essence of successful events by writing about them. Written descriptions characterizing strengths, feelings of success, location, pinnacles of achievement, dialogue, and so forth, allow employees to creatively yet realistically review and relive accomplishments. Once written, the transcript should be read over and over to solidify the event in their minds, as though they were experiencing it anew. Reading the account powerfully inspires employees to further develop their strengths.

Interactive learners and extroverts often need to talk about how they have successfully used their strengths—discussing their proudest moments and how their strengths helped them achieve victory. A strategy useful to developmental managers involves encouraging employees to discuss their heroes to identify skills and abilities they would like to emulate. Heroes inspire employees to develop their personal best.

Managing Weaknesses

Identifying weaknesses is the first step in managing them (Gilley and Boughton 1996). Sadly, our weaknesses are often easier to identify than strengths because others have been pointing them out for years. Because of negative criticism, many people have difficulty discovering good things about themselves, resulting in a self-image that may or may not be accurate. Certain behavioral clues, however, are instrumental indicators of weakness.

Slow learning is the first indication of a weakness (Clifton and Nelson 1992). Repetition of an experience that fails to profit an employee denotes weakness, particularly if no growth is evident after several months of performance. Task completion is the main worry of employees with weaknesses; for them, improving performance is a non-issue at this point. Another indication of weakness is defensive behavior regarding one's performance. Employees feel inferior when they fail to live up to performance standards, which sometimes manifests itself in defensive behavior. In an attempt to overcome weaknesses, some employees become obsessive, engaging in addictive behavior that overtakes them and becoming overly focused on performance. Some employees may work excessive hours because they cannot release the behavior, which can become destructive. Developmental managers guard against harmful behaviors such as these, acting quickly when they see them so as not to risk losing the employee altogether.

Occasionally, employees fearful of or too stubborn to admit weaknesses allow themselves to be placed in situations in which they fail over and over again. The result of this cycle is reduced self-esteem, a high psychological price to pay. If this cycle continues employees will lose confidence in themselves and their abilities, which will ultimately hurt their performance in the form of reduced efficiency, quality, or effectiveness.

Clifton and Nelson (1992, 84–85) illustrate another way of identifying weaknesses—by listening to what employees utter during the day. Primarily, negative statements bespeak underlying weaknesses. Notice the following comparisons:

- "I've got to go to work" versus "I get to go to work"
- "When do I get off work?" versus "What am I to achieve today?"
- "I want to work fewer hours" versus "There are not enough hours to do what I want to do"
- "I have a 'job'" versus "I have a way to 'live'"

- "I avoid work by drinking, overeating, gambling, using drugs, or calling in sick" versus "I think of ways to improve my performance at work even when I'm not actually there"
- "I have to force myself to work" versus "I feel energized from work"
- "I dislike my co-workers" versus "I have friends at work"
- "I have unrealistic expectations of what can be accomplished at work" versus "I have a set of objectives and track record for achieving them"

These eight clues reveal employees' attitudes toward their jobs, potential weakness points, and serve as determinants as to whether employees are in the correct career path within the organization.

Identifying weaknesses is only the first step; their management makes the difference. According to Clifton and Nelson (1992), developmental managers engage in four strategies to help employees minimize their weaknesses, including delegating, partnering, preventing, and accepting alternatives.

Delegating

One of the best ways to manage employees' weaknesses involves delegating responsibility to those in the organization with the necessary strengths. For example, when one of us (J. W. G.) discovered that he did not have a strong talent for editing manuscripts, he delegated the task to his assistant, an outstanding editor. She enjoyed the work, welcomed the challenge, and made them both look good. This was an excellent development process for her—she was able to better understand the work they were doing and the organization. Furthermore, her career was advanced inside the firm as a result.

Partnering

Partnering is *not* matching one person's strengths to another's weakness. Instead, partnering involves combining two employees' strengths to achieve a goal, producing a synergy that results in a better job done together than separately. The scenario just provided is an excellent example of partnering. The person primarily skilled at creative writing and model building had to partner with an individual who could bring his outrageous ideas down to practicality in a clear, concise manner. Complementary strengths overcome weaknesses every time.

Preventing

Many employees place themselves in situations in which they consistently fail. Developmental employees realize their weaknesses and cease to set themselves up for failure. Managers must be willing to support this decision and encourage employees to cultivate those tasks, activities, and jobs they are good at—a process known as preventing.

Accepting Alternatives

Accepting alternatives requires managers to be willing to live with differences. Many managers find this a difficult undertaking, expecting tasks to be done exactly the same way, regardless of employees' abilities. Acceptable alternatives enable employees to accomplish the required work using their strengths. Often, the new way may be a better way. Many of the best quality improvements and performance efficiencies have been illuminated when managers encourage their employees to find alternative ways of getting the job done. Figure 9.2 summarizes the steps in building career development programs that build on strengths and manage weaknesses.

Conclusion

Career development is a process requiring individuals and organizations to create a partnership that enhances employees' knowledge, skills, competencies, and attitudes required for their current and future job assignments. Career development is a quintessential developmental activity of an organization, providing linkage between individual and organizational development, allowing for improved individual proficiencies while concurrently enhancing organizational renewal and improving performance capacity.

Developmental organizations focus career development activities on maximizing employee strengths. Fixing employee weaknesses proves a fruitless strategy that merely makes an employee average, not outstanding. Developing employee strengths leads to high levels of personal mastery and professional excellence that ensure achievement of desired business results. Career development activities that maximize strengths while linking individual and organizational development enhance the firm's competitive readiness while fostering organizational renewal.

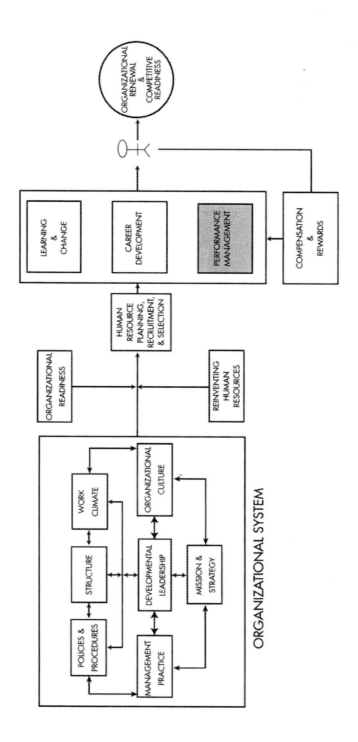

CHAPTER 10

Performance Management

A distinguishing characteristic between traditional and developmental organizations is that traditional firms commonly fail to achieve the results required of them—most notably because they can talk the talk but cannot walk the walk. Historically, they have well-written, meaningful mission statements and strategic plans, but are ineffective in bringing about business results needed to remain vibrant and competitive. They boast that "employees are our greatest asset and most valuable resource," whereas in practice, this could not be further from the truth.

Traditional organizations fail to have or embrace a comprehensive performance management process instrumental in bringing about the performance achievements needed to secure desired business results. Consequently, traditional organizations' strategic business goals and objectives are often unrealized. As expressed in previous chapters, traditional organizations believe that their employees are easily replaced; thus policies and procedures demonstrate a revolving-door philosophy toward human resources.

Traditional organizations often exhibit an attitude of corporate indifference. They "wash their hands of any responsibility for their actions and decisions regarding employee performance and are quickly willing to blame scapegoats for their own failings" (Gilley, Boughton, and Maycunich 1999, 2).

The dilemma facing today's organizations is their ignorance regarding how to manage performance, develop people, and create systems and techniques that enhance organizational effectiveness. In short, organizations must discover ways of transforming employees into high performers who are their greatest asset. This transformation requires performance management to help the firm achieve its strategic business goals and objectives, enhance organizational renewal, improve performance capability, and increase competitive readiness.

WHY EMPLOYEES FAIL TO ACHIEVE DESIRED BUSINESS RESULTS

An organization's competitive readiness is revealed by how well its employees perform. When an organization fails to achieve its desired business objectives, employees may not be performing adequately. Five reasons exist for employees' failure to perform satisfactorily:

1. inadequate job design
2. poor managerial practices
3. inadequate training and development
4. inappropriate corrective strategies
5. inefficient and ineffective compensation and reward programs

Inadequate Job Design

One of the primary reasons why employees fail to achieve their desired performance results has to do with poor job design. A disconnect exists between what employees are required to accomplish and the activities they complete to produce sufficient results. This may be attributable to employees' inability to measure or evaluate their own performance, since they are on their own to determine the level of performance and activities, deliverables, and corrective actions necessary to produce the results required of them. Furthermore, employees may focus on less important activities that do not directly align with the performance required of them. Finally, organizational barriers may prevent adequate performance.

Poor Management Practices

Poor management practices are the heart of inadequate performance, breeding personnel mistrust, fear, and strained manager–employee relations. Employees may be fearful of repercussions for incorrect performance, may not feel safe asking for help, or may fear suggesting better, more efficient ways of doing their jobs.

When managers fail to confront those employees performing inadequately, they inadvertently send the message that the worker's conduct is correct. Managers who do confront employees are often aggressive, abusive, or angry, attitudes resulting in resentment or hostility on the part of workers.

Inadequate Training and Development

Too often, employees fail to perform adequately because they simply do not possess the necessary knowledge, skills, or understanding of job responsibilities as a result of inadequate training and development. Poor quality or insufficient quantity should come as no surprise when abandoned employees are left on their own to gain the knowledge and experience necessary to meet their goals or achieve desired results. One of our former employers (a very traditional organization) somewhat jokingly referred to this as the "throw 'em under the bus method" of training, which essentially meant *no* real training. This phenomenon commonly occurs when managers are inexperienced, do not know the essential job requirements themselves, are poor communicators, delegate training to others, and so forth.

Certainly, many reasons (excuses) are given in explanation for inadequately trained employees. Unfortunately, one of the most common involves *who* bears the responsibility for training and development. Traditional organizations rely heavily on a centralized training and development department to provide employees with the knowledge and skills they need. In developmental organizations, on the other hand, training and development are the responsibility of managers and supervisors, who are ultimately held accountable for productivity and employee development. This approach streamlines the developmental process by eliminating the "middleman" (training and development department) and further solidifies manager–employee relations by increasing their interaction via teamwork and cooperation.

Lack of Corrective Strategy

Occasionally, employees simply refuse or are unable to perform adequately. In either case, organizations must implement procedures that allow managers to take corrective action immediately. Formal corrective strategies permit managers to be proactive, directive, informative, and efficient in their approach to improving personnel performance and achieving desired results. Absent corrective procedures, employees will continue to perform inadequately.

Inefficient and Ineffective Compensation and Reward Programs

Compensation and rewards are powerful incentives, yet when used ineffectively can be just as deterring. For example, employees are often rewarded for completing tasks that are unnecessary, unimportant, and unrelated to their jobs; for their individual contributions even though teamwork is an organizational focus (often sacrificed for personal gain); and for their tenure in a current position. Well-designed compensation and reward programs link achievement with desired results, growth, and development. In this way, organizations continuously reward employees for improving their knowledge, skills, and behaviors—putting into motion a developmental philosophy that enables the firm to achieve long-term success, enhance competitive readiness and renewal capacity, and

improve performance capability. Developmental organizations understand that rewarding employees for growth and development (in addition
to superior performance) is a wise investment in the future of all.

Why Organizations Fail to Achieve Desired Business Results

Organizations fail to achieve desired performance results for a variety of
reasons. They include failing to:

- focus on stakeholder needs
- link organizational performance to strategic business goals and
  objectives
- identify performance breakdowns
- eliminate managerial malpractice
- manage performance
- encourage employee involvement and support
- focus on long-term results (Gilley, Boughton, and Maycunich
  1999, 14)

To overcome these managerial shortcomings and the aforementioned employee failings, organizations must understand the principles of performance improvement and create an organizationwide, strategic, long-term
approach to managing employee performance, growth, and development.

Principles of Performance Improvement

When organizations are confronted with poor employee performance,
they often consider why such behavior exists. Three principles explain
most problems with employee behavior and why organizations fail to secure the results they need or want: performance–reward disconnect, performance whitewashing, and expectation–inspection failure.

Performance–Reward Disconnect

Many employees fail to perform adequately because of a perceived disparity between their performance and the rewards they receive from the organization. The disparity is known as performance–reward disconnect. When organizations suffer performance–reward disconnect, desired behaviors (e.g., loyalty, creativity, entrepreneurship) are ignored or punished in the workplace while other performance is rewarded. Firms send mixed messages by inadvertently rewarding performances they do not desire, such as individualism at the expense of co-workers or other departments. Improving performance requires a direct correlation between desired behaviors and actions and rewards received. LeBoeuf (1985) believes that if people are rewarded for the right performance, the organization will get the right performance. He insists that the things that get rewarded get done. In essence, failure to reward proper performance behavior leads to undesirable results.

Performance Whitewashing

Ineffective managers treat all performance results the same, failing to communicate which actions and results are most important, a behavior that we call "performance whitewashing." Performance whitewashing confuses employees, causing them to treat all outputs similarly when, in reality, some performance outcomes have little value to the organization. Employees permitted (by managers) to continually focus on less important priorities unintentionally sabotage needed business results.

Eliminating performance whitewashing requires that organizations determine (through their managers) which activities are truly important and which are less so. These priorities must then be communicated to every employee and rewarded accordingly.

Expectation–Inspection Failure

Management's failure to prioritize, review, measure, and inspect employee performance often leads to worker inability to meet goals or produce corresponding desired results. To abolish expectation–inspection failure, managers link their expectations of employee performance with an inspection of the results. Communication is the key, both in the manager's expression of expectations and in feedback regarding outputs. Appropriate forums for discussing performance expectations and inspection results include regular one-on-one talks, formal and informal discussions, performance evaluations, and the like.

To perform adequately, employees need to know what is expected of them and in what form or quality their outputs should be produced. Too frequently, managers fail to adequately communicate their expectations or lack the follow-up initiative necessary to guarantee that desired performance occurs in a timely manner. These typically traditional managers mistakenly believe that it is not their responsibility to share expectations or inspect performance outcomes—a tremendous barrier in the evolution to the developmental organization.

PERFORMANCE ALIGNMENT

Every organization faces the performance challenge: to develop management systems that maximize employee performance while enhancing their growth and development. Successfully facing this challenge requires organizational design, development, and implementation of performance alignment. The process is intended to improve performance capacity, competitiveness readiness, and renewal. The performance alignment process addresses the performance challenge while simultaneously transforming the firm from the traditional to the developmental. Performance alignment must incorporate an organizationwide approach that combines the entire performance improvement process into one cohesive operating system. Further, organizationwide performance alignment links performance to compensation and rewards, to the organization's business goals and objectives, and to customer needs and expectations.

Organizational Level

On an organizational level, performance alignment consists of seven interrelated steps:

Step 1: Conducting stakeholder valuations

Step 2: Improving job design

Step 3: Establishing synergistic relationships

Step 4: Applying performance coaching

Step 5: Conducting developmental evaluations

Step 6: Creating performance growth and development plans

Step 7: Linking compensation and rewards to performance growth and development (Gilley, Boughton, and Maycunich 1999, 5)

Each step works in concert with the others, forging an integrative, comprehensive approach to addressing the performance challenge (Figure 10.1).

The performance alignment process separates performance management into two distinct phases. Steps one and two are the responsibility of the organization; steps three through seven are the responsibility of managers and employees. This model embraces the belief that employees are the key to improving long-term business results. Based on this belief, employees understand and align their performance with the organization's strategic business goals and objectives. The performance alignment model provides for such linkage.

Step 1: Conducting Stakeholder Valuations. Identifying clients' needs and expectations is the first step toward achieving desired business results and may be accomplished through an exercise in stakeholder valuation. Stakeholder valuation drives an organization's delivery of goods and services to its clients. Information regarding both internal and external client needs, expectations, recommendations, and suggestions may be obtained through surveys, focus groups, or interviews. Organizations then design processes and procedures to meet or exceed client needs and expectations.

Step 2: Improving Job Design. Performance that does not help a firm achieve its strategic business goals and objectives ceases to be of value. Hence, linking all job design activities to strategic goals and objectives is the nucleus of the job design process, which consists of five interdepen-

FIGURE 10.1   Performance alignment

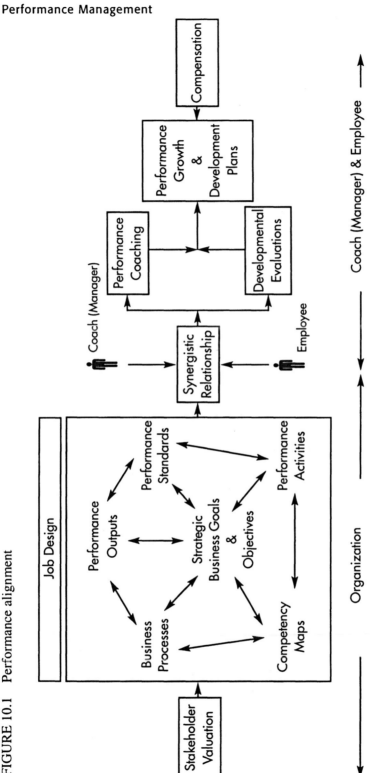

Gilley, J. W., N. W. Boughton, and A. Maycunich 1999. The performance challenge: Developing management systems to make employees your organization's greatest asset. Cambrige, MA: Perseus Books.

dent functions: business processes; performance outputs, standards, and activities; and competency maps (see Chapter 7).

Step 3: Establishing Synergistic Relationships.   Positive working relationships between managers and employees build the foundation upon which firms address the performance challenge and make the transition to the developmental organization. Synergistic relationships benefit all parties—employees, managers, and the organization—by amplifying employee commitment to improving performance quality, increasing productivity, enhancing organizational results, allowing greater worker influence and decision making, and creating work environments dedicated to continuous improvement. When these conditions predominate, employees perform like owners, striving to find efficiencies and economy throughout the firm.

Step 4: Applying Performance Coaching.   Without a doubt, the most common, debilitating problem facing today's organizations is the quality (or lack thereof) of management. Typical managers are untrained in the art and science of personnel management, often lacking adequate communication, interpersonal, listening, and feedback skills. Many managers are often indifferent toward employees, have superior attitudes, and treat employees as disposables—assets to be used and discarded. Overcoming this managerial malpractice requires organizational commitment to transform managers into performance coaches capable of developing their people to the fullest. Developmental organizations embrace performance coaching, selecting managers for their interpersonal skills, and holding them accountable for establishing rapport, enhancing face-to-face communications, and securing results (see Chapter 4).

Step 5: Conducting Developmental Evaluations.   On a regular basis (annually, semiannually, quarterly, or monthly), managers should conduct reviews that enable them to assess personnel performance quality and quantity and to collaboratively create growth and development plans designed to enhance employee performance, both current and future. We call these reviews developmental evaluations, which carry out the following tasks:

1. Determine whether employees are performing acceptably.
2. Generate outputs that meet or exceed performance standards
3. Determine whether the needs and expectations of internal and external clients have been satisfied.
4. Assess employee strengths and weaknesses by comparing their competencies against job requirements.
5. Examine how employee performance helps the organization achieve its strategic business goals and objectives.
6. Design acceptable performance activities.

When these six objectives have been achieved, developmental evaluations prove an excellent tool for assessing employee performance and making recommendations for their continuous growth and development.

Step 6: Creating Performance Growth and Development Plans. Developmental evaluations provide managers with a forum by which to isolate employee strengths and weaknesses and discuss ways to enhance employee growth and development. Growth and development plans must be designed so that employees can apply learning to the job. Unless workers transfer what they learn, the learning is a complete waste of time, effort, and money. Developmental managers, in cooperation with employees, develop growth and development plans that maximize the knowledge, skills, competencies, and behaviors needed to improve employee performance, enhance their developmental readiness, and allow the firm to continuously renew itself.

Step 7: Linking Compensation and Rewards to Performance Growth and Development. Research has shown that performance that gets rewarded and reinforced is repeated (LeBoeuf 1985; Williams and Sunderland 1998; Flannery, Hofrichter, and Platten 1996). Organizations that reward the "right" things (e.g., teamwork, creativity, risk-taking, entrepreneurship, individual growth) improve employee commitment, loyalty, and motivation. From a long-term, organizational growth perspective, rewarding growth and development is far more important than rewarding performance improvement (a short-term focus). This linkage with compensation and rewards acts as a catalyst to continuous employee growth and development while emphasizing the importance of the firm's long-term success. Developmentally focused businesses integrate compensation and rewards as a guiding principle for organizational growth and development.

Performer Level

The performance alignment process, concurrently strategic, macro, and micro in nature, proves to be an effective tool for addressing performance management issues at the organizational and business process levels (large-scale, or macro, level). It is also appropriate and can be applied to help manage each employee's performance at the performer level (small-scale, or micro, level). Rearranging component parts of the performance alignment process (Figure 10.1) assists individual employees with performance management issues.

At the performer level, organizations interface with employees who actually produce the products and services. In a previous book, we discuss the importance of looking toward the performer level:

> The organizational and business process levels may be architectural master-pieces, but if performers cannot execute efficiently and effectively, performance quality and outputs will be negatively affected. Unless organizations create conditions by which their employees can produce adequate products and services, organizational process goals will be jeopardized. Thus, the performer level is critical to the ultimate success of any organization and must be managed accordingly. (Gilley, Boughton, and Maycunich 1999, 42).

Performer Developmental Goals. Performer developmental goals are established for each employee in support of business processes and organizational objectives. Established during the developmental evaluation process, goals provide the focus for employee growth and development plans.

Performer developmental goals encompass a variety of targeted activities, from employee growth and development to enhancement of performance or quality. As the backbone of the performance alignment process, performer developmental goals provide individual targets that are linked to organizational strategic business goals and objectives and that employees strive to meet on a daily basis. These goals may include the following:

- acquisition of new job skills intended to improve performance outputs and activities
- acquisition of new knowledge that will help employees with complex problem solving or decision making
- acquisition or improvement of attitudes associated with one's performance
- targeted performance improvement activities
- improvement in quality or production
- improvement in timeliness of delivery

Applying Performance Management at the Performer Level.   Many organizations use a performance management process consisting of three simple steps (Figure 10.2):

1. Identifying and assembling the material resources (raw materials, component parts, information, product specification sheets and diagrams, tools, equipment, computers, telephones, fax machines, and other resources) required to produce specific deliverables (performance outputs)
2. Engaging in separate tasks
3. Engaging in performance activities—the special arrangements of tasks used to generate performance outputs

In summary, performance transforms material resources into outputs by following a series of predetermined tasks that collectively constitute performance activities. Although the traditional performance process is used in many organizations, several omissions lead to poor performance and

FIGURE 10.2   Traditional performance

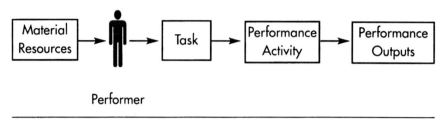

inadequate productivity. First, no performance standards have been identified for the evaluation of the quality of performance activities and outputs. Second, employees are given no performance feedback, which would ensure the timeliness of quality outputs. Third, the traditional performance process does not require or encourage performance appraisals or compensation-and-reward reviews that guarantee long-term performance improvement.

These omissions stem from the traditional organization's belief that employees are self-sufficient, requiring little or no training, feedback, or evaluation to produce desired results. Although this approach is easy to administer and can help firms produce products and services that enable them to remain somewhat competitive or profitable, numerous important steps are missing. Moreover, some assumptions of the traditional performance process negatively impact performance quality and quantity.

Most organizations realize that traditional performance processes have severe limitations; consequently, they employ a modified version to overcome these shortcomings (Figure 10.3). We refer to this approach as performance management since an element of quality control has been introduced to ensure performance improvement. The performance management approach can be differentiated from the traditional approach in three ways:

1. Performance standards are developed and applied to help employees produce outputs and execute activities at the highest possible level of quality.
2. Performance feedback and reinforcement ensures that performers receive specific, timely, and substantive information regarding their work.

3. Performance appraisals and compensation-and-reward reviews are modified to provide employees with formal feedback regarding their efforts and to communicate compensation and rewards for their performance (Gilley, Boughton, and Maycunich 1999, 47).

Performance standards, performance appraisal, feedback, and reinforcement are indicated with dotted lines in Figure 10.3 to emphasize their infrequency and disoriented nature. During this phase of performance management, organizations often approach these activities as options that *may* be implied or used. Hence, managers and supervisors employ them reluctantly, failing to capture the enormous benefits these activities can yield. Additionally, performance appraisals are typically conducted to determine the correctness of performance rather than as a means of enhancing employee growth and development.

Several shortcomings inhibit the effectiveness of the performance management process. First, the process fails to require managers to help employees design growth and development plans useful in improving organizational performance capacity and renewal. Second, it does not encourage formal performance coaching activities to train employees, confront performance, or provide counseling and mentoring opportunities that further develop employees' capabilities. Third, compensation and reward reviews and performance appraisals are not viewed as separate activities, nor are they used to enhance employee growth and development. When compensation and reward reviews and performance appraisals are separated into distinctly different actions, employees approach performance appraisals as developmental opportunities used to determine the amount and type of formal reinforcement necessary to encourage continuous performance growth and development (Gilley, Boughton, and Maycunich 1999).

Figure 10.4 illustrates the application of the performance management process at the performer level. The benefits of conducting activities at the performer level are numerous:

When the process is applied to the performer level, performance standards are in place for employees to gauge the quality of their deliverables and ac-

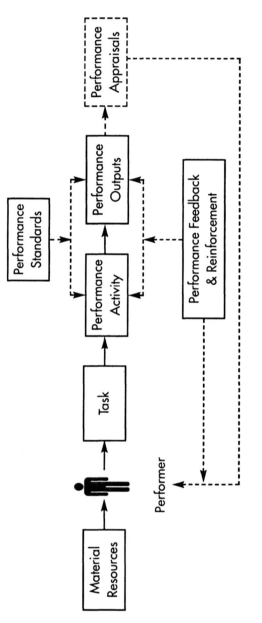

FIGURE 10.3   Traditional Performance Management Process

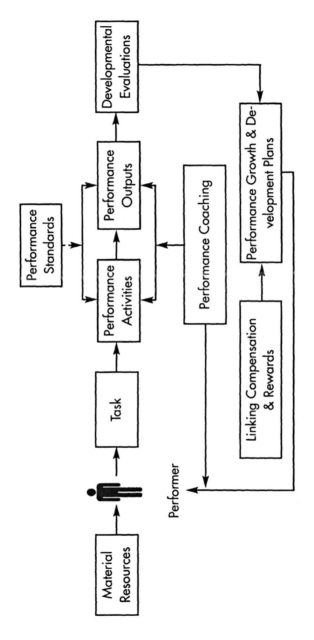

FIGURE 10.4   Performance Alignment Applied to the Performer Level

tivities. At this point, developmental evaluations replace the traditional performance appraisal process, encouraging performance growth and development as well as utilization of learning acquisition and transfer plans. Additionally, informal, sporadic performance feedback or reinforcement is replaced by formalized performance coaching activities that train, confront, counsel, and mentor employees. Finally, compensation and rewards are directly linked to performance growth and development planning actions to remunerate employees for ever-increasing knowledge, skills, and behaviors applied to the job. (Gilley, Boughton, and Maycunich 1999, 48–49)

When the performance alignment process is used at both the organizational and performer levels, it is assumed that stakeholder valuations have been conducted. Duplicating this activity at the performer level is therefore unnecessary. Further, the application of the performance alignment process to the performer level goes on the assumption that job assignments are directly linked to the organization's strategic business goals and objectives.

Although it is often more common to view performance management at a macro level, employee growth and development can best be addressed by applying the principles of the performance alignment process at *both* the organizational and performer levels (Figure 10.5). The principles embedded in performance alignment can indeed help manage individual employees at the performer level. In this way, one organizationwide strategy for addressing the performance and developmental challenge can be applied (Gilley, Boughton, and Maycunich 1999).

Achieving Performance Greatness

Occasionally, we all witness individuals such as athletes, musicians, and physicians who perform at the highest possible level and to the best of their abilities—often demonstrating outstanding performance with apparent effortlessness. Competitions like the Olympics and other sporting events, as well as sudden crises, reveal individuals exhibiting performance greatness. Gelb and Buzan (1992) call this extraordinary performance simply "greatness." Clifton and Nelson (1992) have named this behavior "total performance of excellence." Others (Clifton and Nelson

FIGURE 10.5   The Performance Management Process at the performer level

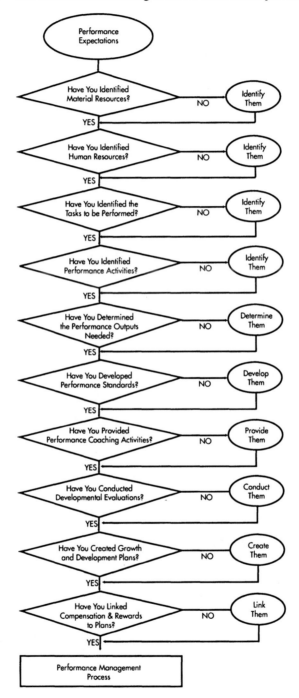

1992; Gilley and Boughton 1996) refer to such efforts as being in the "performance zone" (see Chapter 9).

Individuals who exhibit performance greatness achieve all that they are capable of achieving. The result is great satisfaction, improved self-esteem, and a heightened personal awareness. Those in the midst of great performance report that it is as though time stands still or they are moving in slow motion; behavior is automatic and other people seem to disappear. Spectators watching performance greatness at an athletic event absorb and experience every possible moment, knowing full well that they are witnessing greatness.

Whether at the stadium or on the job, performance greatness does not "just happen." It cannot be "manufactured" or turned on and off like a faucet, nor do individuals wait for the alignment of stars, perfect conditions, or permission from the organization's executive branch. Four activities advance performance greatness, provide opportunities for accelerated learning, and enhance growth and development:

1. failure analysis
2. trial and success
3. encouraging excellence
4. implementing the change process

Failure Analysis

The integration of new skills and knowledge often interferes with employees' current performance. Analyzing long-term effects of interference and its impact on overall productivity is what Gilley and Coffern (1994) call failure analysis. Through failure analysis, employees identify possible conflicts to better integrate learning in the future.

Failure is an integral part of learning and growth for us all. Yet, interference as employees attempt to integrate new skills and knowledge often causes confusion, the loss of confidence, or both. As a result, productivity may temporarily decline while employees integrate new skills and knowledge into their daily actions, and employees may be reluctant to continue applying what has been learned.

Developmental managers and their employees understand that failure is a healthy by-product of performance growth and development—failure does not equal disaster. The important lessons learned involve understanding *why* learning transfer failed to produce desired results and *how* to overcome or minimize confusion, frustration, or a lack of confidence.

Developmental organizations and managers establish safe, supportive work environments in which employees have the freedom to learn from their mistakes (failures) even though productivity may temporarily decline. Safe environments may include work simulations or involvement in case studies whereby employees work in comfortable, secure surroundings as they learn how to integrate new skills and knowledge without becoming frustrated or confused or losing confidence.

Learning failure allows for a quicker, more accurate application of new skills and knowledge; many of us have exclaimed, "I'll never make that mistake again!" Because long-term performance success takes precedence over short-term gains, learning failure allows employees to increase productivity and improve overall job performance while enhancing organizational competitive readiness, performance capacity, and renewal.

Trial and Success

Learning is best accomplished through trial and error. Hence, it is unfortunate that most people perceive errors as poor performance. Gelb and Buzan (1992, 70) believe that the path to accelerating and enjoying the learning process requires employees to view success and failure as equally instructive and valuable. They contend that it is useful to view any learning experience as a fascinating, never-ending journey from the starting point to a continually evolving goal of excellence.

Employees' first attempts to use new skills or apply new learning are often at less than 100 percent accuracy. Instead of considering these as disastrous mistakes, workers should view them as further additions to their data banks of understanding. In other words, errors are an integral part of learning. Over time, employees will adjust their performance sufficiently as learning is incorporated and overall job productivity improves.

People possess unlimited capacities to learn. Both managers and employees must recognize that an error in performance is not a sign of fundamental incapacity but rather an integral part of one's natural path to improvement.

Encouraging Excellence

Performance greatness results when managers encourage excellence in employee performance. Although excellence might be in the eye of the beholder, two specific activities bring about genuine performance success: continuous effort and poise. Successful employees apply the right amount of effort in the right place at the right time, conserving their energy and building adequate reserves for later work. For example, some teams have begun a sporting event with great emotion and enthusiasm, only to become exhausted (and lose) in the fourth quarter when an extra push was needed.

We have all heard the expression, "Never let them see you sweat." Individuals with poise make things look easy and are accustomed to performance greatness, often relying on innate talent or skill. Employees, similarly, must learn to pace themselves—to conserve their energies and take appropriate action that manifests as the natural expression of mind and body working in harmony.

Encouraging excellence requires a lifelong commitment to learning. Whether practicing during a learning activity or performing on the job, employees must learn from every aspect of their participation, gathering new information equally from successes and failures. This commitment to continuous improvement is the key to excellence, the cornerstone of organizational high performance, and the heart of the quality movement (Gelb and Buzan 1992). Employees (and managers) in search of excellence establish high standards for performance and accept personal accountability for their efforts. They are fully responsible for the results they achieve while striving to accomplish more.

Managers concerned with excellence encourage employees to become totally immersed in their self-improvement efforts. Doing so enables employees to focus their passion and achieve their personal best. Finally,

Gelb and Buzan assert that great performers understand that true excellence is achieved via total commitment and consistent discipline—a relentless dedication to the realization of goals through organized, intelligent, consistent planning and determination.

Implementing Change

Performance greatness occurs when employees understand and implement change, reinventing themselves over and over again or making the transition from average to exemplary performance. Four steps constitute the change process:

1. increasing one's self-awareness
2. identifying and isolating inhibitors to change
3. applying visualization techniques
4. committing to lasting change

Increasing One's Self-awareness.   The first step in the change process is awareness, that is, knowing who one is. Awareness exemplifies understanding of one's strengths and weaknesses, tendencies, orientations, likes, dislikes, motivators, "demotivators," encouragers, barriers, satisfiers, and dissatisfiers. In short, awareness is a holistic self-inventory of who one is, created by analyzing one's behavior and performance. Exploring self-awareness involves determining whether one's perception of self is consistent with one's behaviors. If perception is consistent with behavior, then an individual is congruent. However, when a disconnect exists between a person's perception of self and his or her actual behaviors, the person is in disharmony, often referred to as dysfunctional.

Self-awareness is critical to establishing a baseline of behavior or performance, after which a person can determine whether change has occurred. Self-awareness also promotes reflection, which requires an accurate portrayal (twenty–twenty vision) of oneself and one's behavior, thoughts, and actions. Finally, self-awareness is essential in ensuring honest, forthright integration of change. Nothing is more frustrating or discouraging than dealing with individuals who embrace change on the surface while never truly intending to alter behavior or performance. Obviously, misleading behavior damages the relationship between managers and employees.

Identifying and Isolating Inhibitors to Change.   Inhibitors are barriers that prevent change from occurring. Inhibitors can result from past experiences, such as unpleasant schooling, or from early phases in childhood or adolescence in which one may have experienced failure and subsequent embarrassment at the hands of an over-demanding parent.

Fear is a powerful inhibitor, often the result of transferring previously negative feelings to the current situation, causing individuals to panic, mentally detach, or literally shut down their ability to learn. Sometimes these reactions are brought about by tension or fear of failure, causing an individual to freeze during the learning cycle, unable to accept new information, feedback, encouragement, or support. Fearful projections prohibit some individuals' movement away from rigid mental positions resistant to acquiring new learning.

Gelb and Buzan (1992) believe that overcoming fear is one of the most important things an individual can do to bring about continuous and lasting change. They recommend the art of "relaxed concentration." Overcoming fear begins with recognition of the source and manifestation of fear in one's life. Next, one must acknowledge, understand, and accept that such fears exist—which takes courage, energy, and determination. Finally, they contend that people best overcome fear when they combine techniques that enable them to mentally succeed—a process called visualization.

Applying Visualization Techniques.   Visualization involves mentally modeling a performance creation or activity and focusing on the positive steps necessary to achieve acceptable results while mental cues and feedback encourage mastery. Gelb and Buzan (1992) identified two types of visualization techniques: forced analytical and open receptive. *Forced analytical* techniques involve an observation analysis approach that allows individuals to examine the fundamental elements of their performance, analyze whether the steps or tasks are performed adequately, and then improve the execution of each step or task.

Open receptive technique is a multisensory imaging process allowing one to use as many senses as possible (taste, touch, hearing, and so forth) when reflecting upon a performance solution or activity. Visualization techniques can be greatly improved when:

- individuals make an honest, concerted effort to apply visualization techniques accurately
- individuals use multisensory visualization processes
- individuals practice visualization regularly
- visualization is conducted outside-in and inside-out, permitting individuals to improve themselves in action while analyzing the steps and tasks used during a performance
- individuals can distinguish between fantasy and visualization
- individuals remain positive and focused

Committing to Lasting Change. Embracing commitment to success requires employees to clearly understand their learning goals and pure, unbiased data regarding their own performance (comparing desired with actual performance). Commitment to change and growth creates a continuous, positive spiral that accelerates employees toward and beyond their goals. Understanding what one desires to become, coupled with feedback along the way, energizes the learning process and propels employees toward excellence.

CONCLUSION

Organizations and employees fail to achieve their desired results for a number of reasons. Overcoming this failure necessitates organizational willingness to institute an organizationwide approach to employee performance enhancement, one dedicated to simultaneously enriching individual and organizational performance via long-term improvement strategies—the performance alignment process.

The performance alignment process focuses organizations on (1) today's performance challenges, and (2) growth and development activities that bring about individual and organizational renewal, improved performance capacity, and enhanced competitive readiness.

In concert with this activity, developmental organizations embrace the techniques necessary to enable employees to achieve performance greatness. Exemplary performance occurs when employees enjoy caring, supportive environments that allow them to be their best. Great performers own their work, take responsibility for their own growth and developmental, and focus on both current and future obligations.

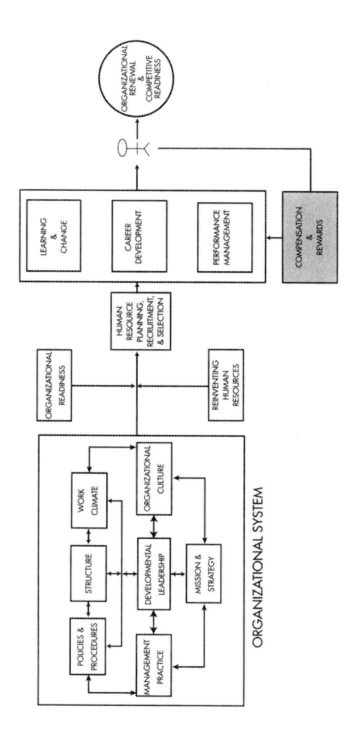

ORGANIZATIONAL SYSTEM

CHAPTER 11

Developmental Compensation and Rewards

The way people are rewarded says volumes about an organization, its culture, and expectations of itself and employees. Compensation and rewards remain one of the most effective tools available for motivating people. An innovative compensation and reward strategy is crucial to developmental organizations.

To effectively propel one's organization to the developmental level, compensation and reward strategies must evolve as well. Like a dynamic, developmental organization, pay and rewards must be flexible, adaptable to change, and aligned with the company's culture, philosophy, and strategic objectives. A well-designed compensation and rewards program fuels employee development, self-esteem, and performance, resulting in a healthier organization.

TRADITIONAL COMPENSATION AND REWARDS

Historically, pay programs often merely compensated employees for showing up and looking busy. Traditional programs such as merit pay attempted to justify employee pay and increases with annual performance appraisals that were skewed, at best. Supervisor biases, inaccurate or un-fair performance measures, difficulty in assessment, inertia, and the like, undermine the intent of rewarding individual performance, particularly when combined with traditional compensation practices that prevent above-average performers from being paid appreciably more than their average or poor counterparts. In essence, traditional pay fails to recognize and reward worker performance differences.

Missing, too, have been links between compensation and reward pro-grams to employee growth and development and organizational goals. Traditional pay rewards performance, but "performance without growth and development will stagnate or even decline" (Gilley, Boughton, and Maycunich 1999, 139). Failure to align pay with strategic company goals sabotages organizational growth and is yet another indicator of outdated, ineffective compensation and reward practices.

Failures and Fads

Antiquated, cumbersome, or obsolete pay programs prevail, unfortu-nately, throughout companies large and small. According to Flannery, Hofrichter, and Platten (1996), compensation strategies have failed to keep pace with the myriad of changes affecting organizations over the past few decades. The General Motors strike, Northwest Airlines pilot strike, and NBA lockout (all in 1998) attest to the importance of pay and benefits, even to those at the upper end of the socioeconomic scale. New organizational processes, procedures, strategies, and philosophies are un-dermined by archaic, ineffective, or "latest fad" compensation programs that often hinder more than help.

We recently worked with a large insurance company that had at-tempted to integrate skill-based pay throughout its customer service de-partment. One department manager spent many hours researching the particular skills needed by successful customer service representatives at various grades, grouping these skills into distinct, measurable modules, and assigning dollar values to each. Implementation of the program proved its downfall. All individuals were tested to determine their skill level, then told that no one would be started above a certain wage, despite their experience on the job. Further, no employee could advance more than two skill levels in any twelve-month period—a practice that completely discounted a representative's learning curve and speed. This company's attempt at a latest fad discouraged an entire department, greatly increased employee absenteeism and turnover, and decreased loyalty and commitment. Fortunately, the company quickly recognized the error of its ways and discontinued the new pay program, learning a valuable lesson in the process.

Changes Affecting Organizations

Organizations, like society, are experiencing profound changes as never before. Traditional, hierarchical, centralized firms resist change, clinging tenaciously to old, comfortable programs and procedures. Developmental organizations embrace change in technology, globalization, socialization of the workforce—and compensation.

For example, computer technology has provided access to a plethora of information, has enhanced employee speed and productivity, and has brought the world closer together. Many tedious, time-consuming tasks, from inventory tracking to document preparation and processing, have been mastered by personal computers. Telecommuting permits many workers the convenience of working at home, a benefit to both employer and employee in terms of cost and time savings.

The Internet links individuals, businesses, and other organizations around the world, mitigating barriers and fostering globalization. Global rivals provide another complex challenge to the already competitive nature of business, yielding new or increased stresses at every level of the organization.

The workplace itself has undergone dramatic change in employee composition as more women and minorities have entered the workforce and ascended to positions of power and authority. The new social and work order faces increased societal pressures and thus demands a response from employers in the form of flexibility of scheduling (part-time positions, job sharing), telecommuting, child care and elder care provisions, and so forth.

Traditional organizations attempt to maximize the benefits of recent change by increasing employee goals, demanding greater output, downsizing, and so forth—all aimed at producing a leaner, more efficient, and profitable organization. Pay strategy has largely been ignored, or forgotten.

Although these changes may have increased employee productivity (and job-related stress), pay and rewards in most organizations have not evolved to effectively compensate individuals for their increased effort, contribution, learning, and development. Fatigued, stressed workers are turning to their employers for relief.

Developmental organizations rise to the challenges presented by the winds of change. They understand that evolution in society, competition, and the workplace necessitates transformation in the boardroom. Instead of fearing change they welcome it. Given the fiercely competitive nature of the dynamic global business environment, organizations must exploit every possible advantage—including that offered by compensation strategies.

BUILDING A DEVELOPMENTAL COMPENSATION AND REWARDS PROGRAM

Developmental organizations epitomize the essence of change—they are dynamic, energetic, flexible, and forward-thinking. They are willing to reengineer traditional processes and programs in favor of revolutionary reflection and rebirth aimed at propelling the organization and its employees forward. Continuous employee growth and development lead to constant organizational improvement.

Williams and Sunderland (1998, 12–13) believe that well-designed developmental compensation and reward programs exhibit the following attributes:

- Rewards are linked to business strategy.
- Program objectives are clearly articulated (participants know what is being rewarded and why).
- Rewards support the organization's culture.

- Pay-outs are related to actual business performance.
- Program design is adaptable to changing business conditions.
- All elements of the program are clearly communicated and fully understood by employees.
- Employees participate in program design.
- Employees perceive that the program has value.
- All elements of the program are regularly reviewed for effectiveness in meeting stated objectives.

Establishing a Developmental Compensation and Rewards Philosophy

The organization's overall compensation and rewards philosophy guides the formulation of long-term compensation and reward strategies. A developmental philosophy aligns compensation and rewards with strategic business goals while encouraging activities, both individual and team, that promote employee learning, reflection, and renewal. Examples include participation in development activities, self-analysis, discussions with performance coaches (mentor and career counselor roles), goal-setting, and entrepreneurship.

An effective developmental compensation and rewards philosophy reflects the importance of change and remaining flexible in adapting to the demands and constraints of a dynamic, ever-shifting business environment. A continuously improving pay program is characterized by constant assessment and refinement, just as with any other organizational initiative or department. Developmental compensation practices remain responsive to organizational initiatives, employee needs, and competitive pressures.

A developmental pay philosophy identifies the participants in compensation and rewards program decision making (human resource, managers, supervisors, employees), their degree of involvement, and their accountability. According to Schuster and Zingheim (1992, 59), "employee involvement in the development, implementation, and monitoring of total compensation programs is clearly a new pay tactic." In addition to promoting developmental objectives, input from all organizational levels provides different perspectives and helps ensure acceptance and participation.

Rewarding the Right Things

Developmental organizations provide opportunities for and reward the right things. Examples of "right things" include long-term solutions, learning new skills, reflection and renewal, working in teams, creativity, entrepreneurship, and leadership.

Long-Term Solutions. Historically, many executives and managers embraced short-term solutions—convenient quick fixes such as downsizing, layoffs, and reducing employee benefits—that failed to satisfy long-range strategic organizational objectives. Customer, investor, and competitor pressures demand immediate results, often undermining the integrity of sound, long-term objectives necessary to maintain viability.

Developmental pay strategies focus on the business horizon and rewarding the long-term activities necessary to reach it. The emphasis on organizational effectiveness forces managers to concentrate on measurable, meaningful initiatives capable of sustaining indefinite long-term growth. Examples of desirable long-range behaviors include investing in leadership training, mentoring programs, encouraging employee entrepreneurship, and new product development.

Learning New Skills. Because employees are a firm's greatest asset, its long-range compensation and reward strategies should encourage its employees to grow and develop through continuous learning. Developmental organizations encourage employee growth at all stages of career and professional progress. These firms assess employee needs and potential for growth, providing abundant, pertinent learning opportunities and application in areas of importance, such as computer and Internet competency, communications, current job-related tasks, and supervisory skills.

Employees are encouraged not only to participate in learning activities, but to apply their knowledge on the job. This long-term compensation and reward strategy should also reward executives, managers, and supervisors for establishing environments instrumental to learning acquisition and transfer (Gilley, Boughton, and Maycunich 1999). A culture of learning and application permeates the developmental organization, instilling in managers and employees the importance of continuous improvement of individual and team skills, ultimately resulting in enhanced organizational performance.

We have had the pleasure of working with a firm in the financial services industry that has gone to great lengths to encourage employee development by offering a host of learning opportunities, coordinated by the human resources department in cooperation with its member divisions and departments. The HR staff works with managers to assess employee needs and provide learning opportunities covering a broad range of topics. Learning events are widely publicized, published in a corporate catalog and regular newsletters, promoted by their developers (often a team of employees, supervisors, managers, and HR experts), and facilitated by department managers, HR experts, or both. Employees have no doubt that their learning, growth, and development are encouraged not only by their supervisors but by the corporation as well.

Reflection and Renewal.   Developmental organizations expand beyond learning organizations in their quest for and support of employee growth. Learning new skills or acquiring additional competencies is not enough. True growth and development require reflection on the part of employees. By reflecting, an individual examines his or her learning and application, assesses victories as well as failures, and alters behavior on the basis of this analysis. Changed behavior as the result of reflection leads to employee renewal—a rebirth of self and a philosophy manifested as permanent growth and development. Enhanced organizational performance capability is a natural consequence.

Collaboration and Teamwork.   On the surface, organizations appear to encourage collaboration and teamwork. In reality, firms continue to compensate and reward employees for their individual efforts. Annual performance appraisals, for example, typically stress individual skills, competencies, and attitudes, rarely taking into account collaboration and teamwork attributes such as loyalty, support, cooperation, or communication.

Developmental organizations identify desirable, effective collaboration and teamwork components, communicate these to their employees, stress their importance, incorporate teamwork skills into the evaluation process, and reward these talents accordingly. Working in teams provides numerous opportunities for employees to learn from each other, assess, reflect, and renew from the experience. A winning attitude disseminates from the team to its individual members, spreading throughout the unit, department, and the organization.

Developmental organizations are serious about enhancing collaboration and teamwork, capitalizing on these moments to improve the organization. Rewarding these activities solidifies the organization's commitment to the employee, team, department, and overall growth and development.

The team that wins together should be rewarded together. Regrettably, although many firms involve their employees in formal and informal group activities, few businesses compensate employees for their team performance. Developmental organizations establish team goals *and* performance rewards. Successful teams may be compensated monetarily or with other meaningful incentives.

Not all employees are members of formal teams. Regardless, all individuals experience opportunities to participate in teamlike settings on a daily basis by virtue of working within an organization. We all interact with co-workers within our own divisions, departments, or units, and often cross-functionally with others. These constant connections offer a multitude of occasions for using teamwork skills. Indeed, our success at work depends upon our ability to function as a vital member of the organizational team; thus, rewarding these behaviors closely aligns with business goals and objectives.

Creativity.   Fear of failure or punishment prevents many employees from expressing their creativity. Organizations that stifle employee creativity neglect the benefits of their workers' experience and expertise. Developmental organizations encourage risk taking on the part of employees, understanding that learning occurs from failure and often leads to ultimate success. Employee ideas and creativity are often credited with cost savings, new product development, improvement of existing products, streamlined processes, or elimination of redundant or unnecessary (and definitely costly) procedures.

Compensation programs that encourage creativity reward the sharing of ideas; promote the free flow of communication between managers, supervisors, and employees; and invite risk taking. Developmental organizations build climates of creativity, encouraging all employees to let their creative juices flow, and include creativity in employee responsibilities. From suggestion boxes to innovation incentives to regular team or unit brainstorming meetings, fostering creativity is a simple concept that can yield enormous benefits for employees and the organization.

Entrepreneurship.   Developmental organizations recognize and reward entrepreneurial traits, which often serve as the catalyst of successful learning, reflection, and renewal, thus sending a powerful message throughout the firm. These entrepreneurial activities improve business performance as personnel operate "outside the box" in search of new efficiencies or processes.

Meyer and Allen (1994, 34) have identified ten personal characteristics of entrepreneurs:

- persistent—tenacious, refusing to abandon a project until it is complete
- creative—willing to try something unconventional; searches for new ways of approaching problems
- responsible—answerable for their own conduct and actions; own their behaviors
- inquisitive—constantly asking questions, searching for answers
- goal oriented—know what they want to accomplish; establish priorities; formulate a plan for making it happen
- independent—autonomous, self-reliant; make up their own minds; set their own schedules
- demanding—unwilling to settle for mediocrity; constantly seeking to improve themselves and their environment
- confident—have faith in themselves and their decisions

- risk taking—not afraid of adversity; put themselves on the line for their beliefs; willing to tackle the unknown
- restless—unsatisfied with the status quo, seeking constant challenge and improvement

The application of these skills within firms is called intrapreneurship (Pinchot and Pellman 1999). Employees in intrapreneurial firms face challenges similar to those encountered by traditional entrepreneurs: how to develop personnel, grow the business, combat and exceed the competition, and prepare for the next century. Just as business owners reap the specific benefits (freedom, creativity, flexibility, income potential) of their motivation and efforts, so do workers of intrapreneurial organizations.

Leadership.   Many employees possess leadership skills, yet lack an available forum to exhibit these competencies on the job. Leadership can be found at all levels of an organization, not just at the top. Flannery, Hofrichter, and Platten (1996, 169–170) have identified the following leadership roles within organizations:

- team leaders—formally appointed team guides, often pulled "from the ranks"
- innovators and creators—knowledge or idea authorities valued for their expertise in important areas
- translators—transform the organization's ideas (particularly those of innovators and creators) into marketable concepts
- producers/orchestrators—are tapped for specific skills, often temporarily spearheading new projects for which their particular leadership skills are most valuable
- change agents—are responsible for transforming some element of the organization; possessing traits such as charisma, authority, or vision, these individuals boldly initiate change

Too many inflexible firms fail to tap into the wealth of leadership available within their own walls, content to pool power and authority among a select few. These shortsighted behaviors prevent talented, qualified employees from making valuable contributions that improve organizational effectiveness.

Leadership traits include advocacy, servancy, vision, initiative, risk taking, results orientation, self-sacrifice, long-term focus, dedication, flexibility, responsibility, accountability, and so forth. Skills include creativity, ability to inspire, and coaching aptitude. Developmental organizations incorporate leadership attributes into job descriptions and responsibilities, provide opportunities for leadership expression and development, and assign mentors to help develop leadership potential among budding managers.

Leadership reward strategies must closely align with the firm's developmental culture, values, goals, and objectives. Developmental organizations bolster and reward leadership talents with base pay, benefits, and incentives commensurate with an individual's effort and results.

ESTABLISHING DEVELOPMENTAL GOALS

Identifying actions or attributes to be rewarded is the precursor to establishing an individual's developmental goals. With the guidance of their performance coaches and mentors, employees develop specific, measurable, attainable, realistic, and time-based (SMART) goals that link their personal and professional growth with organizational goals.

Once developmental goals have been identified, a realistic plan for achievement must be conceived and implemented. Additional learning may be necessary, followed by the exhibition of concepts as proof of ability to transfer new knowledge to the job. Once mastery is proven, the analysis phase reveals an employee's ability to reflect upon successes or failures, evaluating the circumstances and outcomes of decisions made and actions taken. This reflective insight incorporates the learned lessons from each success or failure into the fabric of an individual's essence. Behavioral changes influencing beliefs transcend mere altered actions, resulting in renewed energy and spirit—a rebirth of sum and substance, indicative of true growth and development. Enhanced individual performance capacity results.

Employees must clearly understand the organization's goals, their part in helping accomplish these goals, and the potential rewards commensurate with doing so.

STEPS IN BUILDING A DEVELOPMENTAL COMPENSATION AND REWARD PROGRAM

As the old saying goes, we do not plan to fail, we fail to plan. Obviously, developing a program as critical and complex as compensation requires a strategic plan that is well conceived, designed, implemented, and monitored. Adhering to and championing the process will help master the plan.

Flannery, Hofrichter, and Platten (1996, 247–250) offer the following ten principles of dynamic pay:

1. Align your compensation with your organization's culture, values, and strategic business goals. Pay should be integrated with all aspects of the business.
2. Link compensation to other changes. Pay should support and reinforce organizational change initiatives.
3. Time your compensation program to best support your other change initiatives. Timing is everything. Pay should not force or lag behind change.
4. Integrate pay with other people processes. Pay is not a substitute for developing relationships with employees.
5. Democratize the pay process. Incorporate employee opinions and decisions in compensation and rewards.
6. Demystify compensation. Communication counts, knowledge is power. Share the wealth, so to speak, in more than the traditional way.
7. Measure results. Performance can and should be measured with fairness and consistency.
8. Refine. Refine again. Refine some more. Continually improve the compensation program—analyze and revise. Keep up with the times.

9. Be selective. Don't take to heart everything you hear or read about pay.
10. Don't fall victim to the latest fads. Quick fixes are fantasy.

Schuster and Zingheim (1992, 66) concur that today's organizations are vastly different from those of a century or even a few years ago and thus require new, updated pay programs. As such, pay programs offer the following steps in the development and execution of new, highly involved compensation strategies:

Step 1: Define the project and the expected results.
Step 2: Audit the current compensation and reward program.
Step 3: Establish an involvement process.
Step 4: Design a program that motivates growth and development.
Step 5: Communicate with others and conduct training.
Step 6: Monitor and evaluate.

Step 1: Define the Project and the Expected Results

To define a project and its expected results, organizations must ask themselves a myriad of questions: Precisely what are we doing? What do we want to occur as a result of implementing a developmental pay strategy? Who will be affected? Is anyone left out? What will the organization look like as a consequence? How will the organization and its employees be impacted? When will each party realize results?

Answering these questions clarifies organizational and employee expectation, allowing comparison and linkage to culture, values, goals, and objectives. Organizations, in cooperation with executives, managers, supervisors, and employees, must define realistic expectations that meet SMART criteria.

Step 2: Audit the Current Compensation and Reward Program

According to Williams and Sunderland (1998), knowing exactly where one is helps decide where one wants to be: hence, the importance of auditing one's current compensation and reward program. First, identify all reward and recognition practices currently being used (e.g., merit increases, promotion practices, bonus and incentive programs, profit sharing, stock options, special training or career development, and service awards). Second, calculate the cost associated with each practice. For example, businesses might calculate the percentage of payroll allocated for merit and promotion, the cost of annual bonuses and incentives, the funds earmarked for growth and development, and the like. Third, identify the return in employee productivity and performance associated with each reward practice. Fourth, determine whether current practices effectively reward what the organization values most, such as quality, learning, growth, and development.

Williams and Sunderland (1998) contend that many organizations cannot determine the cost/benefit ratio of their rewards practice and thus are unable to ascertain which rewards motivate employees and which do not. Additionally, they maintain that organizations perceive that their investment in certain reward practices exceeds return. One reason may be that employees do not appreciate or value the investment that their organizations make in specific categories.

Many have echoed the belief that "what gets measured and rewarded gets done" (Gilley, Boughton, and Maycunich 1999; Williams and Sunderland 1998; LeBoeuf 1985). Thus, recognizing and rewarding great performance and success stemming from employee growth and development breeds additional superior performance. Mindful of this reality, developmental organizations guarantee that employee growth and development efforts will be rewarded appropriately and at levels that sufficiently motivate them to produce results valued by the organization.

Step 3: Establish an Involvement Process

Involvement of all organizational levels and representative members in the creation of a developmental compensation and rewards plan must begin early in the process. Neglecting to involve all stakeholders in the planning phase leads to lack of acceptance and support during implementation and execution. Additionally, ignoring employee involvement indicates a lack of understanding of the value and power of employee commitment to company success (Williams and Sunderland 1998, 15). Shared decision making reflects the nature of developmental organizations, which is trusting, risk taking, and committed to building relationships that nourish the growth of its constituents and itself. Given the critical importance and impact of pay decisions, employee involvement makes sense.

Each of us is motivated differently. As such, it is the supervisor's or manager's responsibility to uncover our hidden motivators so that they may be maximized. Doing so requires the supervisor or manager to interact with us; to develop a positive, trusting, supportive working relationship; and to learn what makes each of us tick. For some of us, cash remains the most powerful incentive; for others, company and peer recognition, nonmonetary rewards, and so forth, may be the key.

Healthy, reciprocal relationships established by the aforementioned supervisor or manager are called synergistic relationships (Gilley and Boughton 1996). One component of synergistic relationships critical to the success of a developmental pay program is the free flow of communication. Combined with a spirit of involvement, cooperation, and zest for employee and organizational growth and development, open communication helps ensure a viable developmental compensation and rewards program.

Step 4: Design a Program That Motivates Growth and Development

A well-designed compensation and rewards program supports organizational objectives while nurturing employee growth and development. Keeping all participants focused on desired results, involved, and cooperating will require numerous developmental conditions:

- the understanding and support of the entire organization
- constant and complete communications
- continuous evaluation and feedback
- regular, timely progress reports
- a plan for resolving differences and problems
- well-defined responsibilities and accountability for results

Williams and Sunderland (1998, 14) believe that compensation and reward programs designed only to produce short-term results or to focus at the job or task level, without accounting for the broader priorities of an organization, miss a critical opportunity to align performance in a meaningful way throughout the organization. With this in mind, developmental organizations establish and clearly communicate organizationwide growth and development requirements and demonstrate how these help achieve the business results needed. Organizations must, furthermore, communicate the behaviors and actions that will bring about desired results and link them to the growth and development initiatives most appropriate. Next, organizations tie compensation and reward practices to these critical growth and development requirements, varying the size of the award with the results achieved—the greater the achievement, the bigger the reward.

Developmental compensation and reward programs are designed to support the organization's culture and values (Williams and Sunderland 1998; Flannery, Hofrichter, and Platten 1996; Gilley and Boughton 1996). Further, organizations serious about becoming developmental value employee growth and development, making certain that workers are rewarded for their developmental efforts via public recognition for their efforts, promotion within the organization, and so on (Williams and Sunderland 1998). Failure to do so extinguishes the behaviors and attitudes so necessary to adopting a continuous learning and developmental atmosphere, and prevents organizations from making the final evolutionary leap to developmental.

Organizations that believe that employee growth and development are essential to their ultimate success design compensation and reward programs that ensure personnel "ownership." That is, employees believe that their individual growth and development, which improves their personal performance and productivity, contributes to overall organizational success—for which they will be rewarded. When this attitude is pervasive within a firm, evolution to developmental organization status is promoted.

Utilizing a common problem-solving technique guides the effort to design a developmental pay plan. A well-defined and tested process, which includes the following steps, focuses the team on achieving results: First, define the problem or opportunity. Second, list the alternatives and, third, evaluate them. Fourth, choose and implement an option. Last, assess your results and make appropriate adjustments.

Define the Problem or Opportunity.   A complex compensation program may pose many problems and at the same time offer many opportunities. Each much be accurately identified and handled thoroughly. Examples of problems include high turnover or loss of technical talent, effectively compensating field sales personnel, or motivating part-time employees. Opportunities abound for increasing employee (and organizational) production or fostering employee growth and development (via learning events, encouraging risk taking, and the like).

List Alternatives.   When they encounter a problem, developmental organizations utilize techniques such as brainstorming, nominal grouping, and so forth. They encourage input from all participants, taking care to allow for equal time and full expression of team members. At this point, idea formulation is crucial. Criticism is not useful now; discussion and evaluation will come later.

Evaluate Alternatives.   Open, frank discussion of the advantages, disadvantages, and alignment with organizational goals of each option helps ascertain viability. Assessment may require testing of an alternative on a small population of employees, focus group discussion, simulation, and the like. We hesitate to include cost-benefit analysis in this discussion unless a long-term focus is possible. Cost-benefit analysis as a technique typifies traditional evaluation yet often impedes the goal of a developmental organization. Although cost is undoubtedly an important element, it should not be the deciding factor.

Choose and Implement an Option.   Based on the preceding analysis, the team should reach consensus with respect to a feasible alternative. The choice should reflect the option that best exemplifies the spirit of individual and organizational growth and development.

Assess Results and Make Appropriate Adjustments.   Assessment, as defined by the plan, should occur regularly, for example, monthly (as in performance incentives bestowed on a weekly or monthly basis), quarterly (as in team profit-sharing bonuses if paid quarterly), semiannually (for acquisition and transfer of learning), or annually (employee suggestions resulting in organizational efficiencies or cost savings, and the like). Given the long-term, developmental nature of the compensation plan, some component's evaluation may not be possible in a span as short as a year. For example, some entrepreneurial activities, such as new product development, may warrant a special reward or recognition. Regardless of the frequency, regular progress reports and employee feedback are appropriate barometers of future option success.

A good choice can be made better; a poor one should be altered or discontinued. Designers must set aside their egos and personal biases when implementing or changing a feature—the good of the organization prevails above personal preference or "ownership" of an idea. A well-designed pay plan, its architects, and its beneficiaries must remain flexible, encouraging and allowing for modifications designed to continually improve its impact on employees and the organization.

Step 5: Communication and Training

Thorough, abundant communications are instrumental in the success of any new initiative or program. Compensation, given its importance in all of our lives, is no exception. Unfortunately, communications, or the lack thereof, is the Achilles heel of most organizations. Withholding or gatekeeping information merely causes fear and confusion on the part of employees.

Labovitz and Rosansky (1997) assert that developmental organizations make certain that every employees know why they are in business. This strategic effort enables every organizational member to understand the big picture, which gives employees at different levels of the firm opportunities to see how their piece of the puzzle fits into the whole (Williams and Sunderland 1998, 14). Providing employees with a big-picture orientation facilitates their understanding of where the organization is going, why it is going there, how they contribute to reaching the firm's final destination, and what requirements the business will make of them toward this end. Clear, honest, precise communication motivates employees to adopt growth and development plans in concert with the organization's vision and strategy. Organizations then link compensation and reward programs to these plans, further reinforcing continuous individual renewal.

Developmental organizations share information enthusiastically, devoting significant time and resources to communicate the pay program's objectives and alignment with company goals clearly, efficiently, and effectively. Successful communications require enunciation by three integral groups—top management, program designers, and supervisors. Upper management's responsibility is to communicate their support and the pay plan's alignment with organizational values and strategic business goals. Designers are charged with sharing their support and the specifics about program design and implementation and with addressing questions. Supervisors are responsible for facilitating employee understanding, motivating acceptance, and implementation (Schuster and Zingheim 1992).

Effective communications take many forms. Human resource department communiqués; company newsletters; supervisory one-on-ones; informational meetings and question/answer sessions at the unit, department, division, and company level; e-mails; promotional events; and the like must be utilized profusely. Communications must clearly and honestly convey developmental compensation and reward differences, benefits, goals, strategies, advantages, disadvantages, time frames, and participants. Effective communications invite employee feedback, stressing the developmental nature of the pay program, including its flexibility and continuous improvement.

To be effective, communications may require paired training to solidify or clarify particularly complex aspects of the developmental compensation and rewards strategy. Training event facilitators may include program designers, supervisors, and even top management. For example, we worked with a large insurance company whose telephone sales unit implemented a new sales compensation plan that incorporated base salary plus incentive elements for increasing core product sales, non-core sales, tenure, customer retention, and acceptable (low or declining) claims ratios. This complex plan promised significant rewards commensurate with performance. To reduce confusion and fear, and to ensure employee acceptance, unit management facilitated training in which employees were taught how to calculate incentive pay based on their individual performance (base salaries did not change from current levels). This meeting successfully demonstrated the rudimentary workings of the new program, which employees were able to understand, influence, and embrace.

Step 6: Monitor and Evaluate

Assess, assess, and assess some more. Any new program needs monitoring and routine evaluation to ensure compliance and alignment with its goals and objectives. Flexible, proactive designs demand modification should the new compensation and reward program fall short of organizational expectations.

The design process must include appraisal and review elements in the formal plan. An effective evaluation team includes members of management, designers, and employees—a representation of those influencing and subject to the developmental compensation and rewards program. Further, timely evaluation may need to occur as often as monthly or quarterly; annual assessment permits ineffective systems to do more harm than good.

DEVELOPMENTAL ORGANIZATION COMPENSATION AND REWARD STRATEGIES

Compensation and rewards have been studied, at length, for years. Traditionally, efforts to motivate workers and improve organizational performance focused on universal motivators—a one-size-fits-all strategy. This tactic ignores worker individuality, priorities, and degree of motivation from intrinsic and extrinsic rewards. Developmental organizations recognize the power and importance of individualism, offering a variety of incentives to reward unique employees along their journey of growth, reflection, and renewal.

Rewards for growth and development may take the form of promotions, pay raises, special recognition or rewards ceremonies, additional authority, participation in prominent teams, and so forth. Following are rewards intended to promote developmental organization philosophy and practices:

- cash
- recognition
- noncash incentives
- travel
- responsibility and authority
- personal growth and advancement
- ownership
- freedom and independence
- vacation, leisure time, and sabbaticals
- fun

Cash

Money is the most popular form of compensation and is still a powerful motivator. For example, Hein and Alonzo (1998, 40) reported in an *Incentive Magazine* survey of salespeople, that 79 percent chose cash as the favored reward. Interestingly, as the respondents' salary increased, the importance of cash decreased. Of those who make under $50,000 per year, 83 percent chose cash, compared to 66 percent of those who earn between $151,000 and $200,000.

Money remains a status symbol for many, representing power and prestige. Money, and the things it buys, exhibits to the world our success. Thus, monetary rewards do get results. Developmental organizations link monetary rewards to strategic business goals while encouraging employee learning, reflection, and rebirth. Following are some successful individual and group reward strategies.

Profit Sharing.   Profit sharing, a popular plan, allows employees to receive a portion of the company's profits on a regular basis. Many companies, such as Steelcase, pay on a quarterly basis, some pay annually. Employees are motivated to increase organizational profitability, usually a result of improved company performance and growth (a natural consequence of personal growth and development).

Gain Sharing. Gain sharing differs from profit-sharing in that groups of employees improve productivity via more efficient and effective use of human resources, capital, or materials. Savings from productivity gains are shared with group members in the form of cash bonuses. Gain sharing, as a result, promotes teamwork and cooperation.

Pay for Knowledge. Also called skill-based or competency-based pay, this system ties base pay and pay increases to job knowledge. Multi-skills-based pay remunerates an employee according to the number of different jobs he or she can perform within the organization. Increased-knowledge-based compensation links pay with the amount of knowledge or range of skills an employee has within a single specialty or job classification. Pay-for-knowledge plans encourage employees to increase their learning and acquisition of knowledge and skills.

Individual Incentives. Individual incentives are performance-based rewards linking cash bonuses to measurable outputs such as number of parts processed, customer service calls answered, claims processed, and sales closed. To be effective, incentives must be perceived by employees as significant enough to warrant additional effort. Often combined with spirited competitions within units or departments, individual incentives may adversely impact teamwork as aggressive employees place their own interests above those of the group. Developmental compensation and benefit systems take care to design incentive plans that encourage individual performance that improves—and does not sabotage—overall organizational health.

Group Incentives. Group incentives reward performance of a particular set of employees, either a small group, unit, or department. If group performance improves or reaches a certain goal, its members are rewarded accordingly. This practice bolsters teamwork and cooperation, often resulting in a closeness and camaraderie absent before the inception of the reward program. Group incentives are effective motivators for sales, service, production, customer service teams, and so forth, whenever outputs may be directly impacted and measurable.

Recognition

Recognition is second only to cash. It is impossible to negate the power of praise and the genuine pleasure we feel when acknowledged for our efforts. Recognition boosts our self-esteem and validates our abilities. Developmental organizations recognize not only stellar performance, but goals reached, acquired learning (such as internal or external courses taken), degrees achieved, teamwork, community involvement, promotions, product innovations, new product concepts, cost-savings ideas, and so forth.

Appropriate recognition includes timely praise for a job well done; involvement in major project teams, acquisitions, or strategy sessions; employee-of-the-month or similar awards; honors banquets; trophies, certificates, and plaques; publicity in the company newsletter; formal and informal announcements by supervisors or managers; company gifts such as pens, rings, and watches; membership in a president's club or hall of fame; and so on.

James E. Knight, director of corporate learning and development for Steelcase North America, says, "Recognition is more important than rewards. Any time you throw dollars at things you gum 'em up." One of his employees, Mike Wykes, an acquaintance of ours, recently contributed a chapter to an edited book. Jim highlighted him in a company newsletter, which yielded Mike a great deal of admiration from his co-workers and publicity within the firm. According to Jim, Mike felt that this recognition was worth "more than a five-thousand-dollar bonus."

Noncash Incentives

Noncash incentives such as gift certificates, company merchandise and clothing, and other prizes have monetary value and thus are desirable incentives. These noncash incentives are usually much smaller in value (often less than fifty dollars) and are bestowed more frequently, such as to promote weekly sales incentives, monthly competitions, and to encourage nominations for the customer service representative extra-mile award.

Travel

Certain groups, such as sales personnel, are accustomed to receiving travel awards to luxurious or exotic locations for superior performance. Recognizing the allure of travel, many companies have begun offering similar rewards for departments other than sales. Shopping excursions, day trips, and weekends at local resorts, amusement parks, and golf clubs are popular.

Responsibility and Authority

Employees prove themselves every day, from completing small, routine accomplishments to far exceeding personal and organizational expectations. Those willing and able to assume greater responsibility should be given opportunities to do so. Developmental organizations take care to balance additional responsibility with correspondingly increased authority. Responsibility without authority is a frustrating, discouraging phenomenon.

Personal Growth and Advancement

In developmental organizations, supervisors and managers function as career coaches, helping employees map their professional paths throughout the firm. Workers who have exhibited the desire and talent for additional responsibility and authority are prime candidates for advancement.

Developmental organizations treat personal growth as a routine business function, not an award for doing well. Internal, ongoing training and external education reimbursement send a powerful message that employee growth and development are critical to business success.

Ownership

We work harder, and smarter, for those things we own (such as a share of the business or decision making in initiatives, projects, and the like). Ownership inspires entrepreneurial actions such as improved productivity and efficiency. The opportunity to be a genuine owner is a powerful motivator.

Freedom and Independence

Enterprising employees welcome increased freedom and independence as a reward for good performance. Freedom takes many forms: the ability to work out of one's home, casual dress days, opportunities to work on a pet project, and so forth. Genuine growth and development are by-products of employee creativity set free. Independence may involve working alone on a project or without supervision. Independently working employees feel like trusted entrepreneurs and feel highly valued by their organization.

Vacation, Leisure Time, and Sabbaticals

Hardworking people push themselves to achieve personal and professional growth, often working overtime, evenings, or weekends. Since employers reap the benefits of extra effort and growth, it makes sense to compensate individuals for their endeavors. Too much work can cause frustration or burnout; thus, employees need time to relax and reenergize. Extra vacation or leisure time is an appropriate reward for someone who has devoted long hours to business pursuits. Similarly, sabbaticals provide refreshing "time out" in preparation for the next challenge.

Fun

Laughter is the best medicine. What better way is there to relieve the tension of challenging work situations than to engage in lighthearted, fun activities, particularly with one's co-workers? One of us worked for a division that regularly held golf outings, talent contests, bowling nights, road rallies, decorating contests, and the like. These amusements fostered a sense of teamwork, camaraderie, and goodwill while alleviating the stress that accumulates over time.

Many organizations encourage and support teams of volunteer employees, occasionally called "sunshine," "excitement," or "fun" committees to coordinate motivational activities. Often, service on the committee itself proves stimulating.

CONCLUSION

Compensation is designed to motivate employees to continue or increase production. This is certainly not a new concept. Developmental pay has different aims—to foster individual worker growth and performance by the following practices:

- being an extension of the organization's developmental philosophy
- rewarding the right things
- linking compensation with organizational goals and objectives
- creatively applying existing pay methods, such as individual incentives or profit sharing, in new ways
- being flexible and open to trying new pay methods for existing or novel situations
- constantly monitoring and assessing a pay method's effectiveness and alignment with strategic business goals and objectives

Encouraging the personal and professional growth and development of leaders, managers, and employees ultimately benefits organizations (Figure 11.1). Developmental organizations, functioning at a highly evolved level, rely on fluid, adaptable compensation and reward programs. No singular "right" strategy prevails; compensation and rewards may be simultaneously simple, sophisticated, structured, loose, innovative, proven, or ever-changing. The list goes on. Most important, however, is that compensation and rewards must be responsive to employee needs and organizational aims. In essence, compensation is linked to growth and development.

FIGURE 11.1   Checklist for a developmental compensation and rewards program

Is your organization's compensation and rewards program developmental?

Developmental compensation and rewards:

__ are based on a developmental philosophy
__ are linked to strategic business goals and objectives
__ are clearly defined and articulated to employees
__ are understood by employees
__ support the organization's developmental culture
__ are flexible and adaptable, like the developomental culture
__ involve employees in the program design
__ are perceived by employees to be of value
__ are regularly assessed and modified to ensure effectiveness
__ reward the right things:
    long-term solutions
    learning new skills
    individual reflection and renewal
    collaboration and teamwork
    employee creativity
    entrepreneurship
    leadership
__ link compensation and rewards to employee growth and development
__ employ a variety of compensation and reward stategies to meet employee needs

PART FOUR

The Developmental Organization Blueprint in Action

CHAPTER 12

Building the Developmental Organization

In the first eleven chapters of this book, we outlined the guiding principles that serve as the foundation for the developmental organization. We also identified the outcomes of the transformation from traditional to developmental organization. In this chapter, we provide a simple, straightforward set of steps for building the developmental organization. Thus, this chapter represents a synopsis of the critical information outlined in this book.

GUIDING PRINCIPLES OF THE DEVELOPMENTAL ORGANIZATION

Ten vital guiding principles underpin developmental organizations. These principles represent the infrastructure that supports the developmental organization, without which the firm would certainly crumble under the weight of organizational change. These guiding principles serve as the underlying philosophy by which all business decisions are made—the bricks and mortar that give the developmental organization strength.

335

Continuous Renewal and Performance Capacity

When organizations focus on never-ending growth and development, allowing their employees to take into account new and different information that expands employees' reservoir of performance capabilities, they are applying the principle of continuous renewal and performance capacity. As a result, the organization enjoys enhanced competitive readiness and the ability to constantly grow and develop, avoiding the plateau periods of maturity as well as the slippery slopes of decline.

Servant Leadership

The principle of servant leadership is based on the belief that leaders should serve others by advocating, supporting, and promoting their contributions and efforts. Servant leaders work tirelessly to help employees grow and develop, assisting staff in their struggle to become the best they can be, sharing organizational success, and making certain that other decision-makers are aware of their employees' contributions to achieving business results. They should also accept responsibility for their employees' failures and should celebrate their successes.

Internal Systems Working in Harmony

According to the principle of harmonious internal systems, separate but interdependent functions (i.e., leadership, structure, organizational culture, mission and strategy, management practices, work climate, policies and procedures) must work together to guarantee organizational success. Although the independent functions are entities unto themselves, they either directly or indirectly affect each of the others. Therefore, it is essential that organizations identify breakdowns or failures immediately and take corrective action.

Changeability

The changeability principle indicates that since change is constant, people and systems must change to guarantee long-term organizational success. In developmental organizations, executives, managers, employees, and HR professionals adopt new roles and accept new responsibilities in order to enhance organizational preparedness for growth and development. Preparedness is an essential ingredient for organizational renewal and competitive readiness.

Coachability

The principle of coachability maintains that employees must be selected based on their aptitude and desire for growth and development. As a result, they will be receptive to constructive criticism, suggestions, and honest efforts to help improve their performance. Employees with high coachability are willing to learn, discover, and accept new ways of performing. Additionally, they are enthusiastic about learning, interested in new methods and innovations, receptive to performance feedback, career-focused, inclined to compare themselves with high achievers, and predisposed to reflective and critical thinking skills.

The Right Person at the Right Place at the Right Time

Human resource planning, recruiting, and selection are based on the principle of the right person at the right place at the right time. The principle implies that the type, quantity, and quality of human resources recruited and selected will foster organizational renewal and enhance competitiveness. This principle asserts that an appropriate link with the organization's growth and development strategies (learning and change, career development, performance management, compensation and rewards) must be developed. Thus, human resource planning, recruiting, selection, and growth and development strategies will positively impact one another, providing continuous feedback that ensures improved business results.

Knowledge Construction and Continuous Lifelong Learning

The backbone of the developmental organization is the principle of knowledge construction and continuous lifelong learning, which asserts that employees are responsible for the acquisition, application, transfer, and integration of knowledge. The evidence of knowledge construction is generally demonstrated when employee performance and productivity improves. Employees are accountable for the utilization of knowledge on the job and responsible for continuous growth and development. Furthermore, employees are responsible for becoming career advocates, planners, and personal change agents using their newly acquired knowledge.

Endless Possibilities

The principle of endless possibilities reveals that there are countless career development opportunities for employees who identify their strengths and build on them accordingly. In developmental organizations, a partnership is forged between employees and the firm for the purpose of enhancing employee knowledge, skills, and abilities. Thus, career development is a quintessential organizational development activity, providing linkage between individual and organizational development, allowing for improved individual proficiencies, enhancing organizational renewal, and improving performance capacity.

Performance Mastery

The principle of performance mastery maintains that organizations orchestrate best practices by applying an effective, efficient performance management system. Performance mastery occurs when individuals rely on their strengths and perform without conscious awareness of the steps involved. Employees enjoy supreme satisfaction when allowed to demonstrate performance mastery; they feel invincible and powerful, wanting to repeat the performance over and over again. These experiences enhance employee self-esteem and shape their confidence. Repetition brings improvement, which leads to expertise—a cycle that developmental organizations employ to achieve goals. Moreover, exemplary performance occurs when employees enjoy caring, supportive environments that allow them to be their best. Master performers own their work, take responsibility for their own growth and development, and focus on both current and future obligations.

Continuous Motivation

The principle of continuous motivation is the foundation of all compensation and reward programs; thus, a well-designed program fuels employee growth and development, improves employee self-esteem, and enhances performance, resulting in a healthier organization. Developmental organizations are based on continuous motivation, utilizing strategies, philosophies, and goals to motivate employees to improve their performance and productivity. Most important, the principle of continuous motivation requires compensation and reward programs to be responsive to employee needs and organizational aims. In essence, compensation has linkage to growth and development.

OUTCOMES OF THE DEVELOPMENTAL ORGANIZATION

Applying the developmental organization blueprint generates several important outcomes, including dialogue; harmony through respect; interpersonal reciprocity; collaboration, camaraderie, and teamwork; a sense of belonging; shared reality and purpose; active engagement; and inspired growth and development. Collectively, these outcomes change an organization's culture from a product- and revenue-centered approach to a people-centered one, producing an atmosphere of cooperation, respect, and dignity that yields synergy. These outcomes are essential to enhancing organizational renewal and competitive readiness as well as the continuous growth and development of employees.

Dialogue

Dialogue involves active listening, sharing, high-quality two-way communications, and the free exchange of thoughts, ideas, and feelings. In the developmental organization, such communication is an active engagement between individuals attempting to understand one another's perceptional world. Dialogue is an intense interaction in which people suspend their own views and assumptions in an attempt to better understand another. The artist Bryon, in his 1989 Cubist drawing entitled *Dialogue*, reveals that dialogue occurs when people are in an interlocking embrace, demonstrating their involvement and commitment to one another. They are forever linked together because of their solidarity, affiliation, and association.

Dialogue requires involvement, which is the willingness to care and feel responsible for another person. Involvement requires a manager's active participation in his or her employees' problems and needs, implying that leaders, managers, and employees engage in activities that allow face-to-face contact.

Harmony through Respect

One of the best words to describe a developmental organization is harmony. The Merriam-Webster dictionary defines *harmony* as a pleasing arrangement of parts, an internal calm. This definition describes the work climate and organizational culture found in developmental organizations. Everything works in peace and tranquillity not common in traditional organizations.

Harmony is accomplished through respect—respect for individual performance, achievement, thoughts, ideas, and efforts. In other words, developmental organizations exhibit respect for individuals as persons of worth.

To facilitate harmony, developmental leaders and managers create environments conductive to sharing; they demonstrate acceptance via their willingness to allow employees to differ from one another. This willingness is based on the belief that each employee is a complex being made up of different experiences, values, beliefs, and attitudes (Gilley and Eggland 1992).

Interpersonal Reciprocity

A critical outcome of the developmental organization is a process known as interpersonal reciprocity. It involves the mutual exchange of actions and behaviors between two or more individuals. Interpersonal reciprocity requires empathy, attentiveness, and understanding. Empathy means having the ability to feel and describe the thoughts and feelings of others. Attentiveness involves listening and observing, which allows a person to be heard and observed without interruption or distraction. Understanding means recognizing and correctly interpreting the feelings, thoughts, and behaviors of another person.

Interpersonal reciprocity enables leaders, managers, and employees to treat others the way they themselves are treated. Thus, it is the ability to recognize, sense, and understand the feelings that another person communicates through his or her behavioral and verbal expressions, and to accurately communicate this understanding to that person (Gilley and Eggland 1992, 176–177).

Collaboration, Camaraderie, and Teamwork

When collaboration, camaraderie, and teamwork are present, employee motivation improves, which results in increased productivity, enhanced performance, and improved communication. These environmental factors produce organizational synergy, heightened cooperation, and tolerance.

Collaboration, camaraderie, and teamwork foster open, honest relationships between employees, relationships based on a deep concern for the well-being of others, and active participation on the part of all employees in the projects, tasks, and performance activities of others. Collaboration, camaraderie, and teamwork require employees to have the courage to relinquish control and dominance over their organizational partners. In developmental organization, employees make a gentle shift from authoritarian control to participation, which is less threatening to other employees. Participation allows employees to become agents of change, which helps them support the decisions made.

Sense of Belonging

Dialogue, harmony through respect, interpersonal reciprocity, and collaboration, camaraderie, and teamwork combine to provide employees with a sense of belonging within the organization. This ownership attitude encourages continuous involvement and participation, the results of which include improved quality, increased employee engagement, better performance, and enhanced organizational efficiency and effectiveness.

When employees feel that they are an intricate part of the organization, they are more willing to participate in quality improvement initiatives, change activities, reengineering efforts, and organizational development interventions. Furthermore, they are likely to share their insights and awareness with management to get involved in problem-solving activities, and to participate in strategic planning efforts. In short, employees that think and act like owners are more willing to give of themselves and make sacrifices for the good of the organization.

Shared Reality and Purpose

A common complaint among employees of traditional organizations is that they do not know where the firm is going or how they fit into the overall picture. In other words, they are lost and have no hope of finding their way through the fog of organizational complexity. Consequently, they fail to become actively involved in the improvement of the organization and resign themselves to doing their jobs without the enthusiasm necessary to bring about performance mastery.

In developmental organizations, employees have a shared reality and purpose, knowing how their efforts contribute to the achievement of business results and its respected value. Employees know when their contributions and efforts are appreciated and how their performance outputs fit into the organizational tapestry. Consequently, employees are able to assess their value and contributions, thus enhancing their worth and self-esteem.

Active Engagement

Developmental organizations foster active engagement on the part of their employees by creating conditions whereby employees become totally committed to the organization, its initiatives, and its efforts. Hence, employees are active change agents in search of ways to improve the organization. Employees become absorbed in daily business operations as well as the strategic direction of the firm, sharing their perspectives with management to improve the organization's effectiveness and efficiency.

Active engagement helps organizational leaders increase their knowledge of job-related problems and expand employee levels of influence to solve problems. The successful alignment of these two goals results in more harmonious and efficient organizations. To achieve this end, developmental leaders encourage risk-taking on the part of employees by providing a supportive decision-making climate. Developmental leaders create this climate by the following practices:

- trusting team members with meaningful levels of responsibility
- providing team members with the necessary autonomy to achieve results
- presenting challenging opportunities that stretch the individual abilities of team employees
- recognizing and rewarding superior performance
- standing behind employees and supporting them (Larson and LaFasto 1989, 126)

Inspired Growth and Development

At the heart of every developmental organization is inspired growth and development on the part of employees, which separates developmental organizations from traditional and learning organizations. Unless organizational leaders foster inspired growth and development, the benefits of the developmental organization will not be realized. Performance, productivity, organizational quality and efficiency, organizational effectiveness, and organizational renewal and competitive readiness will not improve. In fact, inspired growth and development is the very reason that developmental organizations exist.

FIFTEEN STEPS FOR BUILDING A DEVELOPMENTAL ORGANIZATION

Building a developmental organization is a challenging task requiring an understanding and commitment to the developmental organization blueprint featured in this book. Making the transition beyond the learning organization is a worthwhile and important undertaking, requiring tremendous effort and energy.

Although there is no single way of building a developmental organization, some clear guidelines and strategies can be presented to organizations desiring to make the journey.

1. *Determine the organization's developmental leadership capability.* Organizations should assess current leadership, scrutinizing its philosophy, talent, roles, responsibilities, and aptitude for change. By administering questionnaires like the *Principles of Developmental Leadership Questionnaire* (Figure 3.1), organizations can assess individual aptitude and readiness for change. Determining a baseline of leadership talent and developmental readiness allows organizations to orchestrate interventions designed to continuously improve developmental leadership capability.

2. *Recruit, select, and train developmental leaders and managers.* Organizations must start at the beginning, with a strategic plan designed to recruit and select the best developmental leaders and managers, then concentrate on training and retaining them. Recruiting and selecting the best allows organizations to concentrate on maximizing leadership strengths while creating an organizational structure that fosters development rather than "fixing" weaknesses of existing management.

3. *Apply the ten principles of developmental leadership.* Developmental leaders are servants of their employees and the organization. Living and manifesting a servantship style of leadership proves to employees that they are, indeed, the organization's greatest asset, worthy of organizational investment in continuous growth and development opportunities. The ten principles of developmental leadership (intrinsically oriented, employee-oriented, performance-oriented, and organizationally oriented principles) provide a blueprint by which leaders may craft their servant talents.

4. *Link growth and development initiatives to the organization's strategic business goals and objectives.* Goals and objectives must drive all organizational operations, directives, processes, and procedures to be successful. Initiatives not linked to the firm's goals and objectives may waste valuable time and resources on expectations not critical to organizational success. Individual growth and development must also be aligned with the firm's ultimate goals to ensure achievement of employee, department, division, or organizational objectives.

5. *Determine the organization's capability and readiness for change.* Prematurely launching into any new venture without adequate research often dooms the project to failure. The same holds true in organizations. Prior to embarking on change initiatives destined to transform the organization, one must determine the firm's capacity for and willingness to change. Absent sufficient indicators of readiness, leaders and managers must motivate and prepare all organizational members for upcoming change—stressing the benefits to both individual employees and the organization itself.

6. *Transform managers into employee growth and development experts.* Managers, given their responsibility for employee growth and development, must become experts in this art. Those unable to develop their personnel are poor managers indeed and are obviously incapable of doing the job for which they were hired. Given today's fiercely competitive business environment, organizations cannot afford mediocre managers unskilled in employee growth and development. The stakes are too high.

7. *Determine the strengths and weaknesses of the organizational system.* SWOT (strengths, weaknesses, opportunities, threats) analysis serves as a powerful tool when analyzing the organizational system, a complex set of interdependent components working in harmony toward a desired common end. Only via critical assessment of the entire organizational system (leadership, structure, work climate, managerial practices, mission, and strategy) will firms be able to improve their

processes, procedures, and management effectiveness along the journey of developmental evolution.

8. *Transform the organizational system into one that facilitates and supports employee growth and development.* The process is simple—grow and develop employees, and the organization will grow and develop with them. Implementation is often another matter. Successfully building an organizational system that supports employee growth, development, reflection, and renewal requires integration of all components of organizational life and manifestation of a developmental culture within each. A feat such as this requires commitment and dedication from all organizational members—leaders, managers, employees, and human resource professionals.

9. *Reengineer the human resource department, its practices, and its professionals.* Human resource professionals in developmental organizations have reached a new plateau—they are fully integrated within the structure of the firm, acting upon new roles and responsibilities that allow them to function as consultants (organizational development, performance management, management development), change agents, and partners within their organizations. These new roles and responsibilities challenge HR professionals to be flexible, adaptive, and benefactors of continuous growth and development themselves.

10. *Apply the human resource planning, recruitment, and selection process to acquire employees with high coachability and growth-and-development readiness.* Some individuals are predisposed to lifelong learning, having long ago discovered the joy and benefits of continuous growth and development. Employees such as these view challenges as opportunities, accept feedback as constructive, seek new ways of approaching problems or situations, and constantly search for new knowledge or meaning. In essence, they are highly coachable. Highly coachable personnel desire continual development, recognizing the importance of growth in their personal and professional lives. Developmental organizations actively seek individuals such as

these, recruiting "best-fit" developmental employees whose ideologies and practices align with those of the firm.

11. *Implement developmental learning approaches.* Developmental organizations, leaders, and managers are learning partners with employees. Identifying and implementing the five phases and seventeen laws of the learning and change process prepares organizational members for developmental learning—a prerequisite to the reflection and renewal necessary to enhance continuous growth and development at the individual and organizational levels.

12. *Create career development programs that build on strengths while managing weaknesses.* Identifying strengths and weakness is just as critical at the individual level as it is at the organizational level. After all, organizations are merely compilations of the collective strengths, weaknesses, talents, and abilities of their members. Maximizing strengths leads to champion performance, whereas "fixing" weaknesses merely makes employees adequate. The choice is clear.

13. *Implement performance alignment at the organizational and performer levels.* Performance alignment in developmental organizations involves understanding why employees fail to achieve desired results. Understanding the numerous causes allows developmental managers to implement the principles of performance improvement and apply the performance alignment process. At the organizational level, performance alignment consists of seven steps; at the performer level, nine. Successful performance alignment leads to performance greatness, a desired outcome for any individual in any firm.

14. *Redesign compensation and reward programs to support growth and development.* Creating a developmental compensation and reward program starts with philosophy and ends with results. In between are rewards for the "right" things (such as leadership, creativity, entrepreneurship, learning new skills, and growth and development), flexibility, goal setting, and responsive compensation and reward strategies.

15. *Evaluate the impact and utility of the developmental organization approach on long-term business results.* Developmental organizations are in a constant state of assessment, reflection, and renewal, particularly of their own performance. A critical foundation of the developmental organization is its ability to remain flexible, adaptive, responsive, and willing to change in order to meet long-term goals. As a result, no single formula exists for making the transformation to the developmental organization—other than the collective desire of all organizational members to be the best that they can be. Dedication and commitment to individual growth and development leads to the same at the organizational level, along with achievement of long-term desired business results. We would wish you and your organization luck in your quest if such a thing existed. Instead, we wish you success in your journey beyond the learning organization.

REFERENCES

Beer, M. 1983. What is organizational development? In *The Training and Development Sourcebook,* edited by L. S. Baird, C. E. Schneier, and D. Laird. Amherst, Mass.: HRD Press.

Berke, G. B. 1990. *How to conduct a performance appraisal.* Alexandria, Va.: ASTD Press.

Block, P. 1981. *Flawless consulting: A guide to getting your expertise used.* San Diego: Pfeiffer.

Boyett, J. H., and J. T. Boyett. 1995. *Beyond workplace 2000: Essential strategies for the new American corporation.* New York: Dutton.

Bradshaw, P. 1981. *The management of self-esteem: How people can feel good about themselves and better about their organizations.* Englewood Cliffs, N.J.: Prentice-Hall.

Brinkerhoff, R. O., and S. J. Gill. 1994. *The learning alliance.* San Francisco: Jossey-Bass.

Brookfield, S. 1992. Uncovering assumptions: The key to reflective practice. *Adult Learning* 16 (1): 13–18.

Burke, W. W. 1992. *Organizational development: A process of learning and changing.* Reading, Mass.: Addison-Wesley.

Carlson, J. 1987. *Moments of truth: New strategies for today's consumer-driven economy.* New York: HarperCollins.

Cascio, W. F. 1995. *Managing human resources: Productivity, quality of work life, profits.* 4th ed. New York: McGraw-Hill.

Chadwick, R. P. 1982. *Teaching and learning.* Old Tappens, N.J.: Fleming Revelle.

Clifton, D. O., and P. Nelson. 1992. *Soar with your strengths.* New York: Delacorte.

Feldman, D. C. 1967. A contingency theory of socialization. *Administrative Science Quarterly* 21 (9): 434–435.

Fiorelli, J., E. Longpre, and D. Zimmer. 1996. Radically reengineering the human resource function: The national semiconductor model. *Organizational Development Journal* 14 (1): 48–49.

Flannery, T. P., D. A. Hofrichter, and P. E. Platten. 1996. *People, performance, and pay: Dynamic compensation for changing organizations.* New York: Free Press.

Galbraith, J. R., and E. E. Lawler III. 1993. *Organizing for the future: The new logic for managing complex organizations.* San Francisco: Jossey-Bass.

Gelb, M. J., and T. Buzan. 1992. *Lessons from the art of juggling: How to achieve your full potential in business, learning, and life.* New York: Harmony Books.

Gibbons, M. A. 1990. A working model of the learning how to learn process. In *Learning how to learn across the life span,* edited by R. Smith and Associates. San Francisco: Jossey-Bass.

Gibson, J. L., J. M. Ivancevich, and J. H. Donnelly. 1997. *Organizations: Behavior, structure, process.* 9th ed. New York: McGraw-Hill.

Gilley, J. W. 1989. Career development: The linkage between training and organizational development. *Performance Improvement Quarterly* 2 (1): 6–10.

————. 1992. *Strategic planning for human resource development.* Alexandria, Va.: ASTD Press.

————. 1998. *Improving HRD practice.* Malabar, Fl.: Krieger.

Gilley, J. W., and N. W. Boughton. 1996. *Stop managing, start coaching: How performance coaching can enhance commitment and improve productivity.* New York: McGraw-Hill.

Gilley, J. W., N. W. Boughton, and A. Maycunich. 1999. *The performance challenge: Developing management systems to make employees your greatest asset.* Cambridge, Mass.: Perseus Books.

Gilley, J. W., and A. J. Coffern. 1994. *Internal consulting for HRD professionals: Tools, techniques, and strategies for improving organizational performance.* New York: McGraw-Hill.

Gilley, J. W., and J. Davidson. 1993. *Quality leadership.* New York: William M. Mercer.

Gilley, J. W., and S. A. Eggland. 1989. *Principles of human resource development.* Cambridge, Mass.: Addison-Wesley.

————. 1992. *Marketing HRD programs within organizations: Improving the visibility, credibility, and image of programs.* San Francisco: Jossey-Bass.

Gilley, J. W., and A. Maycunich. 1998a. *Strategically integrated HRD: Partnering to maximize organizational performance.* Cambridge, Mass.: Addison-Wesley.

————. 1998b. The role of the integrated human resources department in strategic planning. *Quality Observer* 7 (8): 22–25.

Gregory, J. M. 1884. *The seven laws of teaching.* Grand Rapids, Mich.: Baker Book House.

Hardy, R. E., and R. Schwartz. 1996. *The self-defeating organization: How smart companies can stop outsmarting themselves.* Cambridge, Mass.: Perseus Books.

Hein, K., and V. Alonzo. 1998. This is what we want. *Incentive Magazine* 10 (October): 40.

Hesselbein, F., M. Goldsmith, and R. Beckhard, eds. 1995. *The leaders of the future.* San Francisco: Jossey-Bass.

Killion, J. P., and G. Todnem. 1991. A process for personal theory building. *Educational Leadership* 48 (6): 14–16.

Knowles, M. S. 1975. *Self-directed learning.* New York: Association Press.

Knowles, M. S., E. F. Holton III, and R. A. Swanson. 1998. *The Adult Learner.* 5th ed. Houston: Gulf Publishing Company.

Labovitz, G., and V. Rosansky. 1997. *The power of alignment: How great companies stay centered and accomplish extraordinary things.* New York: Wiley.

Larson, C. E., and F. M. LaFasto. 1989. *Teamwork: What must go right, what can go wrong.* Newbury Park, Calif.: Sage.

LeBoeuf, M. 1985. *Getting results: The secret to motivating yourself and others.* New York: Berkeley Books.

Marquardt, M. J. 1996. *Building the learning organization.* New York: McGraw-Hill.

Maslow, A. H. 1998. *Maslow on Management.* New York: Wiley.

Maxwell, J. C. 1998. *The twenty-one irrefutable laws of leadership: Follow them and people will follow you.* Nashville, Tenn.: Thomas Nelson Publishers.

Meyer, E. C., and K. R. Allen. 1994. *Entrepreneurship and small business management.* Mission Hills, Calif.: Glencoe/McGraw-Hill.

Patterson, J. 1997. *Coming clean about organizational change.* Arlington, Va.: American Association of School Administrators.

Peterson, D. B., and M. D. Hicks. 1996. *Development first: Strategies for self-development.* Minneapolis: Personnel Decisions International.

Pinchot, G., and R. Pellman. 1999. *Intrapreneuring in action: A handbook for business innovation.* San Francisco: Berrett-Koehler Publishers.

Preskill, H. 1996. The use of critical incidents to foster reflection and learning in HRD. *Human Resource Development Quarterly* 7 (4): 335–347.

Robinson, D. G., and J. Robinson. 1996. *Performance consulting: Moving beyond training.* San Francisco: Berrett-Koehler.

Rummler, G. A., and A. P. Brache. 1995. *Improving performance: How to manage the white spaces on the organizational chart.* San Francisco: Jossey-Bass.

Saban, J. M., J. P. Killion, and C. G. Green. 1994. The centric reflection model: A kaleidoscope for staff developers. *Journal of Staff Development* 18 (3): 16–20.

Schein, E. H. 1992. *Organizational culture and leadership.* San Francisco: Jossey-Bass.

Schneider, B., and A. Konz. 1989. Strategic job analysis. *Human Resource Management* 28 (2): 51–63.

Schon, D. A. 1983. *The reflective practitioner.* New York: Basic Books.

Schuster, J. R., and P. K. Zingheim. 1992. *The new pay: Linking employee and organizational performance.* New York: Lexington Books.

Schwinn, D. 1996. *The interactive project learning model.* Internal company concept paper. Transformation, Inc., Jackson, Mich.

Senge, P. M. 1990. *The fifth discipline: The art and practice of the learning organization.* New York: Doubleday.

Smart, B. D. 1983. *Selection interviewing: A management psychologist's recommended approach.* New York: Wiley.

Ulrich, D. 1997. *Human resource champions.* Boston: Harvard Business School Press.

————. 1998. A new mandate for human resources. *Harvard Business Review* 76 (1): 124–134.

Ulrich, D., and D. Lake. 1990. *Organizational capability: Competing from the inside out.* New York: John Wiley and Sons.

Watkins, K. E., and V. J. Marsick. 1993. *Sculpting the learning organization: Lessons in the art and science of systematic change.* San Francisco: Jossey-Bass.

Werther, W. B., and K. Davis. 1996. *Human resources and personnel management.* Boston: Irwin/McGraw-Hill.

Williams, V. L., and J. E. Sunderland. 1998. Maximize the power of your reward and recognition strategies. *Journal of Compensation and Benefits* 2 (14): 11–17.

Zemke, R., and S. Zemke. 1995. Adult learning: What do we know for sure? *Training* 32 (6): 31–40.

INDEX

Printed in the United Kingdom
by Lightning Source UK Ltd.
121585UK00002B/50/A